# MULTIPLE
# $\mathcal{B}$LESSINGS

From Pregnancy

Through Childhood,

a Guide for Parents of

Twins, Triplets, or More

BETTY ROTHBART, M.S.W.

FOREWORD BY
PAUL J. WEINBAUM, M.D.

Hearst Books
New York

LIBRARY OF CONGRESS CATALOGING-IN-PUBLICATION DATA

Rothbart, Betty.
   Multiple blessings : from pregnancy through childhood, a guide for
parents of twins, triplets, or more / by Betty Rothbart ; foreword
by Paul J. Weinbaum, M.D.
     p.   cm.
   Includes bibliographical references and index.
   ISBN 0-688-11642-6
   1. Twins.  2. Triplets.  3. Multiple births.  4. Child rearing.
I. Title.
HQ77.35.R68  1994
649'.144—dc20                                     93-36250
                                                         CIP

Printed in the United States of America

6  7  8  9  10

BOOK DESIGN BY PATRICE FODERO

FOR STUART, LILA, AND JACOB,

BLESSINGS IN MY LIFE

# $\mathcal{F}$OREWORD

▨   Over the years that I have practiced high-risk obstetrics, I have assisted many women with multiple pregnancy. As more women use fertility drugs and undergo *in vitro* fertilization and other assisted reproductive technologies, higher order multiple pregnancies are becoming increasingly frequent.

It has always seemed to me that couples expecting multiples are even more excited, and perhaps more anxious, about their pregnancies than those expecting just one child—and with good reason. Multiple pregnancy presents unique challenges to women and their health care providers because of the higher risk of complications. Fortunately, prenatal care by an experienced, knowledgeable, and sympathetic physician can go far toward helping to assure a healthy pregnancy and avoid such complications as gestational diabetes, preeclampsia, and preterm labor.

In my opinion, the physician must assess the need of the "whole" person, and not just the medical requirements of managing a higher risk pregnancy. It is also incumbent upon the parents-to-be to become as knowledgeable as possible regarding the facts associated with multiple pregnancy, so that they can make informed decisions and enjoy a true "partnership of care" with their physician.

Prenatal care for women expecting multiples includes more frequent office visits, attention to the need for proper nutrition and sufficient rest, earlier screening for gestational diabetes and other conditions, use of serial ultrasound scans, and close fetal monitoring during labor. Some women face the need for extensive bed rest or hospitalization during pregnancy, and may feel conflicted between their desire to optimize their pregnancy outcome and their desire to meet obligations to other life commitments including family and career. The couple and physician working closely together can explore ways to help achieve the right balance.

In *Multiple Blessings,* Betty Rothbart has placed a very human face on the many, often difficult issues confronting parents of multiples by providing interesting and sometimes humorous commentary from the numerous parents of twins, triplets, and quadruplets she interviewed for the book. As well as being impressed by the wealth of medical and technical information provided, I am especially taken with the value of the many chapters about parenting multiples, as newborns and throughout childhood. As the father of three daughters, now young women, I found Ms. Rothbart's description of the sometimes trying postpartum period—including the long and often sleepless nights, as well as the sometimes difficult nature of planning even a simple trip to the supermarket—brought back many tiring but wonderful memories. I never cease to be amazed at how difficult it can be to organize the life of only one small child, let alone two or more at the same time!

However, given the excellent suggestions and listing of available resources throughout the book, there is no doubt in my mind that reading *Multiple Blessings* will make the life of new parents easier. Readers will also benefit from Ms. Rothbart's thoughtful discussions of the emotional challenges of parenting, from how to handle stress to how to minimize comparisons and treat children as individuals.

On the basis of this book, if I could make one suggestion to new parents of multiples, it would be to take full advantage of all available resources—from experienced pediatric care providers, to networking groups and publications for parents of multiples—and never hesitate to ask questions. Although all children are unique individuals, there is little doubt that we can all benefit as parents from the experience of both professional care providers and parents who have become authorities by living through the trials and tribulations, as well as the wonders of "multiple blessings."

—PAUL J. WEINBAUM, M.D.
Director, Maternal-Fetal Medicine
Albany Medical Center
Albany, New York

# $\mathscr{A}$CKNOWLEDGMENTS

First and foremost, my heartfelt thanks to the many parents, grandparents, and twins and triplets interviewed for this book for so generously sharing their experiences, wisdom, and ideas, including Jaime Abola, Cathy Adell-Hertzberg, Lela Azatchi, Greg Barrette, Matthew Barrette, Lois Bergman, Miriam Berken-Vidal, Nathalie Bernstein, Jean Bratman, Jane E. Brody, Matthew Brown, Joanne Carbonaro, Michael Cavallo, Carole Charmello, Vicky DeMartino, Linda Doernberg, Barbara Driscoll, Richard Engquist, Cindy Essick, David Ethé, Rosemary Fedele, Laurie Feigenbaum, Arnold Frank, Sara Frank, Bonnie Eisenberg-Greene, George Garcia, Vanessa Garcia, Veronica Garcia, Leah Greenwald, Molly Gutkind, Richard Gutkind, Ruth Hammer, Marlene Hochman, Chaya Horn, Netta Horowitz, Carol Javna, Andy Kaufman, Lolly Kimmel, Mike Kimmel, Jean Klein, Yossi Knoll, Emily Kolker, Janie Krasne, Michael Krasne, Marilyn Lauterbach, Sonia Laudi, Lorraine Levan, Meta Levine, Smadar Levy, Mary Macy, Edward Magid, Fabia Mahoney, Alan Mallinger, Lauren Mallinger, Elizabeth Malloy, Terry McCarthy, Abby Goldstein McDonough, Margie McKee, Debbie Levy McKenney, Nancy Melisses, Beth Melnick, Beth Montgomery, Rosemary Moore, Marjorie Moser, Marlene Nierenberg, Jill Stempler Olin, Frima Peters, Neil Peters, Judy Pohl, Art Powell, Jr., Catherine Tabb Powell, Mark Rice, Linda Richardson, Miriam Schechter, Monica Schurtman, Shelley Smith, Shani Szlafrok, Liz Schiff, Esther Sherman, Nancy Sing-Bock, Chris Snyder, Elyse Spielberg, Jane Greengold Stevens, Ken Stevens,

Barbara Wahal, Pam Haynes Walsh, Renee Woolf, Susie Zeiger, and Grace Zwillenberg.

I have quoted from the interviews throughout the book, changing names and some identifying details to protect confidentiality.

I am greatly indebted to the highly knowledgeable and sensitive medical advisers whom I consulted on various aspects of this book: Paul J. Weinbaum, M.D., specialist in maternal-fetal medicine, who reviewed the entire manuscript for accuracy and wrote the Foreword; Judy L. Aschner, M.D., neonatologist; Ronald M. Caplan, M.D., obstetrician/gynecologist; David L. Rosenfeld, M.D., fertility specialist; Midge Thurin Madsen, R.N.C., C.C.E., and Dory Bronstein Krolick, R.N.C., B.S.N., C.C.E., labor and delivery nurses and perinatal bereavement counselors; Edward McCabe, D.O., specialist in adolescent medicine and former neonatal intensive care unit (NICU) resident; Kathy Whalen, R.N., NICU nurse; and Shoshana Zax, C.N.M., M.S.N., certified nurse-midwife.

Psychotherapists Jane Greer, Ph.D., and Ava L. Seigler, Ph.D., gave me a deeper understanding of the issues multiples and their families face.

Many thanks for the warmth and helpfulness of the National Organization of Mothers of Twins Clubs and their executive secretary, Lois Gallmeyer; Brooklyn Mothers of Multiples and their president, Frima Peters, and vice president, Smadar Levy; Brownstone Brooklyn Mothers of Multiples, Marlene Hochman, coordinator; Manhattan Mothers of Twins Club, Debi Rickard, coordinator; and the South Hills of Pittsburgh Mothers of Multiples Club and their coordinator, Geri Mead.

Rosemary Moore and Judy LeVan Fram were wonderful mentors for the chapter on breastfeeding, offering both valuable information and passionate points of view. Rosemary, who breastfed her own twins and currently helps other mothers of multiples, not only provided a great deal of information and reviewed the chapter, she also advised on the breastfeeding illustrations. Judy, a La Leche League Leader, is a fine source of information. She reviewed the chapter for accuracy and also discussed it with other La Leche League Leaders, sharing their suggestions with me, as well.

It was a pleasure to once again work with Dolores Santoliquido, the illustrator; together we thank the following individuals who, with wonderfully cooperative children, modeled for the illustrations: Matthew Brown, Beth Montgomery, Maria Avila Carballo, Juan Carlos

Carballo, Patricia Lewis-Johnson, Ronald Johnson, and Rosemary Moore.

Jill Stempler Olin was extraordinarily generous with her ideas, time, and contacts. She reviewed the manuscript and offered valuable suggestions, and was always an inspiration.

Jane E. Brody and Richard Engquist were especially helpful regarding how to avoid comparing twins and how to enhance children's autonomy. I have long admired Jane's work as health reporter for *The New York Times,* and was not surprised to learn that Jane and Richard's approach to rearing twins is geared to physical and emotional health and harmony.

I am also grateful for the help of Merle Froschl, codirector, Educational Equity Concepts, Inc.; Nina Otazo and Luisa Menendez, Parents Anonymous, Inc.; Tuula Van Gasbeek, EASE (Empty Arms Support Effort); "Miss Helen" Kirk, statistician; Patricia James, librarian, Squirrel Hill Branch, Carnegie Library of Pittsburgh; and Beatriz Button.

My thanks also to Lou Corti, manager of Ben's for Kids, Inc., a Manhattan baby supply store, who reviewed the chapter on equipment, clothing, and supplies, and made many helpful suggestions.

Many thanks to Megan Newman, my editor, for her dedication to this project and for her on-target and tactfully worded suggestions, and to my agent, Wendy Lipkind, who, as always, was enthusiastic and encouraging.

My parents, Dorothy and David Rothbart, could not have been more loving and supportive, and gave me many helpful comments on the manuscript. Special thanks to my mother for assisting with library research, interviewing several people for the book, and attending a Mothers of Twins Club meeting.

Eleanor Goldman, Irv Rothbart, and Stuart Smith generously read the manuscript and offered wonderfully constructive feedback and steadfast encouragement. I am also grateful for the loving encouragement of Gloria C. Cohen, Judith Kline, Ruth R. Mayer, and Kenneth L. Wampler.

Most important, I could not have written this book without the loving support of my husband, Stuart Smith, whose wholehearted commitment to fatherhood enriches all of our lives, and our wonderful children, Lila and Jacob. This book is about the importance and beauty of family, and I am profoundly grateful for the beautiful and devoted family that is my own.

# CONTENTS

15

# $\mathcal{I}$NTRODUCTION

How lucky to be born a twin, triplet, quadruplet, quintuplet. . .

*Instant playmates!*

Babble, and another child babbles back.

Snuggle under a blanket, and one of the other triplets giggles with you.

Throw a ball, a twin is there to catch it.

Company, company, all the time, for a lifetime. Another person or two or three who really knows you, understands you, has *been there with you all along.*

Sometimes you feel sorry for people who aren't multiples.

How hard to be born a multiple. . .

*Instant competition!*

Speak, and someone else is vying for the same airtime.

Snuggle under a blanket, and another child pulls the cover off your legs.

Get chicken pox, a twin is there to catch it.

Sharing and comparing, all the time. Sharing toys, clothing, friends, a room, blame (even when it wasn't your fault), and *parents' attention.* Sometimes you want the spotlight to yourself.

As a multiple, you learn patience as you await your turn on the swing. You learn to share: the tub, the last cupcake, the backseat of the car. And when you get into mischief, there's someone else to share the blame!

More children means more love to go around, more fun, a close feeling of family. And parents make sure each child feels special.

People call out, "Hey, twin!" You call back, "Hey, I have a name. Use it!" You and your twin laugh, roll your eyes. It's great to have each other.

But it is comparisons that can really do you in: Which twin is smarter? More attractive? More sociable? A sooner walker, a faster runner? Do parents favor one child over another?

It hurts when you and your twin fight. Just because you are twins doesn't mean you always understand each other.

People call out, "Hey, twin!" But you want to be known by your own name, as an individual in your own right. Can't people understand that?

## ⊠ . . . *And Now for the Parents' Point of View*

There is such a feeling of abundance, of overflowing joy, when your arms are full of babies, when you hold a small hand in each of yours, when your family can fill all the positions on a softball field.

"I am twice blessed," say parents of twins.

"Thrice blessed," say parents of triplets.

*And* . . . when you feel worn out by night after night of rocking colicky babies, or when the children are fighting, or when one child gets admitted to advanced science class and not the other, multiples can feel like a *mixed* blessing.

One of the greatest challenges for parents of multiples is simultaneously helping children cherish their status as multiples while nurturing each child's individuality.

And another challenge, of course, is coping with the emotional, physical, and logistical demands of raising two or more same-age children, perhaps in addition to single-born siblings.

## ◙ A Book for Mothers and Fathers

Many men say that an unexpected benefit of having multiples is that they became involved with their care far more than they would have expected. Although active fathering has steadily become more the norm than in previous generations, when parenting was primarily the mother's job, having multiples accelerates that evolutionary process. This book is as much for fathers as for mothers, in recognition of their mutual importance in their children's lives.

And I am speaking in this book both to parents with partners and to single parents. There is no question that raising multiples with an equally committed partner is less difficult and more companionable than savoring the pleasures and shouldering the burdens alone. All parents of multiples need as much help as they can get; single parents deserve a medal, too.

## ◙ With Multiples, There Is Always More to Do

Toy stores sell cute but highly misleading identical-quintuplet baby dolls that drink from five bottles suspended from a single stick. Multiples are not a perfectly synchronized team but a group of children with individual needs and diverse timing. Parenting multiples, especially in the first year, can be a round-the-clock endeavor. Support—emotional and practical—is crucial. Being a parent of multiples means never having to say you are sorry when you ask for help.

And just when you get the hang of parenting baby twins, triplets, or quadruplets, they aren't babies anymore. Logistical issues still have to be worked out (How do you keep twins out of trouble? How do you take triplets shopping and still keep your sanity?). But you also face a host of new, complex issues:

- How can you affirm each child's individual identity?
- Should you dress children alike?
- How can you give enough attention to each child?
- How can you assure each child that you love all of your children equally?

- How should you handle multiples' squabbles, competition, and insecurities?
- What if you find yourself favoring one child over another?
- How can you resist the urge to compare your children?
- Should multiples be in the same class at school?
- Most of all, how can you lay the foundation that will help your multiples to be lifelong friends?

Having multiples is an adventure, and the best adventures are rather messy, free-form, and happily improvised. Childhood is such a brief and precious time. With all the demands of raising multiples, you may never feel perfectly organized or in control. Your home may be cluttered, your free time sparse, your head may feel like a perpetual to-do list, and you may never feel like there is enough of you to go around. But the multiple joys can outweigh such tribulations if you give up some of the perfection and focus on enjoying your children. Adapt your housekeeping standards, reconcile your ambitions of doing it all . . . relax into the lively flow of events as you guide your children's journeys through childhood, lay the groundwork for their lifelong friendship, and treasure those multiple blessings who have entered your life.

## Note

Included throughout the book are quotes from my interviews with parents of multiples, grandparents, and twins and triplets. All names have been changed to protect confidentiality.

# Part One
# PREGNANCY

# ⬣ *Chapter 1*

# ℕEWSFLASH: YOU'RE EXPECTING MORE THAN ONE!

⬣    Excited, tearful, joyful, shocked, thrilled, scared. Overwhelmed. News of multiples inspires many reactions, often mixed. But perhaps underlying them all is awe. Multiples are a sublime coincidence, evidence of the wonder and spectacular variety of life.

## ⬣ *The Benefits of Finding Out Early*

> *"I have always been a highly intuitive woman. One day, after making love with my husband, I knew that I'd conceived. And I had a gut feeling that I was going to have twins."*

*Most* couples get the news well after conception and well before birth, when "signs of multiples" appear (see page 25). It is important to know whether you are carrying more than one. Pregnancy with twins, triplets, or more is higher risk for both mother and fetuses. The sooner you get the news, the sooner you and your doctor can make sure you have good prenatal care, sufficient rest, a proper diet, and any special tests.

Finding out early also gives parents time to make household, financial, work, and birth plans, to select names, to read and talk to other families about multiples, and to get used to the idea of a larger family.

Amazingly enough in this era of sonograms (see "Tests to Confirm Pregnancy with Multiples," page 30), some couples and their doctors do not suspect multiples until the first baby has been delivered:

*"I was so big when I was pregnant, I asked my two doctors and the midwife if I might be having twins. They all said no, they never heard another heartbeat or felt a second baby. They said I absolutely did not need a sonogram. When I went into labor, a day before my due date, I wore a fetal monitor and that did not pick up the second baby either.*

*"We were all set for a LeBoyer birth, with soft lighting and a warm bath prepared for the baby. After she was born, weighing six pounds nine ounces, my husband bathed her and the doctor left the room. But a resident looked at me and said, 'She is still big, get the doctor back in here.' Eight minutes later, the second twin was born. We were so excited. But forget the LeBoyer method. No bath had been prepared for the second baby—and we wanted those lights bright so we could check out our 'hidden baby.' She was fine, all six pounds of her. We were happy the twins were a surprise. It was more fun that way."*

For another couple, the last-minute revelation was traumatic:

*"I didn't find out I was having twins until my water broke in the hospital. They said I had a baby in breech position, sent me up for X rays, and discovered I had two babies inside. I couldn't believe it. All I could think of was how on earth I could manage two babies in our tiny, third-floor walk-up apartment, with no money to move or hire household help. We knew it would be hard having another mouth to feed, but we really wanted the baby. Now, all of a sudden, we had two more mouths to feed."*

Another woman recalls the birth of her twins in the early 1970s:

*"They sent me to X ray when I arrived at the hospital in labor. 'You know, Mrs. Jackson,' the technician said, 'I don't want to frighten you, but you're having twins.'*

*"All I could say was, 'Call my mother!'*

*"My mom raced to the hospital. She was elated because she had always wanted twins. I was in such extreme pain during labor. But my mom just sat there grinning."*

## ⬛ Signs of Multiples

*"When I was ten weeks pregnant, I started staining (I later found out this is common with twins). I was terrified that something was wrong, that I was losing the baby. The doctor ordered a sonogram and said I was having twins! I was thrilled and relieved. I think having twins is an honor. My husband, though, had mixed feelings. He was glad, but afraid, too, about how we could care for two."*

Suspect multiples and contact your doctor if you:

• *are larger than normal for length of gestation.*

In the mid-seventies, before the era of routine sonograms, one woman became large fairly early in her pregnancy, but throughout her first trimester her doctor did not suspect twins. Then one night he dreamed about her; he dreamed that she was having twins. First thing the next morning, he reviewed her chart, had her come in for a special appointment, and broke the news that she was having not one baby, but two!

• *are gaining weight rapidly and early.*

*"At five or six months I got huge. I looked like I was ten weeks further along than I was."*

A woman carrying only one child often has little or no weight gain in the first trimester. But rapid weight gain does not always indicate multiples. It can have other causes, such as water retention.

• *have some spotting* (vaginal loss of small quantities of blood).

*"Five weeks into the pregnancy, on a Thursday, I started bleeding, so they did a sonogram and discovered I was pregnant with twins. The bleeding stopped, but they said if it started again, I might miscarry. My cousin, an ob/gyn, was getting married in Chicago on Saturday, and I didn't want to miss the wedding. So I went, but partway through the wedding ceremony I felt a gush of blood and started shaking like a leaf. My husband and I raced to my hotel room and I held an ice bag to my abdomen to stop the bleeding. We called our own doctor long distance, even though there were all those ob/gyns a few floors below us in the hotel. I didn't want to disrupt the wedding. The bleeding did stop. On Monday, I went in for another sonogram. Both twins were still there, they were fine. The doctor said the bleeding was due to a cervical polyp."*

- **are excessively fatigued or nauseated.** It can be hard to tell what is "excessive" fatigue or nausea if this is your first pregnancy. If it is not, you may realize that this pregnancy is quite a contrast to the last one:

*"With my son, I walked a lot, was active. But in this pregnancy, I was so tired and so sick all during the first trimester."*

- **experience early, intense fetal movement.** Report feelings of movement to your doctor.

The presence of great amounts of certain hormones in your blood or urine can also alert your doctor to the possibility of a multiple conception. Premature labor is also associated with multiple pregnancy.

If you experience one or more of these signs of multiples and your practitioner does not address your concerns, get a second opinion or request referral for a sonogram.

*"Although I had only gained eighteen pounds by my seventh month (of an ultimate weight gain of forty pounds), I was much larger by that stage than during the first two pregnancies. My doctor recommended a sonogram.*

*" 'We may be wrong about the due date or. . .' His voice trailed off as he and the technician studied the sonogram, speaking in low voices. Then I heard the technician mention 'Baby A and Baby B.' I gasped, and she exclaimed, 'Oh, didn't you know you were having twins?' I had always wanted four children, but my husband only wanted two. We had*

*compromised on three. The twins gave me the four children I had dreamed of."*

## ⊠ Who Is More Likely to Have Multiples?

*"I used Clomid [a fertility drug] and knew there was an increased chance of twins, plus I was thirty-eight at the time. Still, I was shocked, elated, ecstatic, scared, and anxious.*
    *"My husband said, 'It's a good shock.'"*

Multiples are more common among:

- *women over thirty.* As more women delay childbirth until their late thirties, the incidence of multiples can be expected to increase.
- *women who already have several children.* The more children a woman has, the more likely her chance of multiples.
- *women who already have fraternal twins.*
- *women who are multiples or have a family history of multiples.* One theory is that the tendency to have simultaneous maturation of several ovarian follicles is inherited; another is that follicles containing two ova is the predisposing genetic trait.
- *women of races that tend to have higher rates of multiples.* Genetic factors affect your likelihood of having *fraternal twins.* Your chances are highest if you are African-American (1 birth per 70) or East Indian, next highest if you are American Caucasian (1 birth per 88), lowest if you are one of the Asian races. (In Japan, the incidence is 1 birth per 150, in China, 1 birth per 300.)[1] In contrast, genetic factors do not appear to affect the incidence of *identical twins,* which is approximately 3 to 5 sets per 1,000 births.
- *women who get pregnant soon after discontinuing birth control pills.*
- *women who have taken certain fertility drugs,* such as Clomid and Pergonal. These drugs increase a woman's chances of multiple conception because they stimulate release of more than one egg at a time. The drugs have especially increased concep-

[1]Waldo E. Nelson, ed., *Textbook of Pediatrics,* 14th ed. (Philadelphia: W. B. Saunders Co., 1992).

tions of not only twins, but also higher-order multiples: triplets, quads, and more.

- *women who have had* in vitro *fertilization,* in which a woman's eggs are taken from her body and fertilized in a laboratory, most often with the husband's sperm but sometimes with donor sperm. Usually several fertilized eggs, or embryos, are inserted into the uterus to increase the likelihood that at least one will implant and gestate successfully. Often two or more embryos prove to be viable.

*"Both my husband and I had fertility problems. We tried for years to get pregnant. Finally, it happened, but it was an ectopic pregnancy, and of course I lost it. I was so depressed that I refused to go to baby showers or get together with people who had kids. When you get pregnant, you think you'll have a baby. You don't think of it not living.*

*"We saved all our money to give in vitro a shot. I traveled five hours a day round-trip to the hospital for my fertility work. They retrieved twenty-one eggs from me. They take as many as they can get. Fourteen fertilized properly. The surgeon advised us to put in four eggs, but another doctor suggested six. I said, 'Put in six, I don't want to do this again.' I was one of the lucky ones. The in vitro worked the first time."*

## ◙ *Types of Multiples*

About 1 in 90 pregnancies includes multiple fetuses, primarily twins.

### Twins

**Identical Twins,** also called monozygotic twins, begin as a single fertilized egg (zygote) that splits in two, creating twins who are genetically the same.[2] Identical twins occur by chance and represent about a third of all twin births. They are always of the same sex, have the same blood composition and many other similarities, and look alike, although one identical twin may be larger because it gets a greater share of nutrients from the shared placenta. (This may result

---

[2]Rarely, the zygote does not split completely, resulting in conjoined twins, also called Siamese twins. Surgeons are often able to separate them, depending on the extent of attachment and the organs involved.

in twin transfusion syndrome. See Chapter 2, page 56.)

Identical twins often have similar temperaments and arrive at developmental milestones very close to each other. For example, within days or weeks of each other, they may begin sleeping through the night, crawling, getting their first tooth, walking, or, during puberty, experiencing bodily changes, including the onset of menstruation.

To see whether twins are identical, doctors examine the placenta after birth to see if it is, indeed, one shared placenta or two placentas that were so close to each other on the uterine wall that they fused, appearing as a single placenta. This is not a foolproof test, however, since some identical twins have separate placentas.

Tests of blood drawn from each twin's umbilical cord can also reveal whether twins are identical. Twins' blood can also be tested later in life to determine if they are identical. This is sometimes done if one twin needs an organ transplant from a compatible donor.

*Fraternal Twins*   began as two eggs, each fertilized by separate sperm. Fraternal twins are also called dizygotic or binovular twins. While identical twins share all the same genes, fraternal twins share only half, just as nontwin siblings do. Fraternal twins may look, act, and mature at the same or very different rates. Half of fraternal twins are a boy and a girl, one fourth are two boys, and one fourth are two girls.

---

### The Five Types of Twins

* identical male-male (one sixth of all twins)
* identical female-female (one sixth of all twins)
* fraternal male-female (one third of all twins)
* fraternal female-female (one sixth of all twins)
* fraternal male-male (one sixth of all twins)

---

## SUPERTWINS

*Triplets, Quadruplets (Quads), and Other Higher-Order Multiples,*   sometimes called "supertwins," may include identical twins, may all be fraternal, or, rarely, may all be identical. They may all be of the same sex or may be a combination of boys and girls.

In the United States, *triplets* are estimated to occur in 1 of 7,396 pregnancies, and *quadruplets* in 1 of 636,056 pregnancies.[3]

The number of twins, triplets, and more born in recent years has risen significantly due to the increased use of fertility drugs and improved prenatal care.

## Tests to Confirm Pregnancy with Multiples

*"I had a sonogram in my sixth month and found out we were going to have twins. My husband picked me up at the doctor's office. When I told him the news, he leaned out the car window and whooped with joy, as if he wanted the whole world to know! In celebration, he decided to give up smoking!"*

**Examination.** The practitioner may hear two or more heartbeats, or feel two or more heads, bottoms, or sets of limbs. Examination is not foolproof, however. Even if examination does not detect multiples, a doctor sometimes recommends a diagnostic test.

*"I gained only twenty-two pounds during pregnancy, but I looked enormous. I was examined by every doctor in the practice, and not one ever heard more than one heartbeat, apparently because one baby was lying on top of the other. They offered me a sonogram, but I did not want one. I had a full-term pregnancy, worked almost up to the day of delivery, and had natural childbirth. After the first child was delivered, the doctor saw a foot sticking out! He found himself delivering a second child— two for the price of one."*

**A Sonogram** enables a practitioner to "see" fetuses through ultrasonography. The woman is asked to drink about a quart of water in the hour before she has the sonogram so that her bladder is full. Sound waves reflect off the bladder, producing an amalgam of echoes. These echoes show on the screen as a series of blips that produce a picture of the fetuses. The use of ultrasonography has dramatically increased the percentage of multiples identified prior to birth.

[3]*Textbook of Pediatrics,* 14th ed.

*"I became pregnant when I was thirty-eight years old and began spotting at about six weeks. I was terrified that I was having a miscarriage and immediately saw my doctor.*

*" 'You're either losing the baby or having twins,' he said, and recommended a sonogram. I was excited when it showed two sacs, but was not surprised because twins run on both sides of my family. My father was a twin, and my aunt had twins. My husband and I had waited to have children and had despaired of conceiving. We felt lucky to get two at the same time."*

Sonograms are not perfectly accurate. For example, in some instances a sonogram has detected twins when in fact a trio was sharing the womb. In May 1993, when a woman who had taken Pergonal and was diagnosed with quintuplets underwent a cesarean, doctors pulled out six babies instead![4]

A sonogram done in the first trimester or early in the second trimester sometimes shows two or more fetuses, while a later sonogram shows fewer fetuses and one or more empty sacs. The absent fetus may have been absorbed into the amniotic fluid or become nourishment for the surviving fetus(es). This is known as the "vanishing twin" phenomenon.

Researchers examining a series of sonograms beginning in early pregnancy reported that "only about 30% to 50% of multiple gestations actually result in all the fetuses being carried to viability. Fetal demise with complete resorption or even miscarriage, manifested only by slight vaginal bleeding, may occur, with survival of the remaining fetuses and continuation of the pregnancy."[5]

*X rays are no longer used to diagnose multiple fetuses because radiation can harm them.* Sonograms are now the diagnostic test of choice despite the fact that they are not perfect, and most doctors believe in informing parents early. The story of one woman who had twins in 1948 shows how times have changed:

*"I vividly remember the day I found out that I was pregnant with twins. While visiting the obstetrician in my seventh month, I sneaked a look at my file while he was out of the room. I was shocked that it mentioned*

[4]Wendy Lin, "And Baby Makes Six," *Newsday*, May 27, 1993.
[5]Allan Killam and Kenneth F. Trofatter, "Multiple Pregnancy," *Obstetrics and Gynecology*, 5th ed., David Danforth and James Scott, eds. (Philadelphia: Lippincott, 1986).

*a strong possibility of twins. The doctor was quite indignant when I told him that I'd looked in the file. But I refused to leave the office until I knew whether I was carrying more than one child. He took X rays and confirmed it. I walked home on a cloud."*

Another woman who had twins in the late 1940s had them confirmed by X ray, too. She, too, confronted the odd veil of secrecy that surrounded twin pregnancy at the time:

*"By the end of my sixth month, I was so huge, I had to sit far from the table. The doctor sent me for an X ray at the hospital where I was to be confined. The technician made me wait in another room while he read the results. He wouldn't talk to me. But I overheard him telling someone else, 'It looks like a doubleheader.'*

*"I had miscarried two previous pregnancies. When I found out I was having twins, I felt so blessed. I thought, God gave me two babies to make up for what I lost."*

## Adopting Twins

There's one more way of "finding out" about multiples: by adopting them.

*"My husband and I went to a large, private adoption agency that involves birth mothers in choosing who will adopt their babies. We both said that we would be quite willing to adopt twins if any were available. Eighteen months later, after going through all the interviews, home visits, seminars, and background checks, we each got a call at work at three-thirty one Friday afternoon: 'Congratulations, you have a new baby girl. Incidentally, she has a sister born two minutes later.'*

*"By five o'clock, we held Alice in our arms. Our other daughter, Dana, had to stay in the hospital an extra week because of apnea and a slight congenital heart defect. But both girls have turned out to be active, robust children.*

*"We were totally unprepared to become parents. No one had told us that a birth mother was considering us for her twins. We felt like the luckiest people in the world. We had been through a lot with infertility treatments that didn't work. Having twins was more than we had ever hoped for. It was the best day of both our lives.*

*"We had no crib, no baby clothes, no diapers. Our next door neighbors had a little doll cradle they kept around for their grandchildren to*

play with. That's where Alice slept that night. She weighed only five pounds; it was fine. The next day, my husband went to Toys-R-Us to shop for baby things, along with a buddy of his who had a one-year-old baby. He guided my husband through the store and told him what he needed. Neither my husband nor I had ever been in Toys-R-Us; for that matter, because of our infertility problems, we had always avoided the baby aisle in the supermarket. We had no clue how to buy or put on diapers, how to mix formula, what to buy. When my husband got home, surrounded by stacks of bags and boxes, I took his picture. He looked like the wind had been knocked out of him!

"People started coming over with offers of cribs, humidifiers, clothing. Friends from my office held a baby shower in our living room. We could not have made it without the support of our friends and family.

"The agency arranged for us to have one visit with the birth mother. Although she didn't say why she had chosen us, I wonder if one reason might be because my brother and sister-in-law have twins, and neighbors have twins. Maybe she thought it would be nice for her daughters to have other twins around.

"She told us that she had briefly considered splitting them up and keeping one of them; she struggled to find a way to avoid placing at least one child. But she really did not feel that she could handle being a parent at this time in her life, and she was very committed to keeping the girls together.

"We use the words adoption and birth mother around the girls, but they are only two now and can't understand the concepts yet. They don't even understand what twins means. I tell them: 'Twins means you were born the same day and came from the same birth mother.'

"They are very close, and really care for each other. Of course, they have the usual two-year-old issues, like problems with sharing. But if one falls, the other comforts her."

One couple "assembled" twins:

"My husband and I tried for a very long time to adopt a baby. One day I received two phone calls announcing a baby available for adoption on the same day. One call was from a doctor on the north end of town, one from a doctor on the south end. We couldn't believe our luck. We adopted them both, and we like to think of them as our twins."

## A Jumble of Emotions

"I called my husband at work right after the doctor said we might be having twins. All he said was, 'We can't afford twins,' and hung up! I *guess he did a double take, because he called me back and said, 'What did you say?' He was happy and said we would find a way to manage.*

*"When the twins were born, my husband did a reprise of his first reaction, just to kid the doctor. 'We can't afford twins. You'll have to take one in payment.' The doctor actually fell for it momentarily, and stammered, 'No, really, you'll love having twins.' "*

On finding out about pregnancy with multiples, it is natural for expectant parents and their family and friends to have many feelings at once. Pride turns into panic turns into excitement turns into research-mania. On getting the news, one woman took off for the library to read every book on twins she could get her hands on, while her husband took off in the other direction—to shop for a minivan.

How you respond to the idea of having multiples can reflect your own family upbringing.

*"I had just moved to New York with my husband, and I missed my family in Minnesota. I was the youngest of seven kids, came from a loving family, was the center of attention. In New York, I felt out in the cold. When I found out I was pregnant with twins, my mom said, 'Now you'll have two dolls of your own.' "*

A woman raised as an only child felt excited but apprehensive. The world of sibling relationships was totally new to her.

Pregnancy is a time of waiting but also a time of preparing (see Chapter 3, "Checklists for Prospective Parents"). Learn what you can about parenting multiples by reading and talking to other parents, and communicate with your partner about fears, concerns, and expectations. Take time together to plan and rest now, for the arrival of multiples is one of life's most thrilling—and busiest—experiences.

# 🔯 Chapter 2

# $\mathcal{P}$REGNANCY AND DELIVERY

" 'Now I will tell you something,' Beate said. . . . 'There are two fetal heartbeats. Paul and I will have twins.'
" 'How wonderful!' Polly said. 'Two little future Supreme Court Justices!' "[1]

Perhaps you have future justices growing inside you, too. Pregnancy is certainly a time of musing about who your children will be. But more short-term concerns are probably foremost on your mind. You may have heard that multiple pregnancies are higher-risk. How can you increase your chances of having a full-term pregnancy? And how can you keep yourself healthy through the months ahead?

This chapter focuses on issues and complications specific to pregnancy with multiples. It does not cover every aspect of pregnancy, labor, delivery, or all potential complications. For a complete description of pregnancy, read one of the many books on the subject, including those listed in the Bibliography.

[1]Laurie Colwin, *Family Happiness* (New York: Alfred A. Knopf, 1982).

## How Pregnancy with Multiples Differs from Single Pregnancy

Women who are carrying more than one child are more likely to:

- *get larger earlier* in the pregnancy.

*"I was in maternity clothes before my third month. In my fifth month, several people said, 'I guess you are due to deliver any minute now.'"*

*"What amazed me was that I could not fit behind the wheel of the car— even when the seat was pushed back all the way."*

- *gain more weight.*

*"I gained sixty pounds. I felt like a walking beach ball. I couldn't sit down without falling off the seat. I had to be perfectly centered on the chair."*

- *have a heavier, more stretched uterus* due to the fetuses, their placenta(s), and amniotic fluid. Carrying this heavy weight is very tiring. The growing uterus presses on the lungs, which can make you feel breathless; on the bladder, inspiring you to urinate more frequently; on the stomach, which can cause heartburn; on the intestinal tract, which can cause constipation; and on the legs, which can cause varicose veins. Physical therapists who specialize in obstetrics may be helpful in relieving pregnancy-related discomforts such as incontinence or lower back pain and in suggesting gentle exercises and positions to relieve pressure.
- *experience nausea, sometimes with vomiting; fatigue; and larger, heavier breasts,* all associated with high levels of pregnancy hormones.

*"No one told me morning sickness is worst when you are pregnant with twins—or that it will ever end. I had a profound lack of support at work. My supervisors were women, mothers themselves. But they had*

*no clue that pregnancy with twins is different. They had not been sick during their pregnancies, so they could not accept that I was. 'Pregnancy is not a disability,' said one supervisor."*

*"I had morning sickness until the middle of my fourth month. I could not work. I lost fifteen pounds my first trimester from vomiting so much. My mother-in-law kept suggesting I chew raw gingerroot or take vita-min $B_6$."*

*"I was depressed for days when I read a book that said morning sickness was a sign of fears and ambivalence. Then I asked my doctor about it. When she told me intense morning sickness was very normal with twins, I was relieved. And then I was angry with the author of that book."*

- *feel emotional stress* due to concern about such potential prob-lems as premature delivery.

*"When I carried one baby, I felt sure everything would be okay. But with the twins, I wasn't sure of anything. I was really afraid, even to take a long walk. I would worry, am I doing everything okay for the two of them?"*

- *develop complications, deliver prematurely, and have smaller ba-bies* (all discussed later in this chapter).

*"There was such a contrast with my first pregnancy. When I was car-rying my son, I was glowing, dancing. With my twins, I had problems from day one. I had to stop work at the beginning of my second trimester because I had two episodes of heavy bleeding and weeks on end of con-stant staining."*

---

## Goals of Prenatal Care
❧

- to keep yourself healthy
- to keep your fetuses healthy
- to get expert advice on diet, exercise, rest, and other concerns
- to increase your knowledge of your body, and to enable you and your partner to make healthy decisions
- to help prevent complications, to detect any complications early, and to treat them promptly, guided by up-to-date medical knowledge
- to help make pregnancy a satisfying and fulfilling experience

---

## ❧ Selecting an Obstetrician and Birth Site

*"We were living outside Boston when I became pregnant with the twins. In my fifth month of pregnancy, I developed gestational diabetes. In my sixth month, I had protein in my urine. It was very traumatic because my doctor, a fairly young man, said he did not want to handle my case any longer because I was seriously high risk. He told me to go to a center in Boston that handles high-risk pregnancy. I was very upset, but then I was glad because the center treated me as if I were perfectly normal. They were handling so many other cases that were in far more serious trouble that they felt mine was very easily treated. That was a very comforting thought to me."*

Excellent prenatal care is crucial. Multiple pregnancy presents more risks for both woman and babies. By taking care of yourself and allowing a doctor you respect to take care of you, you increase the likelihood of a happy outcome.

Your primary caregiver should be an experienced physician whom you can trust to provide top medical care, and whom you feel comfortable talking to, since you will have many questions as your pregnancy progresses. Choose an obstetrician with experience in multiple and high-risk pregnancies. Request a referral from your gynecologist, primary physician, or mothers of multiples who were satisfied with their care.

Certified nurse-midwives can be valuable resources, but only physicians are qualified to handle all medical complications that can occur with twin or other multiple pregnancies. Some physicians have certified nurse-midwives on their staff to conduct or assist with routine examinations, answer patients' questions, teach childbirth classes, and assist with childbirth.

*"When I was pregnant with the triplets, the obstetrician said, 'I tell most women to exercise and not get too sedentary. That doesn't apply to you. And I also tell patients to watch their weight. That doesn't apply to you either.'"*

When selecting an obstetrician, identify your concerns. For example:

**Where to Have the Babies.** If possible, select a physician affiliated with a "Level III" hospital, i.e., one that has a neonatal intensive-care unit (NICU) and specialized obstetrical care. These facilities are also known as regional care centers, to which patients whose care cannot be managed in smaller or outlying facilities are transferred. Since outcomes for care of premature babies are better if babies do not need to withstand the stress of being transported from another hospital, many physicians advise women who are at risk of premature delivery to have their babies at a Level III hospital.

You hope your babies will not need a NICU, but you want one available if they do. Arrange for you and your partner to visit the nursery so the experience will not be entirely new to you if your babies need to go there. If you do not live near a hospital with a NICU, inquire about the means and time it takes to transfer babies to one if necessary.

Inquire about hospital policies that concern you. For example, you may want to know whether your partner may be present at the birth, whether rooming-in for multiples is permitted, whether breast-feeding advice is offered for mothers of multiples, and whether you may move about during labor instead of being required to lie on a bed or be restricted to a birthing chair. If you object to a specific hospital policy, ask the physician to intercede on your behalf to have it waived for you, if possible, or write a letter to the hospital yourself. Hospitals' policies may be flexible. Or your objections, and those of others who voice them, may motivate a hospital to reevaluate its policies—ideally, in time for you to benefit.

Some women dream of having a home birth, and the experience can be a warm and special one if all goes well. However, a hospital birth is strongly recommended for multiples since you or your babies may require immediate access to medical specialists, equipment, and an intensive-care unit. Be optimistic about the outcome of your pregnancy. Be realistic about the need to plan for the unexpected.

*Childbirth.*   Perhaps you feel strongly about wanting a vaginal birth. Some doctors believe that cesarean delivery is best for virtually all multiple births. Others favor vaginal birth whenever possible. Find a doctor whose views are most akin to your own.

Since multiples do not always present head-down at birth, ask whether the doctor is experienced with vaginal breech deliveries and the version technique, a means of turning the baby into position for vaginal birth. Similarly, discuss your views on natural childbirth, the use of anesthesia, and whether your partner may attend and participate in the birth.

The cesarean-versus-vaginal birth issue is a nonissue to some women. "I'm going for a high-tech pregnancy," said one. "If I have a vaginal birth, fine, but I'm not counting on it. I just want to get these babies born."

Many women feel strongly about wanting a vaginal birth, if possible. For more information on cesarean birth, contact C/Sec, or Cesarean/Support Education and Concern (see the Resources section in the Appendix). The goals of this group are "to provide emotional support for cesarean delivery families; to share information and promote education on cesarean childbirth, cesarean prevention, and VBAC (vaginal birth after cesarean); and to change attitudes and policies which affect the cesarean childbirth experience." The organization maintains a referral list of cesarean support groups, advises people on how to start one, and sells books, pamphlets, and other materials.

*Breastfeeding.*   If you wish to breastfeed your babies, choose a doctor who acknowledges the advantages of breastfeeding multiples and who will help you achieve that goal. Contact La Leche League for more information. (See Chapter 21, "Mothers of Twins Clubs and Other Resources," and the Resources section in the Appendix.)

***Weight Gain.*** Rigid limits on weight gain are inappropriate. Select a physician who will assess your weight gain based on your individual needs. While forty-five to sixty pounds is the average weight gain for pregnancy with twins, the optimal amount varies for each woman. You and your doctor need to take into account such factors as the number of fetuses you are carrying, your amount of activity and need for energy, your level of fatigue, and your general state of health. Do not try to base your "ideal" weight gain on anyone else's pregnancy, or even on your own previous pregnancies with multiples. *Every pregnancy is different.*

> *"When I was pregnant with my first child, the trend was to not gain too much weight. Every visit to the doctor, they weighed you and gave you a 'talking-to' if you gained too much. I never listened to them, though. I listened to my body. I believe in the wisdom of the body. That attitude paid off when I was pregnant with my twins. We didn't know it was twins until the day they were born! During that pregnancy, too, though, I was hungry a lot, and I ate as much as I wanted—and had two healthy baby girls, both weighing over six pounds."*

If you were overweight when you conceived, you may—or may not—gain less than the average amount during pregnancy. *Never go on a weight-loss diet during pregnancy or when breastfeeding.*

If you were underweight when you conceived, your doctor may advise an enriched eating plan.

***Diet.***

> *"I had very little energy for cooking during my pregnancy. Every day on my way home from work, I stopped at the deli and put together our dinner from the salad bar."*

Your physician should recommend an eating plan that will assure that you eat a well-balanced diet that provides sufficient nutrients and calories to nourish you and your multiples. A woman pregnant with one child is generally advised to consume about 200 calories more than the standard 1,800 calories recommended for most nonpregnant women. For each additional fetus, a woman should take in 200 additional calories. Thus a woman pregnant with triplets should consume 1,800 plus 200 × 3 calories, for a total of 2,400 calories a day.

Also ask your doctor about taking prenatal vitamin and mineral supplements. Women pregnant with multiples need increased iron, folic acid, and calcium, as well as other nutrients.

Many women recommend materials on diet and pregnancy published by the Triplet Connection (see the Resources section in the Appendix). One woman said that she especially found helpful the Triplet Connection's advice to "eat a *lot,* especially in the later weeks, and not only when hungry." She credits the Triplet Connection's advice with the happy outcome of her giving birth to healthy triplets.

If you have special dietary needs, such as if you are a vegetarian or have diabetes, preeclampsia, or allergies, or if you have other questions about how to eat well during pregnancy, you will find a consultation with a registered dietician to be enormously helpful. Most obstetricians and nurses do not have the expertise needed to tailor a pregnancy diet for women with special needs. Also note that anybody can use the title "nutritionist," for which no special training is required. Only with a registered dietician are you assured that the individual has university training and supervised clinical experience in this field.

## Maternity Clothes

When you are pregnant with multiples, you begin wearing maternity clothes earlier. You also stop wearing them later because it takes you longer to get your figure back after birth. So buy things you will enjoy wearing, and wearing, and wearing. . . .

Borrow whatever you can from friends, especially other mothers of multiples who sewed their own maternity clothes. Why? Because most maternity clothes that are available in stores are designed for women pregnant with only one. They get big. But multiples' moms-to-be get bigger. Dresses and jumpers are more likely to fit as you grow than are pants or skirts, even if they have stretchy panels. They may not stretch as much as you need them to. And the very last thing you should wear is anything that constricts your middle. When you buy maternity clothes, buy larger ones than you think you will need.

Buy a couple of good maternity or nursing bras that support your breasts. Cotton ones are especially comfortable. If you are planning to breastfeed, prepare your nipples by cutting circles from the center of the bra cups so your nipples can poke through. Your nipples' contact with the cloth of your shirt will toughen them up a bit for the coming action. If you do not like the idea of taking scissors to expensive lingerie, buy nursing bras with flaps that unfasten, and wear them sometimes with the flaps down.

Many women find that front-fastening bras are best for simultaneous breastfeeding of two babies. They are easy to unfasten and free your breasts for nursing. Make sure bras are comfortable and that they leave room for you to become even more buxom. You may need larger bras when your milk comes in.

If you have or want to help prevent varicose veins, maternity support hose may be a good idea. Check with your physician.

## Your Sex Life During Pregnancy

Pregnancy can be a terrific time to have sex—if you have the energy and the interest. Some women do, others don't. Sexual interest can fluctuate according to your level of fatigue and stress, feelings about your changing body, and of course your relationship with your partner. Many couples feel closer as they anticipate the birth of their multiples. In some instances, however, if complications have occurred, worry may spin partners into his and hers orbits, each fueled by private anxieties.

Sexual contact can be a way to reconnect. Your increased size and changed shape need not be obstacles, if you are willing to experiment a little and laugh a lot. The man-on-the-top position is probably the first to go. Try other positions as they occur to you.

There is another advantage to sex during pregnancy. You need not worry about contraception. Nor need you worry about trying to get pregnant. Couples who have struggled with infertility have gotten used to the unromantic rigors of sex on a schedule. As one woman said, "We tried every surgery, every drug. Sometimes we made love when we hated each other's guts."

Now, you are finally pregnant. Sex has no other goal than enjoyment. Sexual activity in the first trimester may be difficult to arrange because you would rather be sleeping. In the middle trimester, however, both of you may be surprised by your freshly ignited feelings of lust. Make the most of it. Next trimester you may be napping again.

If intercourse is uncomfortable and a change of position does not help, stop. That does not mean you and your partner cannot be sexually close. Touch, kiss, and explore other erotic stimulation. Enjoy the lushness of your pregnant body. Although some men are oddly unaware of how beautiful pregnant women are, most men appreciate their magnificently curvaceous wives, blossoming with fertility.

If your doctor recommends restricting sexual activity, both partners might want to be present for the explanation and should not be shy about asking questions. Some doctors routinely caution against any sex in the last trimester. But if you have no history of premature labor or delivery, have had no warning signs of early labor in this pregnancy, are getting enough rest, and are healthy, perhaps that rule should not apply to you.

David L. Rosenfeld, M.D., chief of the Division of Human Reproduction, North Shore University Hospital in Manhasset, New York, advises women carrying triplets or more to stay off their feet and in bed as much as possible, and by sixteen weeks gestation not only to stop working, but also to refrain from having sexual intercourse.

"Semen contains prostaglandin, which may stimulate vaginal contractions," says Dr. Rosenfeld. "Semen may also increase the risk of infection and premature rupture of membranes. Orgasm may stimulate uterine activity, which may also increase the risk of premature labor."

Certain rules apply to every pregnant woman: Do not have sexual intercourse if your membranes have ruptured, if you have vaginal spotting or bleeding, or if you have any cramping. Instead, call your doctor.

## How to Increase Your Chances of a Healthy, Full-Term Pregnancy

*Obtain Excellent Prenatal Care with a Physician You Respect and Trust.* Stay in close touch with your doctor about any problems you experience. Ask all the questions that occur to you. Record your questions and the answers in a notebook that can also serve as a pregnancy diary. Invite your partner to attend prenatal visits with you and to ask questions of his own.

*Follow the Eating Plan Your Physician Recommends* to assure that you take in sufficient calories and nutrients to nourish you and your multiples. It is important to eat not only the right foods, but enough of them. Eating foods high in protein is one of the most important ways you can help your fetuses have higher birth weights and survive the pregnancy.

*Take Prenatal Vitamin and Mineral Supplements* your physician prescribes.

*Drink Lots of Water* and other fluids such as fruit juices, vegetable broth, and milk, both during pregnancy and when breast-feeding.

*Get Plenty of Rest.* When resting, lie on your left side as often as possible. This improves blood flow from the lower extremities to the heart by relieving pressure on the inferior vena cava, which is the largest vein in the body.

The need for rest cannot be overemphasized.

*"I thought I was a superwoman. The doctor said to quit work in November. I said, 'Don't be ridiculous. I'll work until February.'*

*"I noticed that my feet swelled during the day, but not at night. I thought it was just an interesting fact. I didn't 'get it' that the swelling signaled possible trouble. If I'd known, maybe I would have gone out on disability. I should have stayed in bed, slowed down, and spent every minute lying on my left side. I also think that everybody who gets pregnant with twins should have to see the neonatal nursery. The sight of those babies would have motivated me to rest much, much more. The babies were born prematurely and had health problems.*

*"I still feel guilty that it was my fault for not slowing down enough. I didn't want my pregnancy to inconvenience people at work or my husband. I wanted to have it all. And after eleven years of trying to get pregnant, I wanted to be out there showing the world I was pregnant. I wanted to prove to myself and the world that I can do everything."*

*Consult Your Physician About Exercise.* If exercise was part of your daily routine before you got pregnant, you may be able to continue, perhaps on a modified basis. However, pregnancy is not a time to begin a new exercise regimen, with the possible exception of a closely supervised and responsibly conducted prenatal exercise class. (Tell the instructor you are pregnant with multiples.) Swimming (but never in a crowded or dirty pool) and walking are two good forms of exercise during pregnancy, but only with your physician's approval.

And remember that your primary goal is to have a healthy pregnancy—not to prove that pregnant women are strong and fit. One woman recalls:

*"I had a hard time walking, I was so big. But I forced myself to go on daily walks. I berated myself for feeling tired. After the babies were born, I was more exhausted than I would have been if I had rested more during pregnancy. My advice to women is to listen to your body and not push yourself."*

*Attend Childbirth Classes with Your Partner.* Perhaps classes are offered at your physician's office. If not, ask for a recommendation about where to go. You might choose Lamaze classes or another type that teaches techniques that will see you through the intense experience of labor and delivery. Tell your instructor that you are expecting multiples so she will be sure to discuss the topic in class. Make sure classes cover cesarean-section delivery, too, so you will be prepared in case you need one. Some couples arrange to attend childbirth classes in the second trimester so that they will be prepared in case delivery is premature.

Good childbirth classes affirm the importance, competence, caring, and connectedness of mothers- and fathers-to-be.

*Remember: Fetuses Live Not Only in You, but Through You.* In the ultimate vicarious experience, they are nourished by your food, they ingest your medicines, they are affected by any noxious fumes you inhale. They can be harmed by drugs you take, cigarettes you smoke, and alcohol you drink. Therefore:

- *do not smoke.* Smoking is hazardous to your own health and to the health of your fetuses. It can lead to premature birth, low birth weight, and placental abnormalities. Smoking constricts blood vessels that lead to the uterus, depriving fetuses of oxygen and slowing their growth. Children whose mother smoked during pregnancy are more likely to have respiratory, learning, and behavior problems.
- *avoid secondhand smoke.* Ask your partner to stop smoking, or to smoke outside the home so you (and the fetuses) do not inhale "secondhand" smoke. Keep up the no-smoking policy after the babies are born, too, for their sake and yours.
- *do not drink alcohol.* Fetuses can sustain severe alcohol-related damage, including low birth weight and size, mental retardation, learning disabilities, and other problems.
- *do not take any prescription or over-the-counter medications without checking first with your physician.*
- *do not take any street drugs, such as marijuana, cocaine, heroin, amphetamines, barbiturates, etc.* They can lead to fetal damage, addiction, or death.
- *refrain from caffeinated coffees, teas, and sodas.* Studies differ in their assessment of the amount of caffeine a pregnant woman may safely ingest, but caffeine is a powerful nerve stimulant, and you and your fetuses are better off without it.
- *avoid or use with extreme caution any household or workplace hazardous substances,* such as pesticides, turpentine, weed killer, aerosol-spray products, etc.

## Home Uterine-Activity Monitors

*"You usually can't feel premature labor, which is the main cause of death in multiples. So when I was pregnant with my triplets, I found the home monitor very reassuring. I'd strap on the monitor and sit or lie down for an hour relaxing and listening to music. Any time I felt what I thought was a contraction, I pushed a button on the monitor. When I hooked up with the remote monitoring station, they read the data, told me how many contractions per minute I had, and chatted with me. I felt very supported."*

Your physician may recommend that you use a *home uterine-activity monitor* (HUAM) to enable early detection of premature labor.

This external device records uterine contractions, usually twice a day, then you transmit the data over the phone to your doctor's office or hospital. A specially trained nurse analyzes the data. The monitor perceives subtle contractions that you may not even feel, but that signal that labor is imminent. If your doctor confirms that you are in labor, he or she may prescribe drugs to stop uterine contractions (tocolytic drugs). Your doctor may also recommend increased rest or extended bed rest, at home or in the hospital, depending on your degree of risk. Some monitors also enable you to check your blood pressure.

A home monitor can help give you peace of mind. While being in tune with your body is always important, the monitor and the nurse become your daily partners in observing how pregnancy is progressing. A monitor may also enable you to delay or avoid extended bed rest, and to continue working longer since you can use it at the office, if you have the time and privacy to do so.

However, the jury is still out on whether monitors have a high enough cost-benefit ratio to justify being used as a routine measure. HUAM systems are costly. An American College of Obstetricians and Gynecologists (ACOG) committee report notes that "the approximate charge for the HUAM system is $90–100 per day. If the system is used between 24–36 weeks of gestation, the cost could exceed $7,000."

Furthermore, ACOG cites some studies that indicate that the primary benefit may not be the monitor, but the regular contact with nurses. ACOG reports that a review by the Food and Drug Administration concluded that there is not yet enough evidence to "determine whether earlier identification of changes in cervical dilation actually translated into prevention of prematurity and improved perinatal outcome."

ACOG concludes that "a prospective, randomized, blinded clinical study of sufficient size is needed to validate the claims made for the HUAM system of care. Until such data become available, ACOG recommends that HUAM devices remain investigational and not be recommended for routine clinical use."[2]

[2]*Home Uterine Activity Monitoring,* Committee on Obstetrics: Maternal and Fetal Medicine, American College of Obstetricians and Gynecologists, ACOG Committee Opinion Number 115, September 1992.

One nurse-midwife admits to having mixed feelings about the value of home uterine activity monitors:

> *"One of the most helpful aspects is the regular contact between the pregnant woman and the nurse. It is a valuable opportunity to ask questions and be in touch, and instruction for use of HUAMs is very individualized. However, some HUAM companies say that any woman should be on HUAM by twenty weeks, and I do not agree that it is universally necessary. A HUAM also encourages a medical view of pregnancy: 'Something bad might happen, so let's plug you in.' Yet it is beneficial because it encourages a woman to rest, especially women in rural areas who might have to travel far distances to see their doctors."*

## Bed Rest

All doctors agree that sufficient rest is fundamental to good prenatal care. Some doctors also recommend extended bed rest for days, weeks, or even months, in order to reduce the risk of premature labor and delivery. Bed rest may be prescribed for women who have warning signs of early labor, such as bleeding or cramping, or who have a history of premature labor or delivery, or who have chronically high blood pressure, or who are carrying triplets, quads, or more. Some doctors routinely advise bed rest during part or all of the third trimester, or even earlier, for virtually any woman pregnant with twins or more.

Busy women may balk at the advice. One woman, diagnosed with a twin pregnancy in her seventh month, was advised by her obstetrician to rest in bed until delivery. She resisted the idea until the doctor said, "Which is harder? Staying in bed for two months or bringing two premature babies home from the hospital?"

If your doctor prescribes bed rest, ask why, and request a detailed explanation of what "bed rest" means. Definitions range from sitting up in bed for a few days or a few months, to lying flat on your back for weeks on end. Bed rest may permit a woman to go to the bathroom or require her to use a bedpan. Some women find it ironic that their doctors prescribe "complete" bed rest—but still require them to travel to the doctor's office for prenatal visits.

Usually, women rest at home. Women with children need to make arrangements for their care. Hannah, a mother of three single-born sons, had signs of early labor when she was six months pregnant with twins. Her doctor prescribed complete bed rest, and she moved into her mother's house so her mother could take care of her sons. Her husband arrived every evening after work to help. She conscientiously stayed in bed except to go to the bathroom. One day at the beginning of her ninth month, she could not stand the confinement anymore and walked down the stairs. "The day I got out of bed was the day my girls were born," she remembers, "at four pounds, eleven ounces each."

Some women must have bed rest in the hospital. Rosa recalls the roller coaster of suspense:

*"They kept me in the hospital for five weeks, one door away from the delivery room. Every couple of days I went into labor, with contractions every four minutes. I called my husband, he would come running, then they would stop labor by putting medication in my IV, and he would go home again to our daughter."*

## ADVANTAGES OF BED REST

***Bed Rest Can Relieve Uterine Pressure on the Cervix,*** and assure that calories that would otherwise be expended on maternal activity will go instead toward fetal growth. Thus it may reduce two major risks of pregnancy with multiples: premature birth and low birth weight.

***A "Doctor's Order" for Bed Rest May Be the Impetus an Active Woman Needs to Give Herself Permission to Slow Down*** and get the rest she needs. It also emphasizes to her husband, family, and employer that during pregnancy with multiples she cannot be expected to conduct business as usual.

A thirty-six-year-old woman never heard sweeter words than her doctor's order for bed rest. "I thought to myself, Oh, thank you, Lord. I'm so tired, tired, tired. Since conception I had been exhausted, but I blamed it on my 'advanced age.' I stayed in bed for two months and enjoyed every minute of it. Fortunately, my husband and I were able to afford help with our two older children."

*Bed Rest May Be an Unexpected Gift of Time with Your Children.*   Mothers on bed rest may not be able to take their children to the playground or make them tuna-noodle casserole. But you can check homework, play countless games of checkers or Monopoly, read picture books, construct fantasy worlds with Legos, help build a model dinosaur, dress dolls, apply fingernail polish, teach children to knit, admire children's drawings, or watch home-produced puppet shows (you are indeed a captive audience!). Once the babies are born, it may be difficult at first to find time for a single game of Chutes and Ladders.

*Depending on Your Type of Work, You May Be Able to Use Bed Rest Productively*   (but do not overdo it). You can make telephone sales calls, review budgets, proofread manuscripts, catch up on reading your backlog of professional journals, sketch designs for the fall menswear line. Home computers, modems, fax machines, and other technological goodies can transform your bedroom into an office, making you wonder why you ever bothered to commute in the first place!

Rosa, a free-lance editor, managed to complete a major project in the hospital on the days between her episodes of premature labor:

> *"I did not tell my client I was working in the hospital. I was afraid he would assign the job to someone else. Any time he called me at home, he got the answering machine, or the baby-sitter would say I was out. I always called back right away. Once or twice I almost got caught when he heard hospital background noise. I told him the radio was on.*
>
> *"After the baby was born, I came clean. I told him I had worked in the hospital. He was pretty surprised. 'How did you do it?' he asked. I replied, 'I felt fine. I just couldn't move!' I wanted him to realize what I had accomplished."*

*Bed Rest Can Be Precious Time for Yourself.*   Read a novel. Learn about parenting multiples by getting in touch with your local Mothers of Twins Club, which may even send a volunteer to visit you while on bed rest. Write in your diary. Speak with friends on the phone or hold court at home. Knit a couple of baby sweaters. Or— radical thought!—do nothing. A working mother of two children treasured the opportunity to lie still and quiet, watching snow drift gently from the sky outside her window.

## THE OTHER SIDE OF THE STORY

Many women tolerate bed rest fairly well, but for others it is a miserable endurance test. Edna, a mother of twins, recalls:

*"I was in the hospital for the last three months. I had no help at home and had to hire a baby-sitter for my daughter at the last minute. I had to give up total control—of my daughter, my home, myself. People talk about bed rest as an opportunity to catch up on reading, but for me, it was an emotional nightmare. I lay there worrying about the babies, my daughter, the toll on my husband. I cried a lot, and I had periods of numbness and denial.*

*"It was a panicky three months. I was in and out of the delivery room so many times. I became so focused on details, I knew everything about these babies, their heart rates, their size. These were medical cases inside me, not people.*

*"The babies were born at thirty-six weeks, one over six pounds, the other less than five. I begged for an earlier birth, but the doctors refused. I couldn't stand bed rest anymore."*

Disadvantages of bed rest include the following:

***Bed Rest May Present an Increased Risk of Venous (Blood) Clots.*** Research shows that 1 in 1,000 pregnant women develops a blood clot, most likely because of the higher concentration of the blood clotting factor in the blood during pregnancy. In some cases of extended bed rest, physicians may prescribe injections of heparin, a blood thinner, to lower the risk of blood clots. But for those women who rest for just a few hours during the day, bed rest should not significantly increase their risk of developing a blood clot.

***Prolonged Inactivity May Highlight or Exacerbate Heartburn, Constipation, Leg Swelling, or Backache.*** Ask your doctor to suggest remedies. For example, heartburn may be lessened by eating smaller meals more frequently, rather than three times a day. To ease constipation, drink plenty of water and eat fiber-rich foods. Laxatives are *not* recommended, but drinking prune juice or taking a stool softener (check with your doctor) is often helpful. Massage may relieve backache and soreness and benefit your circulatory system. Check with your physician.

Contrary to some people's beliefs, there is virtually no risk of bedsores for pregnant women on bed rest; bedsores are far more of a risk for elderly bedridden patients who are in a highly debilitated condition.

*Inactivity May Decrease Your Appetite.*   It is extremely important for you to eat well and to eat enough. If you cannot muster the appetite, discuss the situation with your physician. Consider whether your appetite is reduced because of inactivity or because of depression. If the latter, counseling or spending time with supportive friends may help.

*Bed Rest May Be Extremely Difficult to Arrange for*   women with young children, single parents, or couples with little access to help.

*Bed Rest May Compel You to Forfeit Income You Can Ill Afford to Lose.*   It can be a hardship for women who cannot afford time off from work or who have no disability insurance or maternity-leave benefits.

*Bed Rest May Be Boring or Even Agonizing for Active Women Who Dislike Being Sedentary.*   Madeline, the working mother of a two-year-old daughter, went into preterm labor with her twins in her twenty-third week of pregnancy. She chafed at being in bed:

> *"I wanted to do the right thing, but it is hard to stay put. I'd think, Well, I'll just do a few dishes and tidy up a bit. Before I knew it, half an hour flew by. Then I felt guilty, like I was tempting fate, and I would get back into bed immediately.*
>
> *"I wish I had seen the neonatal nursery during my pregnancy. Then I would never have moved a muscle. I did not understand what 'premature' meant. I thought early babies were just skinny."*

*Bed Rest Requires You to Give Up Some Control and Be Dependent on Others.*   No one else does things quite the way you do. You may need to let go of housekeeping standards, or accept that your three-year-old's shirt and pants do not match.

***Bed Rest May Give You More Time to Worry.*** You may feel depressed, guilty, or resentful of the need to suspend normal life. Try to stay focused on the goal of a positive pregnancy outcome. Read inspirational books or *Twins* magazine. Talk with your partner and close friends. Call your local Mothers of Twins Club for support.

### ALTERNATIVES TO BED REST

*"My first doctor said that by my sixth month I would have to be in bed. I went looking for another doctor. The second one just said to rest every day."*

*"I took a lounge chair to my office and rested for an hour every day at lunchtime. My supervisor was great and let me go home early when I needed to."*

Bed rest is not a uniformly agreed-upon remedy, and for some working women and mothers it is logistically prohibitive. Ask your doctor whether you might try alternatives. For example, you might eat more and take nutritional supplements to increase the number of calories available to your fetuses. Perhaps you can arrange to take several naps throughout the day. Some employers have a "sickroom" or may make available an office with a couch, especially if you present a note from your physician.

Amelia's office was located within easy walking distance of her aunt's apartment. Her aunt gave her a key so she could eat lunch and nap there every day at lunchtime. After work, Amelia went directly home and got into bed. Her husband cooked dinner, served her dinner in bed, and washed the dishes.

Although such alternatives are an option for some women, if bed rest is truly necessary, there is no substitute. If you do not see how you can possibly manage it financially, contact the social-services department in your area. There often are resources available.

## Possible Complications of Pregnancy with Multiples

The following list covers complications to which women and their multiple fetuses are especially vulnerable. It is not a comprehensive list of *all* complications that can occur in pregnancy. Good prenatal care, a nutritious diet, and sufficient rest, discussed earlier in this chapter, significantly reduce the risks.

*Hypertensive Disorders of Pregnancy*   include high blood pressure and preeclampsia, which can lead to eclampsia, formerly called toxemia. When a woman has a hypertensive disorder, her blood pressure rises, tissues swell, and protein leaks out of the kidneys and is present in the urine. Urine is checked at every prenatal visit to permit earliest possible detection.

Eclampsia, the most serious condition, can cause a woman to experience convulsions or fall into a coma and poses severe risk to the fetuses.

Immediately report to your doctor the following symptoms of hypertensive disorders:

- persistent, severe swelling of your feet (edema), especially if swelling lasts longer than twenty-four hours
- excessive weight gain
- swelling of your hands or face
- headaches
- dizziness
- seeing spots before your eyes
- in the second or third trimester: nausea, vomiting, abdominal pain

If hypertensive disorders are diagnosed early, they are fairly easy to treat. But if they are allowed to progress, they can cause life-threatening situations.

*Spotting or Bleeding,*   especially during the first trimester, may indicate multiple pregnancy or potential miscarriage.

Immediately report spotting or bleeding to your doctor. Also report any *cramping,* which may indicate miscarriage whether or not it is accompanied by bleeding.

*Anemia.*   Your blood must be tested to determine what kind of anemia you have. Types of anemia include iron-deficiency anemia, pernicious anemia (caused by a deficiency of vitamin $B_{12}$), folic-acid anemia (caused by a deficiency of folic acid, a B vitamin), and sickle-cell anemia (an inherited disorder that primarily affects African-Americans).

The most common type during pregnancy is iron-deficiency anemia. Avoid it by taking iron supplements that are approved by your doctor and by eating iron-rich foods every day, such as meat, liver, spinach, and other green leafy vegetables, peas and beans, dried apricots, prunes, raisins, and whole-grain breads and cereals.

**Problems with the Placenta(s)**  occur when one or more of the placentas:

- *partially or fully detaches from the uterine wall (abruptio placenta)*, causing bleeding and endangering both woman and fetus(es). The babies must be delivered immediately, often by cesarean.
- *partially or fully covers the cervical opening (placenta previa)*. Babies must be delivered by cesarean.
- *inadequately transmits nutrients, causing intrauterine growth retardation*. Smoking during pregnancy or diseases such as diabetes increase the likelihood of this condition.

**Growth Discordance**  occurs when one fetus grows more slowly than the other(s), perhaps because it is squeezed in the crowded uterus or has placental problems.

**Twin Transfusion Syndrome**  is the unequal transmittal of nutrients to identical twins from their shared placenta. Blood intended for one twin bypasses it and enters the other twin's body. The blood-deprived "donor" may become anemic and be smaller. The "recipient" twin, burdened by the excessive blood supply, may experience jaundice, respiratory problems, or heart failure.

**Polyhydramnios**  (sometimes called hydramnios) is an excessive accumulation of amniotic fluid within the sac that surrounds a fetus. The condition can distend the uterus, causing intense discomfort for the woman, and can lead to premature labor. Polyhydramnios may affect one or more of the fetuses. It can sometimes be treated by removing excess fluid through amniocentesis (see pages 58–59). This treatment relieves pressure on the mother's uterus and surrounding organs and reduces the likelihood that membranes will rupture prematurely.

*Prematurity,* birth prior to the thirty-seventh week of pregnancy, occurs more often in multiple pregnancies, often for no single identifiable cause. Some theorize that the uterus becomes too crowded or too heavy. Yet the combined weight of the fetuses may be less than the weight of a single baby who was delivered at term. Disparate fetal maturation rates may also play a role.

In addition to the risk of having multiple fetuses, risk factors for premature labor or delivery include abdominal surgery during pregnancy (such as for an appendectomy), abnormal uterine anatomy, emotional or physical stress, fibroids (benign uterine tumors), high blood pressure, illness with fever during pregnancy, insufficient rest, kidney infection, maternal age of under sixteen or over thirty-five, maternal *in utero* exposure to the synthetic estrogen hormone DES[3] during her own gestation, placenta previa, polyhydramnios, poor weight gain, previous preterm labor or delivery, smoking, vaginal bleeding.

*Low-Birth-Weight* babies weigh less than five pounds, eight ounces at birth. Low birth weight is common among twins and other multiples. Many are premature. But even those born at term may have low birth weights because of the crowded womb, or if their mother's diet did not supply sufficient calories and nutrients to nourish multiple fetuses.

Premature babies who weigh more than five pounds, eight ounces may still be immature and need special care.

*Presentation Difficulties.* "Presentation" refers to the fetus's position within the uterus prior to birth. *Breech* presentation means that a fetus is not in the head-down (*vertex*) position, which is by far the safest position for vaginal birth. A fetus in breech presentation is vertical, but not in the right direction, because its buttocks or one or both legs are facing the cervix. *Transverse lie* presentation, which is more rare, means that a fetus is horizontal, lying across the uterus.

[3]Diethylstilbestrol, once taken by women to prevent miscarriage, a practice ceased in the early 1970s when DES was discovered to cause reproductive-tract abnormalities in daughters of women who took the drug.

Fetuses' presentations can be ascertained through examination or ultrasonography. Vaginal breech births can be dangerous because of possible damage to the baby, umbilical cord, or placenta during delivery.

In about half of all twin presentations, both babies are vertex; in 25 percent, the first twin is vertex and the second is breech; and in the remaining 25 percent, the first baby is breech and the second is vertex. Occasionally, guided by ultrasound, and depending on the babies' gestational age and the mother's wishes, a doctor can turn the second twin into vertex position by externally massaging the woman's abdomen after the first twin is born (the *version* technique), or, less commonly, by internally manipulating the baby into position. If successful, the second twin can be born vaginally, too. A breech twin sometimes can be delivered vaginally without being turned. A twin in transverse lie must always be turned into a vertical position, either head-down or breech. In some instances, the first twin is delivered vaginally, the other by cesarean.

Although there have been successful vaginal births of triplets, most physicians believe that triplets and more should be delivered by cesarean section since there is a higher risk of umbilical cord entanglement, "locking" of heads, and other complications; it is also virtually impossible to monitor each baby fully.

## Tests to Assess Fetal Complications

Following are prenatal tests used to detect chromosomal and other abnormalities, such as Down syndrome, metabolic disorders, hemophilia, neural-tube defects such as spina bifida, and other serious problems. Sometimes such disorders may affect one fetus and not the other(s).

*Amniocentesis* involves taking a sample of amniotic fluid from the uterus through a needle guided by ultrasound. The test can be performed around the sixteenth week of pregnancy. Make sure the doctor who performs the amniocentesis is experienced with pregnancy with multiples and therefore highly skillful in guiding the needle.

While the ultrasound itself can diagnose multiples, amniocentesis can detect chromosomal abnormalities and neural-tube defects. Late in pregnancy amniocentesis can also determine fetal lung maturity or relieve polyhydramnios, an excessive accumulation of amniotic fluid that may affect one or more of the fetuses. Amniocentesis also reveals the fetuses' gender(s). If you do not want to know the gender(s), tell the doctor and nurse in advance so they will not ruin the surprise for you. Others are delighted to know:

*"I knew from amniocentesis that I was going to have a boy and a girl. My husband and I named them while they were still in the womb, and talked to them. I knew where each twin was located. I already felt very close to them."*

Amniocentesis presents a small risk of miscarriage or leaking membranes. Rarely, the needle can injure the fetus.

**An Alpha-Fetoprotein Test**   analyzes a woman's blood (usually drawn from her arm) or amniotic fluid (obtained through amniocentesis, see above) to reveal any fetal brain and spinal-cord abnormalities (neural-tube defects) such as spina bifida. In some cases, spina bifida can be surgically corrected.

**Chorionic-Villi Biopsy**   detects chromosomal disorders and is guided by ultrasonography. Performed at about the eighth week of pregnancy, it involves obtaining a small sample of placental cells through the cervix. It is slightly more likely to produce miscarriage than amniocentesis and may also contribute to fetal limb or other defects. Infrequently, it may lead to infection or uterine perforation.

**Ultrasonography**   (sonogram) is used to:

- diagnose multiple pregnancy
- determine causes of pelvic pain, vaginal bleeding, and frequent miscarriage
- determine gestational age
- diagnose ectopic pregnancy
- diagnose a missed or incomplete miscarriage, fibroids, or other tumors
- guide amniocentesis, chorionic-villi biopsy, and fetal blood sampling
- determine the position of the fetuses

*Fetal Blood Sampling*   draws blood from the umbilical cord(s) to diagnose such disorders as anemia due to Rh isoimmunization, hemophilia, and sickle-cell anemia.

## When Fetal Complications Occur

If serious chromosomal or other abnormalities are found, a retest may be done to confirm the results. Parents can decide to continue the pregnancy, to abort, or to "selectively" abort only the fetus(es) with the disorder. Such decisions can be emotionally wrenching. A genetic counselor can support the decision-making process. If one twin is aborted or miscarries and the other survives, it is natural for parents, and later the surviving twin, to mourn the twin who was never known. All, however, should bear in mind that the technology that permitted one twin to survive is ultimately life-affirming.

## Pregnancy Reduction

The higher the number of fetuses, the greater the risk of prematurity. Prematurity is the foremost cause of infant death and can also lead to serious, often long-lasting, health problems. Since fertility drugs such as Pergonal can cause a woman to release a great many eggs, she may become pregnant with so many fetuses that none has a chance of survival. Some couples make the agonizing decision to have *pregnancy reduction,* selective abortion of one or more fetuses to increase the chance that the remaining one(s) will survive. Pregnancy reduction, like amniocentesis, poses some risk of miscarriage and other problems, which must be discussed with the physician.

Some women who have had a reduction were pregnant with anywhere from two to eight or more. Pregnancies have been reduced to triplets, twins, or singletons. Pregnancy reduction can give a couple the chance to have the babies they have always wanted. Yet the means to that end is painful and sad. For a couple who have struggled with years of infertility, an overabundance of fetuses is a bitter irony. If the pregnancy is not reduced, it may yield no live children, and they will continue to be childless. In order to have children, they must sacrifice fetuses that, at another time, they would wish to save.

Couples choose reduction not only to increase the chance of live birth, but of healthy children. They may be unwilling or unable to tolerate the emotional and financial hardships involved in raising children with disabilities. By reducing to fewer babies they hope to increase the chance of full-term birth of children who do not have serious health problems.

Recent research has shown that with excellent prenatal care, the outcome for triplets is virtually as good as for twins. Therefore, while physicians who perform pregnancy reductions will reduce four or more embryos to triplets, many are increasingly reluctant to reduce to twins, and virtually no physicians will reduce multiple pregnancies to only one.

One couple, pregnant with triplets, wanted a reduction—but disagreed on how many to reduce. They already had one child; the husband wanted only one more. His wife wanted twins. Their debate turned out to be moot, for their doctor's personal policy was that he would reduce a multiple pregnancy to twins but never to only one.

A mother of triplets, hearing that story, gasped. "But triplets are doable," she said. "I cannot imagine reducing my three to two."

Each woman's risk and personal circumstances are unique. She must consult her husband and doctor and make the decision that is right for her and her family.

## 🦋 Every Day, Nearer to the Birthing Day

*"I was enormous but tried to take a long walk daily. One day, a neighbor cracked, 'Boy, if I looked like you, I'd never leave the house.' I walked home and cried. At first I thought, If I really look so awful, maybe I should stay in. But then I got angry. How dare she say such a thing to me? My body was big, but it was big for the best two reasons in the world. The next day, I went out walking again."*

*"When I was pregnant with the triplets, I was so big I looked like a Volkswagen. On elevators men joked, 'I don't want to ride with you!' "*

When you are pregnant with multiples, you attract attention the way *they* will when they are born. Your growing size affects your life in many ways. As the babies push against your stomach, you may have heartburn and indigestion. You will feel more comfortable eating smaller quantities more frequently throughout the day. Maternity clothes may start to feel snug. Chairs are harder to get into and out of. You may not fit behind the wheel of your car. When you feel the babies move, these inconveniences fade in importance:

> *"I felt so joyful feeling one twin kicking below and the other kicking at the opposite end."*

> *"One day I worried that I didn't feel my girl moving. A friend suggested that I drink orange juice and lie down on my left side. Sure enough, the baby started kicking."*

Unseen but deeply felt, the relationship with your multiples unfolds physically and emotionally throughout the pregnancy. The expectant father, of course, does not have the twenty-four-hour-a-day coexistence with the babies that his partner has, but it is likely that they are never far from his mind.

For many men, thoughts are a revolving kaleidoscope: Will my wife be all right? Will the births go well? How will I feel, seeing the babies get born? How will we afford this? Did I buy the right shade of paint for the nursery? Should I rent a beeper so my wife can reach me when she goes into labor? When push comes to shove (so to speak), will I remember anything at all from childbirth classes? Can I take time off from work? Should I consider paternity leave? Who should go on my list of people to call? Where in the world did I *put* that list!

As the due date nears, every day is remarkable for its similarity to the day before—for its absence of labor. The suspense makes time feel very in-between. There is no going back, but no going forward yet, either. Until one day labor unmistakably begins—with a gush of amniotic fluid, or contractions in a series, or loss of the mucous plug, any or all of these preceded by or coinciding with backache or a general sense of not feeling well.

## ▨ Labor and Delivery

As pregnancy begins to draw to a close, you probably are anxious about how this pregnancy will transition into parenthood. Will you have a vaginal birth? A cesarean? One mother said, "I wanted my doctor to be in 'both worlds'—let me labor naturally, but be prepared if there are complications."

At the onset of labor, call your doctor for advice on whether you should continue labor at home for a while or go to the hospital right away. Much depends on whether your doctor classifies you as high-risk, how close you are to your due date, and how many babies you are having.

Every pregnancy is different. Every birth story is unique. There are so many variables. Labor may be spontaneous, induced, or accelerated. You may rely solely on Lamaze breathing and have no anesthesia, or you may request pain relief. Labor may be relatively brief or lengthy. Babies may be born vaginally, perhaps with no medical intervention, or perhaps with episiotomy (an incision from the vagina toward—but not into—the anus to ease birth and prevent tearing of vaginal and perineal tissue).

While the average interval between vaginal births of twins is twenty-five to thirty minutes, there is no specific "upper limit" on what the interval "should" be. Much depends on each baby's presentation, its condition as revealed by fetal monitoring, the position of the placenta, and other factors.

One or more babies may require forceps (large, gently curving tongs), or vacuum extraction (a process in which a cap is applied to the baby's head to create suction and help the baby slide out). Or they may need to be born by cesarean.

*"At thirty-seven weeks, I told the doctor, 'I can't take it anymore!' I was so physically uncomfortable, and I thought one of the triplets had stopped moving. My doctor agreed to do amniocentesis to measure the amount of lung surfactant in the fluid. The more surfactant in the fluid, the more likely the babies would be able to breathe adequately and do well outside the womb. He was able to get to two out of the three sacs, and each was okay. The next day I had a scheduled cesarean. The delivery room was like the state room scene in* Night at the Opera. *There were three neonatologists, three pediatricians, the obstetrician and some residents, nurses, and of course my husband. I thought we should sell tickets to all the observers.*

*"Because of the epidural, I felt, oddly, like I was being painlessly disemboweled. It didn't seem completely real until we heard the babies cry. One of the babies was snuggled so far inside my rib cage that the doctor had to really reach in for him.*

*"Sometimes I regret not experiencing labor. It is such a rite of pas-*

*sage. A cesarean is not equivalent. But I felt strongly that it was the right thing to do."*

Most women want a vaginal birth, so that they and their children have the experience, and so that they avoid the added recuperation time needed after a cesarean. Many do give birth to multiples vaginally, but it is important to be flexible about your expectations. Of course you want the best birthing experience—and ultimately *the "best" birthing experience is the one that gets the babies out safely and protects you as well.* During pregnancy, delivery often seems like *the* defining event, yet it is just one important part of the continuum of your children's lives and your own.

*"I was told that 'locking heads' was a potential problem because one twin was head-down, the other had feet-down, and neither was engaged. The doctors were worried that whichever twin moved to get born first could 'lock heads' with the other twin, and neither would get through. I would not believe them. I had my heart set on a vaginal delivery. I insisted on an X ray. Only after I saw the X ray—the two heads, the feet—did I consent to the cesarean, and I cried all the way through it."*

*"One twin was born vaginally with the midwife's help. The other was born by cesarean due to a problem with the heart rate. I just wanted them born."*

*"I had a full-page birth plan I was so proud of—requests for no IV, no anesthesia, and so on. One by one I had to cross off each item. I was so angry at first, but then I realized the bottom line: Save me and save the babies. Just let us all be healthy."*

Because of the higher possibility of cesarean with multiples, many women mistakenly assume that they will *not* get the birth they want. It is so common for twins to be born early and at low birth weights that some women are shocked to discover that this is by no means inevitable:

*"My due date was March 15, but I was so sure my twins would be delivered early that I had my bags packed in January. They weren't born until the end of March! I had a vaginal delivery with no painkillers.*
*"Even though they were late, I was still afraid they were underweight. Nervously, I asked the doctor if they were over five pounds. He*

*sounded so proud of himself: 'They are well over five pounds. One boy is eight pounds six ounces, and your little one is seven pounds ten ounces!'*

*"I was like a celebrity in that hospital! All the nurses came into my room to see the petite woman who had the huge twins."*

*"One of my babies was transverse, so they wheeled me into the delivery room in case I needed a cesarean. After the first twin was born vaginally, the doctor reached up inside me, broke my daughter's water sac, and moved her into position, while another doctor helped by manipulating from the outside. She was born vaginally, too."*

*"One twin was vertex, the other was breech, butt-first. The breech twin was born first, vaginally. It worked out great because the water bag was wedged in my cervix. The doctor joked, 'Watch out, everybody, it's going to blow!' When the water bag burst, the baby slid right out! Then the vertex baby was born."*

If you have had a baby before, you will probably notice that giving birth to multiples is a much more public event. A "three-ring circus" is how one nurse-midwife describes delivery of multiples:

*"Delivery of twins or more is not the calm, quiet, peaceful scenario that many parents of singletons experience. Even with vertex-vertex twins [who are both head-down and well-positioned for vaginal birth], there are usually two nurses for each baby, an anesthesiologist, a fetal monitor, an ultrasound machine, and so on. Sometimes women feel like they are surrounded by people who are waiting for something to go wrong.*

*"And then once the babies are born, everyone leaves! It's such a contrast! It's the woman's greatest moment, but the only people left are the woman, a nurse or two, and the dad—unless the babies have been taken to the nursery and he has gone with them."*

One couple described their own "three-ring circus":

SHE: *There was such a contrast between our son's birth and our twins' births. We had our son in a birthing suite at the hospital. It was a nice room, with a TV, a radio. It was a laid-back birth.*

PREGNANCY

*With the twins, they put us in a room on a ward right across from the nurses' station. The nurses kept coming in, one after another, checking the fetal monitor. We didn't get such attention the first time. I felt so dehydrated, I asked them to hook me up to an IV. It was the first time in the pregnancy that I really felt my thirst quenched. I had a tingly, cool feeling as the liquid from the IV pulsated through my veins.*

*At first, I went on Stadol to get me through the contractions. Then the pains were so irregular, they ordered Pitocin. But as soon as it arrived, the pains became regular! The doctor came in and said, "I see the Pitocin is working well." The nurse turned around and said, "I never gave her any."*

HE: *When she was ready, I stuck my head out the door and told everybody, "She's ready to push." Six people jumped up at one time. They gave me a suit to put on, and I met her in the operating room. They put her in stirrups. It was bright as a sunny day. There was equipment everywhere. My wife was laughing at how many people were there. I was at her right arm, a nurse was at her left. There were two doctors to deliver the babies, two pediatricians (one for each baby) and four nurses to assist them, an anesthesiologist, his assistant, and nurses to assist the obstetricians.*

SHE: *I couldn't stop laughing, even with the contractions. I asked for more Stadol, and they said, "No way." Our girl came out pretty quickly.*

HE: *I got to cut the umbilical cord. It was neat. I hadn't gotten to do that with our first child.*

SHE: *They put Pitocin in the IV to get the contractions going again for the second twin. The umbilical cord came down beside him. They had to move real quick to get him out. They used vacuum extraction. The doctor said, "Okay, you'll feel just a little pressure." He stuck a suction cup the size of my hand in my vaginal area, and I jumped and yelled, "Whoa!" But it worked so quickly, the baby crowned and was born.*

HE: *This time the doctor cut the cord. Our boy was definitely bluer than the girl. But everything was okay. Both babies got an eight or nine on the Apgar score [an assessment of newborns' appearance, reflexes, and breathing].*

*I was walking around, looking at the babies. I was just part of the crowd. Then I looked back over at my wife. The placentas had come out, and she was looking at them with the doctors. They were handling the placentas like children in a toy store playing with Play-Doh!"*

## ▩ Meeting Your Children

It took all these months for these babies to move from inside to outside. Now you finally get to see them (and not through sonogram). They may seem skinny, fragile; they may seem sturdy, able nursers from the start. One twin may be stronger than the other; two triplets may be larger than the third.

You have all been through so much together already—but as you hold them in your arms, or begin to breastfeed, or watch them being tended to by a nurse, or ponder whether they look alike, you realize: This is just the beginning.

# ✪ *Chapter 3*

# CHECKLISTS FOR PROSPECTIVE PARENTS: PLANNING FOR THE BABIES' BIRTH AND HOMECOMING

## ✪ *Checklist for the Expectant Mother*

- ☐ Get plenty of rest, eat well, and follow your doctor's advice about prenatal care, diet, and exercise.
- ☐ Keep a list of questions to ask your practitioner at prenatal visits. In addition, you may enjoy keeping a diary of your pregnancy.
- ☐ Buy nursing bras and loose-fitting postbirth clothing. If you plan to breastfeed, choose two-piece outfits and button- or zip-front blouses, nightgowns, and robes.

## ✪ *Responsibilities Both Parents Can Share*

There's a lot to be done. Along with the heightened physical and emotional stresses associated with bearing multiples will come the inevitable disagreements with your partner over issues large and small. Together, acknowledge the supreme importance of avoiding unnecessary strains that sap strengths and darken mood. Resolve to work together to plan and arrange the many details listed below. When you feel overwhelmed, remind yourselves that you are about to become members of an elite group who take much pride in being parents of multiples. Focus on the prize, and the details won't seem so endless.

## PLAN FOR YOUR OTHER CHILDREN'S NEEDS

☐ Help your children prepare for the new babies, arrange care for them while you are in the hospital, purchase gifts, etc. (See Chapter 4, "Preparing Children to Become Siblings of Multiples.")

☐ Ask if the hospital provides a tour for siblings-to-be.

## PLANNING FOR UPCOMING CHANGES

☐ Register for childbirth classes to attend together (ask your doctor for a recommendation).

☐ Select baby names. (See Chapter 8, "Naming Your Babies.")

☐ Spend some time discussing your respective feelings, concerns, and ideas. Speak with other parents of multiples.

☐ Try to anticipate and estimate expenses and plan for any potential reduction in income.

☐ Take advantage of this pre-babies time to enjoy being together, whether you go for a walk, dine at a romantic restaurant, or check out baby-supply stores.

## HOME PLANNING

☐ Plan the babies' room or space. Decide where you will place cribs, changing table, rocking chair, etc. Add a couch or cot if possible.

☐ Discuss whether painting, wallpapering, new carpeting, picture hanging, window coverings, or other preparation of the space is needed. (Moms-to-be: Do not paint, refinish or move furniture, or engage in strenuous physical labor unless you check with your doctor.)

☐ Make and freeze meals for the weeks following the births.


## AT WORK

☐ Get information on your employer's maternity, paternity, or family policies.

☐ Discuss with your supervisor and coworkers who will take over your work while you are on leave.

☐ Make contingency plans in case you need to stop work earlier than planned.

☐ Clarify what your health insurance will and will not cover.


## SHOPPING

☐ Shop for baby furniture, equipment, clothing, and supplies. Have purchases delivered now or ask the store to delay delivery and billing until the babies are born. Remember that they will need car seats, clothing, and hats for the drive home from the hospital. (See Chapter 11, "Equipment, Clothing, and Supplies.")

☐ Sign up with a "baby gift registry" at a local store or through a mail-order catalog that offers this service.

☐ Find out which neighborhood pharmacies, grocery stores, and other stores and restaurants deliver. Collect take-out menus.

☐ Stock up on camera film and videocamera cassettes.

☐ Buy thank-you notes.

☐ Purchase or order birth announcements (phone in the babies' names to the printer after they are born). Remember to include your older children's names on the announcements. Prepare mailing labels in advance, or check off names in your address book and have a friend do the labels.

☐ If you are interested in a diaper service, call several for information and to compare prices.

## ARRANGING EVENTS

☐ Have a relative or friend throw a "babies' shower" now or plan one for after the babies are born. (See Chapter 19, "Getting Help from Family and Friends.")

☐ If you plan any religious ceremonies for the babies, get information on what arrangements will need to be made. (See Chapter 17, "Siblings of Multiples," for information on how to include older siblings.)

## ARRANGE FOR HELP, SUPPORT, AND SERVICES

☐ Select a pediatrician. (See Chapter 13, "Selecting and Visiting the Pediatrician.")

☐ Line up as much help as you can from friends and family. (See Chapter 19, "Getting Help from Family and Friends.")

☐ If possible, hire a baby nurse or a baby-sitter to assist you. (See Chapter 20, "Baby-sitters and Other Parents' Helpers.")

☐ Find out whether there is a Mothers of Twins Club in your community. Call for information and names of members you can talk with for advice and support. Ask if you may attend a meeting. (See Chapter 21, "Mothers of Twins Clubs and Other Resources.")

☐ If you plan to breastfeed, contact La Leche League and/or a certified lactation consultant. (See Chapter 9, "Breastfeeding.")

☐ If you plan to use a day-care center when you return to work, research which centers are available, at what age they accept children, their licensing, cost, staff, facilities, parking, etc. Some day-care centers are so popular that they have a waiting list, and you should sign up early in the pregnancy. One woman, after taking a home pregnancy test, called her town's best day-care center even before calling her doctor.

## THE HOSPITAL

☐ Tour the hospital where you will give birth. Ask to see the nursery. Many parents whose babies were born prematurely also recommend visiting the neonatal intensive-care unit, so you can be prepared in the event that your babies will need it.

☐ Find out visiting policies.

☐ Consider preparing a "birth plan" for your doctor and the hospital to keep on file. List your preferences about such issues as:

    ☐ the presence of your partner at delivery

    ☐ prepping (e.g., Would you rather not have an enema? Do you have any objections to being shaved?)

    ☐ mobility (Do you want to be able to walk around during labor and try different positions during pushing and childbirth?)

    ☐ anesthesia (Do you want to avoid or take pain medication?)

    ☐ rooming-in (Do you want full- or part-time access to the babies?)

    ☐ breastfeeding (Do you want the babies to be exclusively breastfed, to receive formula, or both?)

    ☐ allowing the babies' sibling(s) to visit, if this is not standard hospital policy

☐ If possible, complete admissions and health-insurance paperwork in advance.

## ARRANGE TRANSPORTATION TO THE HOSPITAL

☐ Have a backup plan. Even if you plan to drive to the hospital, arrange in advance for a ride with a neighbor in case your car breaks down. Have the phone number of a taxi service handy, too.

☐ Plan your route to the hospital.

☐ Work out a way to contact your spouse. Some couples use beepers.

## PACK THE HOSPITAL BAG

Include:

☐ phone numbers of people to call from the hospital
☐ a robe (easy to open for breastfeeding), socks, slippers (perhaps a bed jacket, for an extravagant touch)
☐ comb, brush, toothbrush and toothpaste, other toiletries and makeup
☐ book or magazines
☐ checklist of things to add just before you go (e.g., eyeglasses, camera, film, batteries, camcorder)
☐ a notebook and pen (Use these to record thoughts, feelings, questions for doctors, lists of things to do, tasks to delegate, and gifts to acknowledge. You may even wish to have one notebook for each baby.)
☐ quilts or receiving blankets (depending on the weather), two sets of clothing per child, including a warm hat or sun hat
☐ nursing bras
☐ maternity or other roomy clothes to wear home (Do not expect to fit into prepregnancy clothing just after giving birth; it takes time for your figure to return to normal.)

# Chapter 4

# PREPARING CHILDREN TO BECOME SIBLINGS OF MULTIPLES

*"... certain courtesies are owed to existing children. One of them is not the senseless but ubiquitous inquiry 'How would you like a little brother or sister?' to which an honest answer would be 'Like a hole in the head." Propaganda is what is required here ... until the child is actually half convinced that the project is partly his idea, and will be to his advantage. After the birth, this is sustained by giving the older child as many ceremonial duties and honors as possible."[1]*

You were their parents first. They have laid claim to you—to your lap, to your morning kisses, to your attention. When the new babies arrive, the number of children having claim to you will increase—exponentially!

But there is much you can do to prepare siblings for the new arrivals and to ease their adjustment once the babies are born. Honoring their status as older siblings helps them come to accept and love the newcomers.

[1]Judith Martin, *Miss Manners' Guide to Rearing Perfect Children* (New York: Atheneum Publishers, 1984).

## ▣ When to Tell Children About the Pregnancy

Children can be charmingly, flabbergastingly oblivious. With each month of your pregnancy, you see your belly mushrooming large, larger, even *larger,* like an astonishing *Alice in Wonderland* transformation. And all your little child notices is the pretty new barrette in your hair!

Yet the fact remains that while you have been observing your children all their lives, they have been observing you right back. So even if they do not seem to notice the watermelon under your T-shirt, they may sense that something is up. Many children read their parents' faces with the keen-eyed know-how of farmers scanning the ever-changing sky for news of the weather: "Something is way far out there on the horizon. . . . Hard to tell yet just *what* it is, but no doubt about it, I can just *feel* that the atmosphere around here is going to change."

Well, that something on the horizon is a big old wing-flapping, babies-toting stork. Change in the family atmosphere *is* imminent, and at some point the children must be told.

Just when to tell them about the babies on the horizon is a decision on which families differ greatly. Many parents tell as early as possible, for several reasons:

*The Pregnancy Affects Everyone in the Family,* and all family members need time to assimilate the news and express their feelings about it. And if labor happens prematurely, it is better for children to know what is happening than to learn at this time that Mom is pregnant.

*Parents Don't Want the Pressure of Having to Keep Such a Major Matter Hushed.* They want to be able to take a phone call without huddling in a closet.

*One Cannot Count On Adults to Be Oblivious to Your Extravagantly Blossoming Shape.* The first time you step out in maternity clothes, some well-meaning neighbor is sure to cry, "Oh, you're pregnant again! When are you due? You're so big, I bet you're having twins." There! The news is spilled, and your child is taken aback, confused, and reproachful. Better to give your child a well-thought-out, loving explanation early on in the pregnancy—and to avoid the risk that someone will spill the news.

> *"We knew we were having twins by the fifth week of pregnancy. We told our son first—and we knew as soon as he knew, he would tell everyone. We showed him the picture from the sonogram. 'See these two little circles? These are twins!'*
>
> *"It never crossed our minds not to tell him as soon as possible. It wouldn't be fair not to tell him. We wouldn't want the problem of other people blurting it out. If anything had gone wrong with the pregnancy, we would have dealt with it."*

Other parents prefer to delay delivering the news until they absolutely have to. Their reasons include the following:

*Young Children Have Little Sense of Time.* Nine months (or eight, or seven) may seem an eternity to them. To mitigate the suspense, some parents would rather wait until some time in or closer to the third trimester, when birth is more imminent. (One solution: Mark a calendar to help children understand how much time is—probably—left.)

*Parents May Wait Until They Are Sure the Pregnancy Will Proceed Well.* Perhaps they have a history of miscarriage and want to make sure the pregnancy is strongly established before announcing it. Or, as Barbara Katz Rothman described in *The Tentative Pregnancy* (see the Bibliography), some couples do not allow themselves to feel emotionally attached to a pregnancy until prenatal tests are completed and the results found favorable. If they are not certain the pregnancy will be carried to term, they do not want to announce it to their children.

*Parents Expecting Multiples Often Worry That the Babies May Be Born Prematurely, or That One Twin Will Survive and Not the Other.* They wish to spare their children the ups and downs and anxieties that they fear may lie ahead.

Other factors in the decision of when to tell are the ages and maturity of the children and what is happening in their lives. If a child has just started nursery school, moved to a new home, or gotten chicken pox, it is probably better to wait until things settle down a bit before divulging another major change to come.

## ▨ *Pregnancy: A Family Experience*

*"When I was pregnant with the twins, my daughter couldn't believe I was pregnant with two! She asked, 'How do they fit in there? Do you have two babies kicking? Isn't it tight in there?' I said, 'It sure is!'"*

So you have told your children that two (or more) babies are growing in your uterus, and that they will be joining the family— and that your current children will always be your beloved babies, too. This is just the beginning of many talks you will have over the coming months, for there will be many new things to get used to and learn about. Spend as much time with your children as you can, making yourself available for questions and ruminating about what life with multiples will be like.

Try to involve your children in the pregnancy:

- Let them place their hands on your belly and feel the babies move.
- Have your children join you for a prenatal visit and listen to the babies' heartbeats.
- Take them with you to shop for baby furniture, layette, or maternity clothes (plus maybe a small toy for each child), then go out for lunch together afterward.
- Have children make or buy a gift for each new baby, such as an undershirt they decorate with fabric paint or a small stuffed animal. They can bring the gifts with them when they visit the hospital.
- Let them help decorate the nursery and make paintings to hang on the wall.
- Together, cook meals and bake muffins, cupcakes, or a "welcome home" cake to freeze now and eat after the babies are born.
- Sign up for a siblings tour of the hospital, if one is offered.
- If you need extended bed rest during pregnancy, anticipate your children's disappointment that you cannot drive them to school or walk them to the park. Make your bedroom a welcoming

family meeting place. Set up a card table for the children's puzzles, crayons, and storybooks.
• Look through family albums and reminisce about when your children were babies. Describe how excited you were when pregnant with *them*.

## ▨ Advance Planning

Pregnancy is a time to plan ahead for the babies *and* for the children you already have:

***Decide Who Will Care for the Children When You Go to the Hospital and Whom You Can Ask to Spend Special Time with Them Once the Babies Are Born.*** You will be very busy. Consider arranging with a friend, relative, or neighborhood teenager to spend regular, scheduled time with your children, such as twice a week after school or every Saturday morning. They can visit the playground or library, go for a walk, or just play with toys at home. If the person is not familiar to your children, begin the arrangement while you are pregnant to make sure your children enjoy and feel comfortable with their "playmate."

***If Possible, Anticipate and Minimize Upheaval in Your Children's Lives Around the Time of the Birth.*** For example, try not to have them switch schools or teachers, wean from a bottle, toilet-train, change bedrooms, or give up a crib at the same time they are coping with this major change at home. Work on such changes while you are pregnant or postpone these goals until at least six months after the babies are born.

***Make or Buy Small Gifts to Take to the Hospital to Give Your Children When They Come to Visit the Babies.*** Also have gifts ready at home, both to celebrate your homecoming and to balance the gifts the babies will receive.

***Buy, Wrap, and Label Gifts Early*** so you will not be caught unprepared if your child's birthday or Christmas or Hanukkah falls within a couple of months of your due date.

Amid the atmosphere of pleasurable anticipation, be realistic with the children about what they can expect. You do not want them to get the impression that bouncy, laughing, TV-diaper-ad babies are coming home from the hospital with you—and then be disappointed by the delicate newborns.

Yes, talk about how much fun it will be to have new brothers and sisters. But also explain that new babies are very little and fragile. Unlike big children, infants cannot talk. They will need to cry to let their family know that they need to be fed, changed, or held. They will have to eat more often, so they will wake up at night. They will not be able to sit or stand or run and will need to be handled very gently. However, with your support, children *will* be able to cuddle and stroke the babies and hold their hands, sing to the babies, and be your helpers.

Prepare your children—without unduly alarming them—for the fact that babies keep everyone in the family very busy. Sometimes you might have to tend to the babies when your children want you to play. But reassure them that you will still—will always—have time for them, too. And to the best of your ability, when the babies come, make sure that promise comes true.

# ❦ Chapter 5

# ℐF BABIES ARE PREMATURE

*"I bought so many premie socks, and bows to Velcro to my daughters' hair. That's all they wore, socks and ribbons, until there was enough room between the tapes and the wires to start dressing them in clothes."*

❦ Prematurely born multiples (born prior to thirty-seven weeks gestation) may need the special medical care and equipment of a hospital's neonatal intensive-care unit, or NICU (pronounced *nik-you*). Here, specially trained staff—neonatologists (physicians who specialize in the care, development, and diseases of newborns), nurses, respiration therapists, social workers, etc.—work as a team to address the unique needs of "premies" and their families.

Parents, of course, as the most important people in their babies' lives, are a crucial part of the team. Depending on the babies' condition, either from the beginning or during the course of their stay in the NICU, parents can stroke, speak to, hold, and cuddle their babies, bottlefeed or breastfeed or express breast milk for tube- or bottlefeeding, diaper, and assist with babies' care under the supervision and instruction of the NICU staff.

81

*Under supervision of staff . . .* hardly the beginning to parenthood that most people envision. It can be distressing and disorienting to see your babies in isolettes, the incubators that provide controlled temperature and humidity. What can help counterbalance your anxiety is the knowledge that medical advances such as surfactant replacement therapy and other treatments (described later in this chapter) have dramatically increased the odds that low-birth-weight premature babies will survive and enjoy long-term health.

Only a couple of decades ago, just 10 percent of babies weighing less than three pounds survived. Today, in a stunning reversal of that statistic, more than 90 percent of these babies survive, according to Judy L. Aschner, M.D., associate professor of pediatrics, Albany Medical College, and attending neonatologist at Albany Medical Center. The chances of survival for even the tiniest babies have improved. About 50 percent of babies weighing 500 to 750 grams (about 1 pound, 2 ounces to 1 pound, 10 ounces) will survive. Of these, about 20 to 25 percent will have a chronic medical problem or disability; the majority will go home with intact neurological exams and good prognoses.

The types of treatments and lengths of stay in the NICU vary depending on the gestational age of the infants and the development of complications of prematurity or complications related to the therapy they receive. Most supportive therapies prescribed by neonatologists are temporary, such as aid with breathing, feeding, and temperature regulation, until the child "catches up" developmentally within days, weeks, or months, and can do these things independently. Sometimes medical or surgical treatments are needed to remedy or ameliorate problems associated with prematurity. By the time the majority of premies are ready for discharge to home, they do not need special equipment or medical care. They can be treated like normal, healthy infants.

## ▨ Risks and Resources

Twins are more likely than single fetuses to be delivered prematurely, although most twins are delivered at or close to term. With triplets, quads, and more, the incidence of prematurity rises almost exponentially: the more fetuses there are in the uterus, the higher the risks of premature birth.

Some parents consult with a neonatologist if they know they are at risk of premature delivery; most meet the neonatologist during premature labor. The neonatologist can explain the types of difficulties prematurely born babies may experience and the treatments available.

Many parents have found it valuable to have a tour of the NICU during pregnancy. One mother said that the tour motivated her to get more bed rest; a woman in labor at thirty weeks was reassured when a nurse held up a thirty-week-gestation baby for her to see.

A mother who did *not* see the NICU in advance expressed regret: "The NICU should be part of every hospital tour. Seeing it would have helped to prepare me for this experience." Like many women, she did not see a neonatologist until the onset of premature labor, and her first exposure to the NICU was when her own babies were in it.

Expectant parents who know or suspect birth will be premature should also explore the possibility of delivering at a regional care center. Usually found at teaching hospitals, RCCs are Level III hospitals, i.e., they have all of the supportive services that might be needed, such as a NICU, the capability of neonatal surgery, consultive services, pediatric anesthesiologists, etc., as well as the added capability of transporting newborns to the hospital. Whenever possible, advises Dr. Aschner, extremely premature babies (less than thirty weeks gestation) should be delivered in these hospitals, since outcomes are better for "in-born" infants than for babies who had to endure the stress of being transported from another hospital. And since the mother may not be transported along with her babies, giving birth in the regional care center hospital ensures that the mother will be able to visit her babies, and that her husband and other family or friends will not need to shuttle between two hospitals.

"When I first found out I was pregnant, I went to a local ob/gyn who has a small birthing center in a beautiful Victorian house. I thought it would be a lovely place to give birth. But when we learned I was having triplets, the doctor insisted on referring me to a high-risk pregnancy specialist in a Level III hospital that had a NICU.

"At first I was upset, but later I realized that if I had delivered my kids at the birthing center, or even at the local community hospital, I don't think they would have lived to be transported to the Level III hospital. And they certainly would not have had the team of four—for each *baby—that the Level III hospital provided.*

*"Even if the babies could have been transferred, I would have been left behind. They usually don't transport the mom, just the babies. I'd have been left alone, while my husband was with the babies.*

*"My advice to women is that if you know you are at risk of delivering prematurely, make sure you deliver at a Level III hospital—even if you have to get into an ambulance or a helicopter in order to get there."*

## ▣ *Where to Stay*

When babies need to stay in the NICU for extended periods of time, parents may need to consider how to handle the logistics of visiting them if they live far from the hospital. Three couples who had premature twins at around the same time, same hospital, had three different solutions.

One couple, who lived an hour from the hospital, chose the long daily commute. "The drive gave me thinking time," said the mother, "and being home with my husband gave us some semblance of normal life."

Another couple stayed at a Ronald McDonald House near the hospital:

*"The Ronald McDonald House was like staying at a second home, within walking distance of the hospital. It's a real good resource. We live in a rural area, and it was great to be able to stay there, for a very low fee. Occasionally local businesses would come by and donate food—some pizzas, or some rolls and Danishes for breakfast."*

A third couple, discovering that the Ronald McDonald House was full, asked the hospital social worker to help them find a low-cost bed-and-breakfast. (Some families have also discovered that when a Ronald McDonald House is full or restricted to families of children with specific medical problems, such as cancer, nearby hotels often give discounts to parents who explain the situation.)

## ▣ *The NICU Experience*

Parents of multiples in the NICU may feel like they are on two or more emotional roller-coaster rides simultaneously, as they follow each baby's progress. Joys and fears overlap when parents find themselves celebrating one child's improvement while worrying about another's continued struggle. It takes all of parents' faith, strength, and optimism to cope with the stress of waiting to see how their babies will fare in this brand-new world of medical marvels.

One challenge parents face, at a time when they struggle with fear and fatigue, is the need to take a "crash course" in the new technology on which their children's lives depend. They must quickly learn a new language, a new vocabulary, so they can communicate with the physicians and nurses in whose hands their children's futures lie.

For example, parents must learn to decipher such jargon as:

*"What's the Baby's Gas?"*   This refers to a test to find out the levels of oxygen and carbon dioxide in the arterial blood, commonly performed when babies have signs of respiratory distress.

*"We Need to Do a Dextrostick."*   This refers to taking blood from a baby's heel or finger—a "heel- or finger-stick"—to find out the level of sugar in the blood.

*"The Baby's Having A's and B's."*   "A" refers to apnea, a twenty-second pause in breathing. "B" refers to bradycardia, a drop in the baby's heart rate.

*"The Baby's Having Decels and Desats."*   A "decel" is a deceleration, or drop, of the baby's heart rate, a condition called bradycardia. A "desat" refers to a drop in the oxygen saturation revealed by an oximeter, a noninvasive device attached to a baby's hand or foot. The device is often used for babies who have apnea.

Parents learn to ask many questions: "What is that tube called? What does that device measure? How is this chart set up? What is that fluid? Why does the baby need this monitor?" By the time babies are ready to come home, some parents can decipher charts and handle certain equipment almost as expertly as the staff.

Yet the intellectual challenge of learning "NICU talk" does not hold a candle to the emotional challenge of coping with the suspense, loss of control, and anxiety of the NICU experience. Parents often express such feelings as:

*"I Feel Like They Are Not Really My Babies."*   When babies are in the intensive-care unit, there is always at least one nurse around—and it is the nurse's turf, not yours. Parents often feel frustrated that they cannot do what they want, when they want to. They must check their spontaneous impulse to hold their babies or change a diaper. They may not feed their babies until given the okay.

However, when parents are able to hold or stroke their babies, it means the world to them—and to the infants, who thrive on the contact and closeness.

> *"The NICU staff was very positive. They said our triplets were doing as well as any twenty-seven-week triplets they had ever seen. To help me realize that the babies were not totally fragile, a NICU nurse had me slide my hand underneath the babies' bodies just so I could feel that they had weight. Two pounds does weigh something. I began to feel that two pound babies didn't look small—it was just that normal babies looked enormous.*
>
> *"The staff really made us feel that our children were human beings, were even feisty. One day a nurse said that my daughter had a 'temper tantrum' earlier that day; when they tried to do a medical procedure she didn't like, she held her breath.*
>
> *" 'You mean she had apnea?' I asked.*
>
> *" 'No, she actually held her breath!' the nurse said. 'She was mad!' "*

*"It Pains Me to Feel the Babies' Pain."*   Parents witness their babies' pain, whether from blood sampling or disease processes. Parents suffer to see their babies subjected to invasive treatments, even though they know they are necessary.

But do not feel you must watch procedures that make you squeamish, uncomfortable, or afraid. You do not need to watch in order to prove your love. Some parents feel more comfortable than others around medical procedures. Also, in some cases, parents who get very emotional may distract physicians or nurses and interfere with their ability to complete a procedure.

*"It Is Hard to Entrust My Children to Strangers."*   For months the babies were inside you. Now they are in strangers' hands, and you have no choice but to trust them. A parent of babies born at twenty-eight weeks gestation cried, "My babies are so small, they

can't even cry or eat. I have to entrust them to these people I do not even know and hope they will love the babies, too." Most parents develop good, even close, relationships with neonatologists, nurses, and other staff, but people's personalities differ. Some staff can be more likable, helpful, and encouraging than others—and some parents can be less trusting, more possessive, and less patient with hospital procedures. In the NICU, as in the world at large, both medical personnel and parents can display a range of human emotions.

*"I Am Desperate for Reassurance and Support."* When a child or adult is ill, relatives and friends usually know how to offer support. But when babies are premature, many people feel uncomfortable, scared, and unsure of how to respond. Not knowing the "right" thing to say, some say nothing. They leave the parents alone, not to isolate them, but because of their own awkwardness. One mother was especially upset by those who sent no baby gifts:

> *"It makes you feel like your kids don't exist when people send nothing. It's like they're waiting to see if the kids die. I feel like saying, send gifts when kids are born, send condolence cards if they die. If one child dies, then the other will get two outfits. If both kids die, I can always give the gifts away to other babies. At least I would have had the pleasure of having their births acknowledged."*

If only people realized that there are so many ways they can help. They can visit; if NICU rules restrict visitors to only parents (and perhaps grandparents), friends can still offer to meet them for coffee or dinner in the hospital cafeteria to provide a much-needed respite.

Friends and family can also drive parents to the hospital, offer assistance with the couple's other children, buy groceries, provide meals, run errands, send flowers, cards, gifts, or just make a phone call—and leave an encouraging message on the answering machine if the parents are not home.

The right thing to say? All people need to do is congratulate the parents on the births, ask how the parents are doing, ask how the babies are faring. It is especially nice if, instead of asking, "How are the twins?" people use the babies' names. This acknowledges that each is a special individual.

What people say is less important than their willingness to listen. Some avoid talking about the babies so parents don't get upset. But most parents love and need to talk about their children—whatever their age, whatever their situation.

*"I Rely So Much on My Relationship with the NICU Nurses. They Really Understand What Is Going On."*   In most hospitals, when a child is in the NICU, he or she is assigned a primary nurse. Every time that nurse is on duty, she cares for *that* baby. This is done for consistency, for the family's sake, and for the nurse herself—so she can develop an attachment, see the benefits of her care, and witness the baby's growth and strength. The nurse really gets to know "her" baby.

For example, premies are often "difficult feeders." Even at this very young age, these children have individual temperaments and preferences. It is important to learn how an individual child likes to eat. A NICU nurse described how babies vary:

> *"One baby may take five cc's and burp, while another takes a full ounce. There are different types, sizes, and textures of nipples, and babies often have a preference. If we run out of breast milk, it is important to know what type of formula the baby tolerates best. We also need to know how well a baby tolerates being held, and what length of time the baby can tolerate away from a heat source."*

The nurse's knowledge affirms the baby's specialness. A parent feels more confident when the nurse knows this child's individual "ways." Details mean everything.

But sometimes a parent can feel intimidated or upset when a nurse knows the child so well. Nurses sometimes overhear parents mutter, "She thinks *she* is the baby's mom!" Other parents, however, simply feel relieved that their baby is in competent, caring, and knowledgeable hands.

When parents chafe at the nurse's intimate knowledge of their child, nurses often encourage, even push, parents to become more involved themselves. A nurse might say, "She needs a diaper change," or "How do you want to feed him this time?" For example, many mothers pump and store breast milk. Depending on age and weight, a baby may be able to nurse or bottlefeed, then finish feeding by tube, or be cuddled while tube-fed. By giving the parent some say in the matter, when possible, a nurse can affirm that the parents, after all, are and will always be the most important people in that child's life.

Conversely, if parents do not feel involved enough, they should feel free to express this feeling to the nurse, who may not be aware of their desire to participate more in their children's care.

In some cases, the main reassurance parents get is from the nurses. One neonatologist, in fact, said she rarely gets a chance to give parents good news because nurses are so eager to convey it first!

When problems arise, however, the parents are usually referred to the neonatologist in charge of the babies' care. The more complicated or serious the problem, the more important it is that consistent information from a single authority be provided to the family. Usually this person is the attending neonatologist. Parents who think they are receiving mixed messages from other hospital staff should request a conference with the attending neonatologist and establish a single line of communication.

A kind of symbiosis sometimes develops between parents and their babies' primary nurses: Parents crave the nurses' attention to their babies, and the nurses in turn are warmed by the parents' concern. The nurses explain the medical care and offer encouragement; the parents deepen their knowledge, become more involved in the children's care, and develop an appreciation for the nurses' dedication and skill.

The relationship with each baby's primary nurse may be especially intense because attending physicians and residents often rotate, perhaps changing month to month, while the nurses remain constant. Especially in a teaching hospital, where having so many different faces around can be confusing, parents often latch onto the primary nurse as a source of familiarity and comfort.

One NICU nurse described the "NICU nurse personality":

*"Other nurses and doctors think of us as overprotective. They gossip about us. They say we baby our parents too much, and spoil them. A lot of premies come back as pediatric patients, but it's just not the same. In the NICU, there is such close contact. In pediatrics, it's a little looser."*

After "graduating" from the NICU, many parents stay in touch with the nurses:

*"We often hear from parents through their babies' first year. They call us with questions, send photos. The contact usually wanes after the first*

*birthday, except for Christmas, holidays, birthdays. It is very special for us to keep up friendships with parents."*

Many parents, with their babies, go back to visit the NICU from time to time:

*"Every three months, I have to go back to the hospital with my children for a medical test. I always take the babies to the hospital nursery. I love keeping in touch with the nurses—and I also want other parents to see my 'success stories' so they can keep their hopes up for their own babies. I tell them my kids were born at twenty-eight weeks, weighing two pounds, two ounces each. And now look at them walking, talking, and carrying on!"*

One couple developed such a close relationship with NICU nurses, and became so aware that the nurses themselves needed appreciation from both parents and hospital, that after their babies' homecoming they donated funds to refurbish the nursing staff room, complete with microwave oven and new, comfortable furniture. The couple also donated their daughters' outgrown "premie clothes" to the NICU, where the nurses kept a clothing bin for low-income parents who could not afford premie outfits.

**"I Can't Believe It. The Comparisons Have Already Begun."** Parents who vowed they would never compare their multiples may feel chagrined that the comparisons begin in the nursery. Parents find they are labeling one twin as the "big, strong one" and the other as the "delicate one," and comparing their progress.

Nurses, too, sometimes compare babies' progress. They sometimes joke, "Ha, mine gained an ounce," or "Well, *my* baby graduated from the respirator." While a little banter can lighten things up for everyone, if it is habitual, it can cause the parents also to get into the habit of comparing the children.

**"I Am So Frustrated. They Put the Babies in Different Nurseries!"** Many hospitals have the policy that premature multiples should be separated to assure sufficient focus on each baby's care. Often there is not enough space or staff in a single nursery to handle two or more very fragile babies. If there are three nurses per room, one is assigned to a particular baby, but the other two nurses can come to that nurse's aid if their own babies are more stable. If multiples are in the same nursery, it may not be as possible to give each the same attention.

It can be hard for parents to shuttle between different nurseries, and the inconvenience may even seem cruel. Yet there are unexpected advantages. For example, parents are not usually allowed in the nursery when nurses do bedside reports, when shifts change, when doctors do rounds, if another baby in the nursery is in critical condition, or when certain medical procedures are being done. If their babies are in different nurseries, the parents can visit one baby while another is temporarily off-limits.

Parents also get to see different nurses and gain different perspectives, insights, and knowledge. And as one parent said, when one baby is doing better, it is easier to rejoice if the more frail twin is in a different room.

*"I Feel Overwhelmed by the Loss of Control."*   Some parents who are used to being in control feel upset that the neonatologists and nurses are the people in charge. Some parents overreact. One parent watched a nurse's every move and picked apart her actions: "Can you please not slam that door!"

In this way, parents may take out their fears and apprehension on the staff, but always, a cooperative and collaborative approach is best for everyone, especially the children.

*"It Is Hard to Leave."*   A NICU nurse said, "Ninety percent of parents worry about leaving the NICU." When babies have been on apnea monitors, parents get used to that little mechanical baby-sitter checking the heartbeat. And when expert nursing care was present twenty-four hours a day, parents about to take their babies home cry, "Oh, my God, I'm on my own here!"

Do not hesitate to call the nurses. They are accustomed to calls, and they know your children. One nurse said:

> *"Parents call us with all sorts of questions: 'No bowel movements in two days, what should I do?' Or, 'The baby has been sleeping for five hours now, should I wake her?' Or, 'The baby is screaming. I fed and changed him. Is he in pain?'*
>
> *"Many parents don't really know their babies yet. We can ask the*

*parents questions about eating, sleeping, and so on, and we may be able to say, 'Oh, that baby never had a B.M. more than every three days anyway.' If we feel any doubt, we refer the parents to their pediatrician. Some parents worry about asking their doctor 'silly questions' and feel less reluctant to ask the nurse. Or they don't want to awaken the doctor at night, but they know we are awake and at work! After the first couple of weeks out of the hospital, most parents bond more with their doctor and call us less. But we are always happy to take their calls."*

## Bonding

"Love at first sight" is a captivating notion, but it is neither a sound basis for lasting romantic love nor a requirement for parent-child bonding. The popular belief that there is one right time and way to bond—in the hours and days after birth—is an unfair burden for parents denied the opportunity for such requisite cuddling. For example, if their infants are premature, parents snared by such a bonding theory may fear they have missed out on some magic "click," as if it were a phenomenon that happens on a fixed schedule. When a child is connected with lifesaving equipment, parents may not be able to hold and feed the child for quite a while. But there is no magic time period for bonding, and there is no expiration date on bonding opportunities.

If one baby comes home first, parents may feel a stronger bond with that baby and fear they will never bond equally with the baby whose homecoming is delayed. You may, in fact, need to concentrate more on the child who comes home later, in order to get to know that child and feel close. But do shake free of the idea that there is one right time and way to bond with your baby. All intimate relationships grow and deepen on the basis of cumulative shared experiences.

*"I had no problems through my pregnancy until the ninth month, when I developed very high blood pressure and was ordered into the hospital. A few days after a successful cesarean section, my blood pressure sky-rocketed again, causing seizures. Eclampsia was not diagnosed promptly; if it had been, it could have been alleviated by the proper drugs. I was in the hospital several weeks but was transferred out of the maternity wing. Meanwhile, the twins were released in seven days, cared for at home by their father and grandparents. My mother took the day*

*shift, my husband and father took the night shift. The twins were always waking up. It was bedlam.*

*"My separation from the babies was agonizing for me. I was concerned about whether we would bond, given the time apart. When I came home from the hospital, I grabbed both babies, one in each arm, and burst into tears. In that one moment it was clear: Together again, our bond was unquestionable."*

## ⚙ The Ups and Downs of the Long Haul

A fortune cookie once yielded this wisdom: "Nature, time, and patience are the greatest healers." In the NICU, where neonatologists try to provide what nature cannot, and to buy time for tiny patients who were born too early, parents must provide the patience—and it is not easy. Dr. Aschner says:

*"One of the things many families are not prepared for is their changing expectations. At the beginning, when the issue is life or death, parents are relieved to just get through each day. Once the major problems are resolved—the babies have been weaned from the respirator, are tolerating some breast milk or formula, and have avoided serious complications such as intraventricular hemorrhage—we refer to the babies as 'gainers and growers.' The parents, at that point, expect daily weight gain and progress. Every day should bring the babies closer to going home.*

*"Yet the course is rarely one of continued, steady improvement. There are still ups and downs, maybe not as high or as low, but almost predictably, very premature babies develop feeding intolerance, or have apnea episodes, or develop an infection, or some other problem comes up. Although these problems are usually not as life-threatening as those faced in the first few weeks of life, they are often just as upsetting to families. And every day the parents leave the hospital with empty car seats is just as hard as the day before. To get through the little ups and downs in the latter part of the hospital stay, it helps to remember how far you've come. Don't compare today's weight or problem to yesterday's, but to last week's or last month's.*

*"After a while, parents' patience may grow thin as they become increasingly exhausted with their constant vigil. It is important for parents to take a break, to take care of themselves by getting enough sleep, and to do some of the things they enjoyed before the birth. Sometimes parents feel it is unfair for them to go out to dinner or to a movie when their babies are still in the NICU. Or one parent will feel this and the*

*other won't. People cope differently. But many find it helpful to take time out and do some special things as a couple or with their other children. Once the babies come home, the parents may not have time for these things for quite a while."*

A father of identical twins born at twenty-nine weeks gestation, now almost three years old, describes his family's experience:

*"Our son Nathan was two pounds, twelve ounces. He was off oxygen in about three weeks and came home one month after birth. Our other boy, Noel, weighed eight ounces less at birth, didn't come home until he was six months old, and needed oxygen until he was a year and a half old. You would think Noel would still be sickly, yet although he gets ear infections and colds now and then, he recovers pretty quickly.*

*"He's been sort of intimidated by his brother—Nathan is five pounds bigger—but yesterday they had a knock-down-drag-out fight and Noel won. But most of the time they get along pretty well.*

*"We stayed at Ronald McDonald House when the babies were in the NICU; we are still using the Ronald McDonald House, this time in a different city, where Noel is getting a cochlea implant. That's one thing parents need to know, by the way: Once kids are out of the NICU, it's not always over. Some of them need surgery down the line. And you can't assume that the same hospital where they were in the NICU is the best hospital for whatever surgery they need later on."*

## ▣ Discharge from the NICU

Before babies are discharged from the NICU, their neonatologist communicates with a written discharge summary and often by telephone with the pediatrician who will take over their care. The neonatologist relates each child's medical problems, medications, feeding history, immunizations (if any) and any special recommendations, such as a need for eye or hearing exams. Most babies who leave the NICU do not need a specialist, but even those who do need to be followed by a cardiologist, neurologist, or other specialist still need a primary care pediatrician. (See Chapter 13, "Selecting and Visiting the Pediatrician.") In fact, neonatologists will not discharge a baby from the NICU until the family has identified a pediatrician, a family practitioner, or a health care clinic that will provide routine well-baby care.

### ▨ "Adjusted Age"

It takes some time for prematurely born babies to catch up developmentally to full-term babies. Even if the babies' development was not adversely affected by prematurity, brain maturity is a continuum that cannot be hurried. A baby born two months early will simply not demonstrate developmental milestones at the same time as a full-term baby born on the same day. (Developmental milestones are achievements by which babies demonstrate progress, such as smiling, rolling over, sitting, crawling, walking, speaking, etc.)

Therefore, to help premies' parents be realistic about when their babies will reach developmental milestones, neonatologists usually advise parents to "correct" for prematurity until children are two years old by calculating their age not by when they were born, but from their due date. Thus if babies are born on the first of January, but were due on the first of March, on the first of June they are *chronologically* five months old, but their *adjusted age* is only three months—and they are likely to have the skills of a three-month-old, not a five-month-old. By the time children reach the age of two, any difference associated with prematurity is rarely significant.

### ▨ Special Services

Your premature multiples may be entitled to free or low-cost special programs and services, such as occupational and physical therapy and early intervention programs that can enhance their development. Such programs are often in great demand and fill up quickly, so find out about them as early as possible. Ask your pediatrician for recommendations or obtain referrals from the hospital social worker. Some social workers are on top of such matters, and others are not. If the social worker does not seek you out, take the initiative to ask as many people as necessary about what services are available and how you can apply.

Some parents hesitate to take advantage of special programs because they do not want their children "labeled" as "special education kids." That will not necessarily happen. Find out about procedures in your community. In many areas, by state law records of early intervention programs are sealed, and youngsters may qualify for a regular kindergarten.

And if they *are* "special education kids"? It just means that these special children, like all children, require and deserve an education tailored to their needs.

## Categorizing Low-Birth-Weight Babies

Low-birth-weight babies in need of special care are categorized as follows to aid in diagnosis and preparation of a treatment plan.

*Premature and Appropriate for Gestational Age (AGA).* The baby was born early but is of normal size for the amount of time spent in the womb.

*Premature and Small for Gestational Age (SGA).* The baby was born early and appears to have suffered intrauterine growth retardation (IUGR). One cause is maternal diseases such as chronic or pregnancy-induced hypertension or kidney, lung, or heart disease. Cigarette smoking, which causes contraction of blood vessels, thereby interfering with normal nourishment of the fetuses, can also increase the risk that a baby will be SGA. Other problems that prevent sufficient nourishment through the placenta can also cause IUGR. Identical twins who share a placenta may experience twin-to-twin transfusion, wherein one baby becomes the other's blood donor. The recipient receives too much blood and may become hydropic (suffering from fluid buildup); the donor loses too much blood and may become anemic. Survival of the twins depends on the severity of the condition, how early it was detected, and whether the babies could be delivered before the condition became dire.

Another possibility with low birth weight is that the due date was miscalculated, meaning that the baby has a younger gestational age than has been assumed but is of appropriate size for the actual gestational age.

*Premature and Large for Gestational Age (LGA).* The baby was born early but high maternal blood sugar levels due to diabetes may have caused the baby to put on extra weight *in utero*. The child may have a problem maintaining blood sugar, may have high insulin levels, or other problems such as jaundice or respiratory distress syndrome.

Or the due date was miscalculated, meaning that birth was not premature.

*Full-Term but Small for Gestational Age.*  The baby had the normal length of gestation but may have suffered intrauterine growth retardation.

## 🎴 Some Problems of Premature Babies

A baby born prior to thirty-seven weeks gestation may have an immature circulatory system, respiratory system, liver, brain, immune system, and digestive system that can make the child vulnerable to such health problems as:

*Respiratory Distress Syndrome (RDS)—Formerly Called Hyaline Membrane Disease (HMD)*—is the most common reason for admission to the NICU. It is caused by the immature baby's inability to manufacture sufficient surfactant, a substance required for healthy lung functioning. Surfactant is formed by cells within the lungs, then secreted into little air sacs called alveoli. The surfactant coats the alveoli, decreasing surface tension and keeping lungs from collapsing.

Dr. Aschner compares lung surfactant to another kind of surfactant: dishwashing liquid. While plain water may form bubbles that quickly burst, dishwashing liquid decreases surface tension on the water and enables bubbles to linger longer. Surfactant within the lungs keeps air sacs partially expanded, even during exhalation. It enables the lungs to expand and contract more easily by reducing the surface tension on pulmonary alveoli.

Babies without surfactant must struggle so hard to breathe that they soon tire as their air sacs collapse. Surfactant replacement therapy, which Dr. Aschner terms the most important advancement in neonatal medicine in the last decade and a half, has been shown to improve survival rates and decrease complications.

Most babies with RDS improve as their lungs begin to make surfactant. They can then be withdrawn from the respirator and breathe on their own. Most have no serious lasting lung damage. However, some babies whose RDS is treated with oxygen and respirator therapy may develop bronchopulmonary dysplasia, a chronic lung disease.

A steroid given to the pregnant woman a minimum of forty-eight hours before delivery may accelerate lung maturity and reduce the possibility of RDS.

*Dehydration*   is a decrease in total body fluid from one or a combination of reasons, such as losing fluids too quickly or not being able to take in enough fluids to replace lost fluids.

Dehydration is treated by administering fluids orally or intravenously. It is a common complication during the first few days of life for the most prematurely born infants (born at twenty-three to twenty-six weeks of gestation) weighing under 750 grams. Dr. Aschner explains that the skin of these infants "is like a thin sheet of cellophane—you can see the veins through it. The skin is not a good barrier against loss of fluids."

Babies can experience "insensible" (unmeasurable) loss of moisture through the skin. Therefore, it is important for them to be in a humidified environment. Parents are sometimes surprised to see their child loosely wrapped in a tent of plastic wrap, under which a hose emits moist air. Condensation that forms inside the tent attests to the humid climate within. Sometimes, a similar "hat" of plastic wrap is also fashioned for the baby.

*Hypothermia*   is abnormally low body temperature requiring an infant to be placed in an incubator. Most babies over four pounds can maintain a stable body temperature and be transferred to a crib.

*Jaundice*   is a yellowish tint to skin indicating the immature liver's inability to adequately process bilirubin, a yellow organic compound derived from hemoglobin during normal and pathological destruction of red blood cells. This is a common problem and can usually be treated with phototherapy, exposure to special lights of a particular wavelength. The lights help break down bilirubin and allow a chemical conversion in the skin, converting bilirubin into a form that can be excreted without first being conjugated (processed) by the liver.

*Susceptibility to Infection.*   Most full-term newborns are protected by their mother's antibodies to various viruses and bacteria.

However, since most antibodies cross the placenta during the third trimester, prematurely born babies do not have the same amount of maternal antibodies as full-term babies do.

Furthermore, white blood cells in premature babies do not combat infection as efficiently as white blood cells in full-term babies and older children. Yet the very care of premature babies may expose them to bacterial infections; when an IV is inserted, for example, the normal bacteria on the skin may have easier access to the bloodstream or underlying soft tissue. Once bacteria enter a baby's bloodstream the infection is more likely to spread and cause such problems as meningitis or osteomyelitis.

*Apnea* occurs when breathing ceases for at least twenty seconds. This condition can be nerve-racking, sometimes leading parents to misinterpret a normal sigh as apnea. Physicians are not always sure of the cause, but apnea appears to be more common among very small babies, babies with systemic infection (sepsis), or babies whose mothers took certain street drugs, such as cocaine, during pregnancy.

The younger the gestational age at birth, the more likely a child is to have apnea, since it is associated with the immaturity of the respiration center of the brain. Infants literally "forget" to breathe. As babies mature and reach the equivalent of thirty-four to thirty-six weeks of gestational age, apnea usually goes away, and relatively few need to be sent home with an apnea monitor.

Apnea is usually treated with medication, most commonly theophylline (a common asthma medication) or caffeine (yes, the same substance found in your morning coffee!). Both theophylline and caffeine are potent respiratory stimulants and well-tolerated by babies. Apnea may also be prevented with "nasal Continuous Positive Airway Pressure," or "C-PAP," short prongs placed into the nostrils that blow air into the nose with gentle but sustained pressure and keep the lungs expanded.

Although premature babies are at slightly higher risk of Sudden Infant Death Syndrome (SIDS), it is believed that babies who have apnea of prematurity are not at greater risk of SIDS than premature babies who have not had apnea. SIDS is death of an infant in apparently good health, usually under six months of age, due to unknown causes.

*Anemia* is abnormally low levels of red blood cells or hemoglobin. Red blood cells in newborns have a shorter life span than those in older children and adults, and premature babies have lower iron stores than full-term babies. Anemia may be exacerbated by withdrawing of blood for tests.

If the anemia is mild, it can be treated by giving the baby iron. A transfusion is given if the baby shows symptoms of anemia, such as poor weight gain or increased oxygen requirement.

*Necrotizing Enterocolitis (NEC)*   is a potentially fatal disease of the bowel in which air forms in the wall of the intestine and can cause perforation or necrosis (death of the bowel wall). The condition is sometimes associated with, but not directly caused by, infection.

NEC, which occurs more often in premature infants of very low birth weight and in SGA infants, is almost always diagnosed after feedings have been initiated. NEC must be ruled out—or ruled in—when an infant experiences feeding intolerance, such as becoming bloated or having residual food within the stomach after the stomach should have emptied. Food must be withheld until a diagnosis can be made.

In most cases, NEC can be treated with medications, although surgery is sometimes required to remove damaged bowel.

*Intraventricular Hemorrhage (IVH)*   is bleeding inside the ventricles of the brain (reservoirs of spinal fluid). IVH can occur spontaneously; the younger the gestational age, the more common is this complication. Almost all babies who will experience IVH will do so within the first seven to ten days of life, and usually within the first three days. IVH is diagnosed by cranial ultrasound, and parents are relieved to learn that two normal ultrasounds within the first couple of weeks of life generally mean that the child will avoid IVH.

There are different levels of IVH. A small IVH may cause no lasting problems; however, a large blood clot may obstruct the flow of spinal fluid, exerting pressure on the brain. The clot can even extend into the brain tissue itself. At its most serious, IVH can cause such problems as developmental delay and cerebral palsy.

IVH can sometimes be "waited out," or medications may be given to limit the excess production of spinal fluid. In severe cases, surgery is needed in order to drain fluid through a shunt.

IVH should not be confused with cephalhematoma, which is a

collection of blood that occurs between the scalp and the skull. Cephalhematoma is self-limiting—it goes away by itself and requires no treatment.

*Hernia* caused by incomplete closure of the abdominal wall often occurs in premature babies. A hernia is a defect in the muscle wall that lets an organ slip out of place and protrude.

- *Umbilical hernia* is a protrusion of the navel. Surgery is not recommended for infants since this condition often heals by itself within the first year of life.

   *At no time should coins, trusses, or other objects be placed over the bulge and taped or banded in place.* This practice does *not* fix a hernia and can interfere with the baby's ability to breathe deeply enough, chafe the skin, interfere with blood circulation of the skin, and cause scarring.

   When diapering a baby with an umbilical hernia, fold down the top of the diaper so it rests below the navel.
- *Inguinal (groin) hernias* require surgical repair. Inguinal hernias frequently occur bilaterally (on both sides).
- *Undescended testicles,* common among premature boys, are also associated with incomplete closure of the abdominal wall. Testicles usually descend by themselves within the first year of life. If testicles have not descended by age two, they should be surgically descended, since undescended testicles are susceptible to cancer and cannot manufacture sperm at the onset of puberty.[1]

*Patent Ductus Arteriosus (PDA)* is the failure of closure of the ductus arteriosus, a blood vessel which, in a fetus, connects the pulmonary artery with the aorta and conducts most of the blood directly from the right ventricle to the aorta, bypassing the lungs. This circulatory route works well *in utero,* since the fetus obtains its oxygen from the placenta and the fetal lungs do not require much blood because they are not yet functioning. Once the child is born, the ductus arteriosus is supposed to close in order to allow sufficient

[1] *The Hernia Book,* by William P. Homan, M.D., with Betty Rothbart, M.S.W., provides full information on the causes and treatments of umbilical, inguinal, and other types of hernias as well as undescended testicles and related conditions. (See the Bibliography.)

blood flow to the lungs. If the blood vessel remains patent (open and unobstructed), it continues to afford free passage of the blood, causing the lungs to get too much blood, or not enough.

PDA is usually diagnosed when the physician hears a heart murmur. It is important to understand that murmurs result from a turbulent blood flow pattern and do not necessarily indicate a heart defect. An echocardiogram (ultrasound of the heart) may also be used to diagnose PDA.

PDA can usually be treated with indomethacin, an anti-inflammatory drug. Sometimes, however, the blood vessel must be surgically ligated.

*Retinopathy of Prematurity (ROP)* is a disease of the blood vessels in the retina. The blood vessels grow out of control, in all directions, and can pull the retina away from the back of the eye (retinal detachment), a cause of blindness in 1 to 1.5 percent of premature babies.

Prematurely born babies should be examined by a specially trained ophthlamologist to facilitate early diagnosis of ROP, which generally cannot be diagnosed until a baby is about six or seven weeks old.

*"We were just getting ready to take Billy home when ROP was diagnosed. It was so frustrating, after all we had been through, to have to deal with a new problem. We thought we were 'in the clear,' but Billy needed to stay in the hospital for surgery."*

Treatment consists of stopping the growth of the out-of-control blood vessels through freezing (cryotherapy) or laser therapy.

---

## Parent Care, Inc.: Offering Support During and After the NICU Experience

*Parent Care, Inc.* (See the Resources section in the Appendix), is an international organization for parents and professionals concerned with infants requiring special care following birth. Parent Care supports the establishment of parent support groups in neonatal intensive-care units. It also publishes educational materials and a newsletter, holds an annual conference, and serves as a referral source for parents and health care providers.

For additional sources of information and support, see Chapters 19, 20, 21, and the Resources section in the Appendix. For information on how to obtain clothing, diapers, and other supplies for prematurely born babies, see Chapter 11.

---

## Looking Ahead to Brighter Days

A wonderful tradition at some hospitals is the annual party for "NICU graduates." An ebullient crowd of parents and children from one year to eighteen years of age celebrates how far they have come since those early, nerve-racking days. Babes-in-arms coo. Toddlers giggle and run around. School-age children play games. Teenagers munch cookies and hang out.

All of these children had rocky beginnings, but they are on solid footing now. And their parents, who once could not have dreamed of this day, who once kept anxious vigils, remember.

Parents whose children are currently in the NICU take a break from their own vigils. They go downstairs to the cafeteria and join the party, exhilarated to think that their children will one day be there, too.

# COPING WITH THE LOSS OF A CHILD

ॐ   Sadly, not all prematurely born or full-term babies survive. And unfortunately, some people do not understand why you grieve so deeply for an infant who barely had a chance to live or for a fetus who died *in utero,* never to draw a breath. You think, Of course I grieve. I struggled to have this child, I wanted this child to live, and to outlive me. Mourning is painful enough without having to justify it to others.

Some people say, "Count your blessings. At least your other twin is fine." Yes, you are grateful for your living child. But one twin is not the other's "spare." Human beings are not replaceable.

If all of your multiples have died, your arms are empty and no fraction of your dream of parenting them survives.

Guilt may be mixed up in your grief: Did I take good enough care of myself during pregnancy? Should I have eaten more, rested more? Should we even have attempted pregnancy with this many fetuses? Could we have saved this child, somehow?

Guilt focuses on the failure of your own small power to prevail over the great matters of life and death. You surely did all you could. Even if you were perfection itself, your child was vulnerable and succumbed to forces you could not control.

If you are able, name all of your children, whether or not they live, to give them dignity and to enable their family to remember and speak of them by name. You may wish to hold your child in your arms and say good-bye. Let yourself cry. If the hospital would deny you this closure, have your physician or a family member intervene on your behalf.

Honor the deceased child and surviving ones by speaking openly about the loss. Acknowledge that the child's death affects both parents and siblings. Surviving twins or triplets, or "twinless twins," can have an acute awareness that their twin or triplet is missing, both in infancy and later in life. Contact the organizations described in the following section (or see the Resources section in the Appendix) for important help in how to remember your loved one while moving on with life.

## Perinatal Bereavement Services

To help comfort those who have lost a child through miscarriage, stillbirth, or neonatal death, some hospitals have established perinatal bereavement programs. Labor and delivery nurses, trained and certified as bereavement counselors, acknowledge the parents' loss and offer support. They also refer bereaved parents to support groups in the community; some groups are led by parents who have themselves lost a child.

After delivering a stillborn twin and a living twin, one mother wrote to Midge Thurin Madsen, R.N.C., C.C.E., a nurse-counselor at Benedictine Hospital in Kingston, New York:

*"To go into labor and delivery and be faced with death and loss rather than birth and life is always hard to accept. Perhaps there's even a small sense of failure mixed in. So the 'moments of truth' such as a final sonogram, a printout from a monitor, or a doctor's reluctant assessment are moments of vulnerability which need responses which are consciously sensitive as well as honest. . . . And that's where you come in, with your steady support which is not 'pushy' but always lets others know: 'We're here, caring about you.' "[1]*

[1]Reprinted by permission of the letter writer.

To parents who wish them, the nurse-counselors make available keepsake remembrances of their child: a lock of hair, a hospital I.D. bracelet, the baby's footprints, a photograph, to commemorate the quiet dignity of the life that once was.

Sometimes the nurse-counselors are called upon to do more. On behalf of a mother who was upset that she had never received a birth certificate for her child who died shortly after birth, one nurse-counselor called the county clerk's office to see what was holding up the certificate. Although in many locales, parents must request (and even pay for) death certificates, parents are supposed to receive a birth certificate for any child born alive. The nurse-counselor learned that a clerical worker who had heard about the baby's death had prevented the birth certificate from being mailed, on the basis of a mistaken, albeit well-meaning, assumption that the parents would rather not be "reminded" about the baby.

If and when parents try again to conceive a child, memories of the loss may be especially sharp. Some parents change their doctor, change hospitals, hoping it will change their luck not to do anything the same. Some form intense relationships with nurses. One woman who had lost a child came in once or twice every week to hear the heartbeat of the child she was now carrying. She gave birth to a healthy child.

In every birthing room at Benedictine Hospital is a rocking chair donated by a family who had experienced a loss. Each chair bears a small memorial plaque engraved with the child's name and birthdate. Some of the families who donated the rocking chairs have later used those birthing rooms to deliver healthy babies.

One mother said of the experience: "It is good to be able to speak of [the deceased child], to say to our new baby, 'This is where your sister was born, too.' This helps us heal and come to closure."

On the hospital grounds, a heart-shaped monument, donated by a local merchant and designed by the hospital's perinatal bereavement coordinators, is inscribed, "In loving memory of all babies who have so briefly touched our lives."

Members of a community bereavement support group hold a memorial service at their annual December holiday gathering. Parents celebrate their children's lives by sharing poetry, playing music and singing, and reading text from several religions. At the conclusion of the service, white ribbons are tied on the branches of a Christmas tree by the families, in memory of their babies.

*Selected Resources for Help*

*in Coping with Loss*

- *Center for Loss in Multiple Birth, Inc. (CLIMB)* "is by and for parents who have experienced the death of one or both of their twins, or one or more or all of their triplets or higher multiple-birth children, during pregnancy, at or after birth, in infancy or childhood, and also adult survivors of these losses." The center provides a support network and publishes a newsletter.
- *The Compassionate Friends* refers people to local support groups and publishes a newsletter and pamphlets on bereavement in the death of a child.
- *Twinless Twins International* was founded "to serve in support of twins (all multiple births) who suffer from the loss of companionship of their twin." The organization facilitates networking, maintains a resource library, and publishes a newsletter on bereavement issues for all ages.

For addresses and phone numbers for each of these organizations, see the Resources section in the Appendix.

# Part Two

# LIFE WITH MULTIPLES

# $\mathcal{T}$HE PARENTS' PARTNERSHIP

*"Early on we took turns taking primary responsibility for the twins. All the juggling helped in keeping each other fresh."*

Traditionally, child care has been a mother's domain, with occasional "help" from the father. In some families, that still holds true. But increasingly, men reject the role of a remote dad who refuses to change a diaper. Today, both men and women are far more likely to believe that parents conceive or adopt children in partnership and should raise them the same way. In other words: When a father is with his children, he is not "baby-sitting." He is fathering.

Some men acknowledge that they became more involved in child care with multiples than with their single-born children, simply because there was so much to do:

*"I worked all day—then the minute I came home, my wife thrust a baby or two into my arms and said, 'Here, you take them! I need a break.' I could understand that, and I wanted to be with the children, but I was tired, too. I figured out a solution: Before heading home, I closed my eyes for ten minutes in the car, in the parking lot near my office. It was*

*Mom breastfeeds one baby while Dad bottlefeeds the other. These quiet moments give the parents an opportunity to catch up on the day's events.*

just enough to refresh me and give me a transition between work and home."

If the father is working but the mother is home full time or on maternity leave, obviously his time for the family is more limited. And just as no woman should be expected to be Supermom and do it all, neither should a man need to be Superdad. If only more men could and did take paternity leave! If only *both* parents could be free to give their all to their babies, without worrying about jobs, money, or other pesky realities.

Even given time restraints, however, the father's participation is vital—not only to give his wife support and relief, but for his own sake and the children's. They need to get to know their father and to have him get to know them. When both parents are employed, the need to coordinate a joint effort is all the more compelling.

Many men—and women—feel awkward, even scared, caring for tiny babies for the first time. As time goes by, it is tremendously satisfying to feel ever more comfortable and confident handling and comforting the babies. Parents discover that all infants, even identical twins, have unique personalities. One baby plays with the bottle nipple before feeding; another fastens on immediately. A third makes funny faces or likes to be carried in a particular way. To the uninitiated, such details may seem insignificant. But to parents, they are ways babies reveal who they are. Parents who know their children's special ways understand their individuality. They can soothe them, please them, and before long even make them smile. Both parents deserve these pleasures.

*"We are closer since we had the twins. We went through wars trying to conceive them."*

*"My husband is comfortable and calm when he talks, when he changes the kids, even when the five-year-old is running around crazy and the twins are screaming. He just laughs and says, 'Children will be children.'*
*"Recently, he took all three children to the nursery-school picnic. He had the [five-month-old] twins on a quilt on the grass—and all the while he didn't lose sight of Andrew for a minute!"*

Collaborative parenthood brings parents closer together. The truth is, with the possible exception of grandparents or a devoted aunt or uncle, no one cares about the events of children's daily lives as much as their parents do. Most other people are not particularly riveted by the news that Johnny finally tried the pureed carrots, or Ginger pulled herself up on the coffee table, or Camilla said the cutest thing today. But parents find these events the most entrancing and important news of the day.

## ▧ A Time of Transition

*"Twins are a great contraceptive!"*

*"We are like two ships passing in the night. We have a fantasy of visiting a hotel with thick walls and dark curtains."*

Some couples say that while having multiples is thrilling, it is also so overwhelming that a marriage's strength can be put to the test.

The family's equilibrium is thrown off balance; everyone has to adjust to a new family order and find new ways of relating to one another. The babies need so much attention that exhausted parents may not get much of a chance to focus on each other's emotional and physical needs. The mother is recovering from vaginal birth (perhaps with an episiotomy) or cesarean birth. Breastfeeding continues to place demands on her body, which is going through postbirth transitions, possibly including postpartum depression—a condition aggravated by fatigue. Sex can seem like a distant memory of something nice you used to do "before." Add older siblings' needs for attention to the mix, and a family can feel like they are clutching the sides of a boat on a very rocky sea. Parents need to anticipate and plan for ways to navigate through these turbulent times.

It can help to realize that upheaval is normal and temporary. It will not be long before the family settles into new routines. Parents eventually find the time and energy to make love again, and resistant older siblings can come to accept and love the family's newest members. But first, parents must accept that there is an inevitable transition between pregnancy and the creation of a new equilibrium.

For some couples, the difficulty of the early months of parenthood is a poignant contrast to intimacy during pregnancy, labor, and childbirth. Together, they had learned of and planned for multiples and gazed in astonishment at the sight of babies' limbs poking against their mother's ever-rounder belly. When multiples are born, parents may need to tear the to-do list in half and go in separate, though complementary, directions for a while. If one twin needs to stay in the hospital, the father may stay there while his wife recuperates from birth and cares for the other twin at home. Or while the mother is busy with the babies, the father may devote himself to making sure older children do not feel left out.

Some new fathers feel left out after the birth of a single-born child; their wife and the new baby develop such a tight bond that they may seem to exclude him. "Breastfeeding?" one father recalls. "It was great for the baby. Great for my wife. But it left *me* out." Although caring for multiples is certainly more demanding than caring for a single-born, a man is more likely to be part of the action, less likely to feel like a third wheel.

*"I felt completely engaged in caring for the girls. Having twins called for greater involvement. I was in awe of the nursing relationship, but*

*there was plenty for me to do. I diapered them, held them, soothed them when they cried, and maintained the functioning of the household."*

## ❧ Finding Time for Each Other

Children and jobs require so much energy, there may seem little or none left to spare for your partner, let alone yourself. Unless you have the money and desire for baby-sitters, going out together may be rare, and until *all* the children sleep through the night, you may be able to manage only small amounts of uninterrupted time. Yet staying in touch with each other, communicating about these all-important days in your lives, cannot be postponed for a year. Some parents have met success with the following strategies:

**Turn Off the TV.** Turning on the television is often a reflex action, a signal to others and to oneself that this is "relaxing time." But you might be surprised at the talking time that opens up when you do not have to compete with the TV for airtime.

**Arrange Phone Dates.** If one or both of you are at work, call at lunch hour or at another prearranged time during the day.

**Take Family Walks.** Sometimes couples who take turns with the children realize that they only see each other when shifts change. Taking children out in their stroller, a time when they may be inclined to be less demanding, can give you a chance to catch up.

**Take Advantage of Mothers of Twins Club Family Events.** Attending "Couples' Night Out" or going with the children to holiday parties can give both parents a chance to compare notes with other couples with multiples.

**Shower Together.** It is only five or ten minutes, but it's time together naked and talking, and you save water, besides!

**If the Going Gets Tough on Your Marriage, Get Help.** As one woman said, "My advice to other parents of twins is, don't be shy about going to a counselor. That forty-five minutes every week is like a date. It gives us a chance to talk."

New parents of multiples confront so many issues: acknowledging the need for help, deciding whether to breastfeed or bottlefeed, coping with night feedings and fatigue, responding to the needs of your other children, managing logistics and finances. Creating breathers, together and separately, is essential.

> *"One night, I felt like I would go out of my mind if I stayed home another minute. My husband cared for the children while I went swimming with a friend. That was great. But even better was coming home and seeing that my husband had put away the toys and laundry that had been strewn all over the living-room floor. Seeing the rug with nothing on it was like seeing a clean slate, feeling like the next day would really be a fresh start."*

Expect to give your negotiation and stress-reduction skills a workout, and to call upon (or pretend to have) reserves of patience. Sometimes the most loving thing you can do for each other is to give your partner the night off: to go out, regroup, talk things over with a friend or support group, relax at a movie or restaurant or work out at a gym. Recognizing each other's needs for togetherness *and* individual recharging can go a long way toward getting you through the stressful times.

# Chapter 8

# Naming Your Babies

Like parenthood itself, naming children is both a privilege and a responsibility. Names are gifts that last a lifetime; those passed down through generations even bridge lifetimes.

Parents signing birth certificates are saying to each child, "This name has special meaning for us. We take pleasure in giving it to you. With this name, we celebrate and commemorate your birth."

Expectant parents try to imagine the future. Which names will do right by the babies, make them happy, do no harm? Parents circle around names like museum-goers checking out sculptures, exploring them from every angle:

- Do the first and middle names sound good with the surname?
- Do initials spell out distinguished monograms? (Donna Ursula Morgan is smart, but her initials aren't.)
- Are names difficult to spell or pronounce? (Chloe, Dwanda)
- Are names so unusual they will be hard to remember, or so common that your child will feel like one of a batch? (One nursery-school classroom boasts four Zoes and five Michaels.)

- Which names best reflect your personal style and expectations? (Joy? Ringo?)

## ▣ *Special Concerns for Multiples*

In addition, parents of multiples need to think about how their children's names will sound together. Some parents want names to accentuate twinship, while others prefer diverse names that emphasize individuality. Four approaches to naming multiples are:

### SOUND-ALIKE NAMES: VARIATIONS ON A THEME

*"Naming our triplets took months of negotiation. It was tough not knowing their genders; we had to choose six names. Just for fun, we referred to them as Huey, Dewey, and Louey, characters in our older son's favorite book,* Mickey Mouse's Pluto Pup.*"*

Sound-alike names have been such a tradition for multiples that many parents automatically look for a set of names that "go together." Such names rhyme (Tad and Chad) or repeat the same syllable (Marla and Marvin). These names can be cute but hard to tell apart. People confused by who is Donny and who is Johnny often end up calling them "the twins." Many twins resent this catch-all label because it makes them feel like components of a category, rather than individuals.

Names that are nearly identical (Michael and Mitchell, or Janet and Jeannette) challenge people's abilities to recollect who is who. Children feel exasperated by the constant need to remind people, "No, *I'm* Michael."

### NAMES THAT SHARE A FIRST INITIAL

Nonrhyming names that begin with the same letter (Jillian, Jennifer, and Janine) are more distinctive than sound-alike names. On occasion, however, they can cause mix-ups. If a letter comes addressed to J. Jones, to whom does it belong? If a sweater is monogrammed *JJ*, is it anyone's in particular?

## EQUIVALENT NAMES: THE SEPARATE-BUT-EQUAL APPROACH

Some parents prefer "equivalent" names that do not sound alike or share a first initial but do have similar characteristics. They may have the same number of syllables (Rebecca Ann and Jennifer Lee), the same degree of fanciness (Katarina and Anastasia) or plainness (Joe and Max), or a similar meaning (Opal, Ruby, and Jewel).

Equivalent names are sometimes given so that children will not have any reason to suspect that one child's name is better. One mother said, "I love the name Meg, which the baby-name book said is Greek for 'pearl.' But I could not give one twin a one-syllable name and name the other Christina."

Surely it is unlikely that the one-syllable daughter would someday cry, "She has more syllables than I do! You must love her more!" Yet equivalent names are some parents' way, even unconsciously, of "proving" equal love.

## DIVERSE NAMES: TO EACH, HIS OR HER OWN

Diverse names are not chosen because they go together, but because they differ. If they have the same number of syllables or the same first letter, it is by happenstance rather than design. Parents may choose names they like or names that honor family members (Grandma Celia, Grandma Blanche, and Uncle Roger) or carry on family history (John Alton Johnson III), or traditions (Lowell, named after Great-grandfather Lowell). Either name all multiples after important family members, or none.

Many parents select diverse names in order to declare, "You are multiples, but we regard you as unique individuals—and we want other people to treat you that way."

"Twins have to share everything," one father said. "They go through every day, every experience, together. They share parents, a room, most clothes and toys. We did not want them to have to share a name, too."

### 🌐 Signing on the Dotted Line

When choosing names, project ahead to a moment five years from now, and imagine this scene: It is dinnertime, and your children are dashing about the house. You summon them to the kitchen by cupping your hands like a megaphone and calling out each name. The names resonate, lingering in the air. Every day, you utter those names a hundred times, but tonight, unexpectedly, you seem to hear them as if for the first time . . . and you feel a small thrill of pride that these were the names you chose.

# $\mathscr{B}$REASTFEEDING

*"We didn't know until the girls were born that we were having twins. Once we got over our initial shock, the first thing my husband thought was, How will I support two babies! And the first thing I thought was, How will I breastfeed twins!"*

*"It is so important to understand that many doctors, many nurses, just don't know the truth about breastfeeding twins. You have plenty of milk for both! But you have to be committed. If you don't really, really want to breastfeed, it's hard to keep it going."*

*"My mom tried to discourage me: 'Be prepared. It might not work out. Have the bottles and formula ready.'*
    *"To appease her, I said, 'I'll just play it by ear.' But I knew I would breastfeed. I was determined."*

Not so long ago, every new mother was advised to bottlefeed. Today, increasing awareness of the substantial benefits of breastfeeding has inspired many mothers to nurse. But while the mother of a single-born child merely has to state her intention to breastfeed, a mother of twins, triplets, or more sometimes must wage a crusade to convince her obstetrician, her pediatrician, her husband, and other family members that yes, breastfeeding the babies is a very good idea. Multiples' moms confront discouraging statements such as:

"Well, I guess you can try it at first, see if it works."

"You might not have enough milk."

"Your babies are small. Are you sure you don't want to supplement?"

"You won't get as much help with the babies if you breastfeed."

"Have some formula on hand just in case."

One woman's pediatrician was so pessimistic about her ability to breastfeed twins that she felt vindicated, even triumphant, when each twin gained half a pound during their first week home from the hospital.

Rebecca Grunberg, a mother of triplets, described the need to hold fast to the nursing goal in *New Beginnings: La Leche League's Breastfeeding Journal:*

*"[As I nursed my triplets in the neonatal intensive care unit] and I could look up at the faces of the nurses on the floor, I sensed a strange tension in the air, instead of smiles or nods of approval. . . .[The] nurses did not understand my insistence on nursing my three tiny babies, because they are used to dealing with critical babies and having total caloric and medical control. . . . [Many] of the nurses came up to me one by one while I was nursing the babies and voiced their very negative opinions. I lost hope for a moment; then I immediately realized I had the babies at my breast where they belonged and had to get back to the big job I had ahead of me."[1]*

Each woman must make the choice that best suits her and her babies. As described in Chapter 10, bottlefeeding is also a valid choice, and both bottlefeeding and breastfeeding mothers deserve support.[2]

[1]Rebecca Grunberg, "Breastfeeding Triplets," *New Beginnings: La Leche League's Breastfeeding Journal:* September/October 1992, Vol. 9, No. 5.

[2]NOTE: If you are infected with HIV, speak with your physician about the advisability of breastfeeding, as some researchers state that HIV may be transmitted from an infected woman to her child(ren) through breastfeeding.

## ▧ Advantages of Breastfeeding

*"I breastfed my twins, and I highly recommend it. . . . I find that nursing provides a wonderful reminder (and excuse!) to sit down, relax, and spend quiet, focused time with my children. . . . My husband and I still find ourselves enthralled as we watch our babies nurse together and reach out to hold each other's hand or stroke each other's hair."*

—*Anjelina Citron, "Dear Parents of Twins,"*
American Baby, *October 1991*

**Mother's Milk Is the Healthiest Food for Babies.** In quality, quantity, composition, and temperature, breast milk is made to order. It is not only nutritious but also easily digestible. Breastfed babies are much less prone to colic and are not allergic to their mother's milk. Breast milk contains maternal antibodies that help babies resist infections—an especially significant bonus for vulnerable premature or small babies. Pre-term milk, which is higher in protein, calcium, and phosphorus, is specially suited to the special needs of premature babies (although extremely premature babies of less than thirty-two weeks' gestation may also need "breast milk fortifiers," nutritional supplements added to breast milk to help meet these infants' additional requirements.) Full-term milk is suited to the needs of full-term babies.

Colostrum, the yellowish first milk, has high concentrations of nutrients and maternal antibodies that help protect babies from disease. It can be especially valuable for premature babies who have missed out on some of the maternal antibodies they would have received over the course of the third trimester.

Colostrum also serves as a natural laxative. It helps the baby to pass meconium, the dark greenish mass of mucus and bile that accumulates in a fetus's bowels and is eliminated soon after birth, and to eliminate the excess bilirubin that can cause jaundice.

**The Milk Supply Increases According to the Babies' Needs.** Breastfeeding is the perfect example of the law of supply and demand. As long as a woman stays well nourished and committed to breastfeeding, she usually can produce enough milk to satisfy her babies' growing appetites and nutritional needs—even during growth spurts, when they seem to want to nurse around the clock. Breast size does not affect how much milk a woman can produce.

*Suckling Is Important Exercise for Babies.*   Sucking at the breast contributes to healthy development of the palate and facial structure.

*Breastfeeding Is Less Expensive Than Bottlefeeding.*   Its costs? Ample nutritious food and beverages for the mother, purchase or rental of a breast pump, storage containers and bottles for expressed milk.

*Breastfeeding Is Convenient.*   In the middle of the night, you don't have to stumble into the kitchen to prepare bottles. Breastfeeding frees you from having to sterilize, prepare, or wash bottles, except when your children are drinking expressed milk. When you are out, your babies' refreshments are automatically with you. However, it is indisputably more difficult to nurse multiples discreetly than single babies, unless you breastfeed one child at a time and have a companion hold the other(s). A U-shaped breastfeeding pillow (described later in the chapter) can be helpful when you are alone.

*Breastfeeding Helps Your Uterus Contract*   and helps control postpartum bleeding.

*Breastfeeding Burns Calories*   and mobilizes fat stores, so eating a healthy diet actually often results in a gradual, easy weight loss. Since many women look forward to returning to pre-pregnancy weight, breastfeeding helps them accomplish that goal while at the same time helping babies gain weight! If you want to lose more weight, or lose weight more quickly, consult your physician.

*Breastfeeding Is an Intimate and Tender Way to Bond with Your Babies.*   Through breastfeeding, you offer the bounty and warmth of your body and the security of your arms. You can breastfeed two babies at the same time. Babies not only bond with you, they also enjoy being close to each other.

You can also feed babies one at a time. This lets you give each child undivided attention and may even give you greater insight into each child's unique personality.

*Breastfeeding Is Pleasurable.*   It is lovely to feel your babies sucking. Some women have sexual feelings when they nurse. Such feelings are normal and certainly nothing to feel guilty about, though some women do. Consider these pleasurable feelings Nature's way of providing the mother with an additional incentive to breastfeed!

*Breastfeeding Is Something You Alone Can Offer to Your Babies.*   Through breastfeeding you continue the relationship established in pregnancy: Your body sustains theirs.

*Breastfeeding Multiples Does Not Preclude Your Partner's Involvement or Outside Help.*   While bottlefeeding is often thought of as the method that most involves the father in child care, many women say that their spouse's support was crucial to their successful breastfeeding. To build up your milk supply, especially in the first months, you need enough rest and the ability to focus on feedings. Your partner's involvement can make all the difference. He can help you get the babies into position, especially if you have delivered by cesarean section. While you breastfeed one baby, he can burp, diaper, walk, rock, dress, gently massage, or bathe another one, or tend to the myriad of other child-care and household tasks.

When he is not available, a friend or baby-sitter can help in these ways. It is a myth that women who breastfeed cannot take advantage of outside help. There is always lots to do!

*Both Physically and Emotionally, Breastfeeding Is a Vital Way You Can Give of Yourself to Your Children.*   Breastfeeding requires stamina and determination, especially in the early weeks. But it also can be extraordinarily rewarding as your investment pays off. What a contented feeling it is to gaze at your blissfully satisfied babies. Their hands rest on your breasts like starfish on the sand.

## ▧ Preparing to Breastfeed

*"I had to be aggressive when I was pregnant and seek out people to talk with about breastfeeding. I called the Mothers of Twins Club, spoke with a lactation counselor at the hospital, and with a woman at the community health center."*

*"I was very insecure about breastfeeding. I never felt that I had a good milk supply. The resident I spoke to was not helpful or knowledgeable—*

*and he never told me that the hospital had a lactation specialist on staff! When I finally heard about her from someone else, I was so relieved; she had so much information.*

*"I was furious with the resident and I confronted him. Otherwise he might neglect to tell other women about her, too."*

Consult your obstetrician or nurse-midwife, a lactation consultant, La Leche League, or other parent support organizations for information on breastfeeding, support groups, and services. If possible, attend a La Leche League meeting or two prior to having the babies. (See the Bibliography and the Resources section in the Appendix.) Select a pediatrician who will be supportive of your desire to breastfeed your multiples. Buy nursing bras that will support your breasts and be easy to unfasten. When your milk comes in, your breasts will be larger, so buy a bra with room to grow.

When you are in the hospital, have the nurses bring all of your babies to you for each feeding so you can begin to build up a sufficient milk supply. You may want to have the babies "room in," i.e., stay in your room all or part of the time, particularly if your spouse or another family member or friend is there to help you.

If one or more babies is in a neonatal intensive-care nursery, ask the neonatologist and lactation expert about the possibility of breastfeeding while your babies are in the NICU. Even if at first your babies are too weak to suck, they may show signs of breastfeeding readiness while still in the NICU. Until babies are ready to breastfeed, you can express milk. Ask a nurse or the hospital's lactation consultant to help you learn how to express milk and to breastfeed multiples.

*"I don't think the NICU nurses had much experience with breastfeeding of twins, and they were not encouraging. I felt like I was on my own. Then I thought of calling the hospital operator and asking if there was a breastfeeding adviser on staff. It turned out that there was—and her office was on the same floor as my room! She marched into the NICU with me and spent a lot of time talking with the nurses and showing me what to do. They listened to her and became much more supportive of me. If not for her, I would have given up."*

## 🕮 Getting Comfortable with Breastfeeding

Many women, especially those who are breastfeeding for the first time, worry if they feel anxious. Nourishing babies is so crucial that

it is not uncommon for a woman's mind to race with "what ifs"—
What if I don't have enough milk? What if the babies don't get
enough?—even as she is breastfeeding just fine and the babies are
getting the best nourishment in the world. One reason that one La
Leche League Leader is so committed to helping other women breastfeed is her vivid memories of the anxiety she felt when she began
breastfeeding her first child:

> *"I was scared that if the nursing didn't go well my baby would starve.*
> *He had nipple confusion and could not nurse efficiently. Each nursing,*
> *I was so anxious and my nipples were sore. Armed with suggestions*
> *from a La Leche Leader, I retrained him. Within days, he nursed well,*
> *the soreness went away, and breastfeeding became the relaxed feeling it*
> *should be."*

Paradoxically, some women are especially uptight because they
have heard that milk supply is dependent on how relaxed the mother
is. So prevalent is the myth that every nursing mom must be a par-
agon of smiling calm, that some women despair of breastfeeding success because they feel so uncalm and awkward at the beginning.

Tension *may* delay letdown but in no way need sabotage breastfeeding, especially if you recognize that as you and your babies become more experienced with breastfeeding, you will all feel
increasingly comfortable and at ease. As with any new skill, practice
and patience are key to long-term success. (There is, of course, a
difference between normal anxiety and paralyzing panic; if you feel
the latter and nothing—even consultation with a lactation consultant
or La Leche League Leader—seems to help, consider consulting a
mental health practitioner for support and assistance.)

Until you feel that breastfeeding is truly "in gear," there are several
things you can do to make it a more comfortable experience:

*Make Sure You Are Physically Well-Supported.* Pillows are
nearly as important as breasts to successfully breastfeeding multiples!
Make sure your back and shoulders are adequately supported; a back-
rest pillow with arms is especially helpful. Place the babies on bed
pillows or a U-shaped nursing pillow so that they are raised to your
breasts. That way, babies can latch on to your breasts more easily
and you do not have to lean over. To help prevent or relieve any
strain on your lower back, rest your feet on a stool when nursing on

a couch or chair, and place a pillow under your knees when nursing in bed.

*Create a Calming Ambience.*  Let the answering machine pick up calls. Play soft music. Perhaps the dimmer light of your bedside lamp is more restful than the bright overhead light. Welcome company if the individuals are helpful and make you feel relaxed (your husband, your mother, a lactation counselor or a helpful member of your Mothers of Twins Club); avoid being with people with whom you tend to feel more nervous.

*Find Ways to Relieve Predictably Stressful Times of the Day.*  Perhaps, like many women, you find the most difficult period of the day is sometime between 4:00 and 7:00 P.M., when your energy seems to subside with the afternoon light.

Yet just as you are ready to wind down, the babies seem wound-up—stressed-out and fussy, whimpering or yowling—which is why this time is often called the "witching hour." Often all that will comfort babies is burrowing close for constant nursing—just when you think you really must think about dinner.

Perhaps babies are fussy because they sense a shift of household pace, as older children come home from school and Dad is awaited, or simply because energy builds up throughout the day and needs to be released.

One woman dealt with this daily pattern of low energy and babies' fussiness by taking the babies for a walk every day at four-thirty; the fresh air seemed to restore them all, and she craved the sight of other adults. When she returned home, her husband was there and they could share the babies and dinner preparation.

Hiring a teenager, perhaps even a young one, to come over after school for a couple of hours to work as a helper alongside you may be just the extra help you need. Some teens love babies so much, they are eager to work just for the experience, and whatever you can pay is icing on the cake. It can be a relief to have someone else to hold or rock a baby while you nurse another, or to bring you a glass of water or run to the corner market for a carton of milk.

If you begin to think of dinner as a dragon that rears its terrible head every day, an obligation demanding to be fed, then clearly that is a signal that something more predictable needs to happen at dinnertime so that dinner feeds *you*. Making some food ahead on week-ends, or asking friends or family to donate casseroles, or making simple weekly dinner menus with your spouse may give you more of a feeling of being in control of these dusky hours that can try your soul.

## Simultaneous or Sequential Nursing

*"After the first month or two of feeding the babies at the same time, I decided I was more comfortable feeding them separately. Sometimes I rocked one baby with my foot while I nursed the other one. If both babies were really hungry, I would nurse each one for two minutes, just to take the edge off the hunger. Then I would rock one while I fed the other, and then I'd switch. I got a lot of reading done at the same time!"*

For the first several months of life, most mothers breastfeed two babies simultaneously at least part of the time. With triplets, this results in only two feeding sessions rather than three, so breastfeeding does not take as much time as nursing each child separately.

Some mothers prefer to nurse their twins sequentially: one baby at a time. An oversized chair can allow you to feed one baby and hold the other nearby. This is easiest if one twin is sleeping. If he or she awakens, a pacifier can help calm the child until the other twin is finished nursing. The twin who wakes and cries first is the first to get fed. However, mothers who are trying to get their children on a schedule may awaken one twin and then the other at "feeding time," alternating the one who is awakened first.

*"I found it hard to nurse simultaneously. I would cradle my daughter between my feet while I nursed my son, then switch."*

One mother's secret to successful sequential nursing was to "run a tight ship." She did not allow her babies to "hang out" at the breast as long as they liked. She gave a pacifier to the waiting twin and limited the nursing twin to no more than twenty minutes total per feeding.

"They were always fat little babies," she said. "My doctor told me that as long as they had six soaking-wet diapers a day and continued to gain weight, they were getting enough milk."

She had not enjoyed simultaneous nursing and felt she could

develop a closer bond with each baby by nursing one at a time. While she breastfed one baby, her baby-sitter or husband held or walked the other. If you have no one to assist you, you can still nurse sequentially with the help of pacifiers and toys to occupy babies while they wait for their turn.

Other mothers feel it is easier, timesaving, and enjoyable to feed simultaneously even after the first few months. To get twins on a schedule, some mothers let the hungrier twin set the pace for both. They awaken the second twin and nurse both together. Babies can be surprisingly agreeable when awakened from a sound sleep to nurse.

*"I fed my babies on demand, but I tried to get them to take as much milk as possible at each feeding to help stretch out the time between feedings. Usually, in two hours they were ready for more."*

Since the phrase *feeding babies on demand* may sound as though babies are demanding, imperious people, many people prefer the gentler, more accurate phrase *feeding babies on cue*. Mothers who favor on-cue feeding opt for individual recognition of each child's personal rhythms and preferences over the convenience of a schedule. They feed each baby when the child awakens and cries and do not awaken children for feedings. This choice can be exhausting but rewarding. However, some women who practiced on-cue feeding with their single-born older children abandon it with their multiples, feeling that the advantages of the increased rest permitted by a regular schedule outweigh the advantages of feeding on cue.

Ask your pediatrician for advice about whether always to nurse each baby at the same breast or to alternate. To stimulate your milk supply, many doctors advise alternating breasts at each feeding. Keep track of which baby was on the right or the left. Some women make a chart. If one twin has a markedly different appetite from the other, some doctors prefer assigning each twin one breast that is always his or hers. Each breast will "customize" to the needs of its assigned baby. Your breasts may end up being different sizes. When you finish nursing, they will return to their original, symmetrical size.

*"I assigned a breast to each of my twin girls, but in retrospect I do not recommend it. Why should each twin get only one view of the world? Every time a baby nursed, her head was turned the same way, her eyes*

*gazed in the same direction. They should alternate breasts—and their views of the world—too."*

## 🌀 Supplementing with a Bottle, Cup, or Solids

*"My pediatrician kept asking how often I was feeding the babies. Their weight kept going up, so obviously we were successful. The doctor said it was okay if I wanted to supplement with formula. At first I resented him saying that."*

Most breastfeeding mothers of twins, and some mothers of triplets, find they are able to nurse exclusively for the first four to six months, until solids are introduced, while mothers of quadruplets or more are most likely to require supplementation.

However, many mothers of twins and triplets do choose to combine breastfeeding with bottlefeeding. Even so, most babies need a solid four weeks of exclusive nursing. This helps stimulate a good milk supply, especially for multiples, and prevent the soreness that develops from a confused latch-on technique (how the baby fastens on to the nipple).

When you are ready to do so, there are many ways to combine bottlefeeding with breastfeeding: choose the pattern that is right for you. It is generally best to alternate breast and bottle at different feedings, instead of offering the breast first and then the bottle during the same feeding. The drawback to the latter method is that babies may come to prefer the bottle, and wait for it, going through the mouthing motions at the breast but not effectively nursing. Therefore, they may end up weaning from the breast sooner than you would like. Or, they may feed fully at the breast, then because the urge to suck is so strong, still take the bottle, resulting in overfeeding and spitting up. Some recommendations about how to supplement with bottles:

**Breastfeed During the Day; Have Your Husband Bottlefeed at Night.**

**Breastfeed Exclusively at First, Then When You Go Back to Work, Nurse Only in the Morning and at Bedtime.**

*Breastfeed for the First Few Months, but Have Your Spouse Give the Babies a Bottle of Expressed Milk, Formula, or Water Two or Three Times a Week,* from age three or four weeks, to make sure the babies can and will take the bottle. Even taking just a few ounces this way lets babies develop the "bottle skill," so that the mother knows she can count on "future freedom," as one woman put it. But babies should not get the bottle before the age of three weeks, since they may develop "nipple confusion," a situation in which a baby refuses to breastfeed or breastfeeds unsuccessfully because breast-feeding and bottlefeeding require quite different mouth and tongue coordination. Nipple confusion results in unsuccessfully short or long, dragged-out feedings, often with severe nipple soreness due to the baby's confused attempts to treat the mother like an artificial nipple, such as that on a bottle or pacifier. Nipple confusion, and its accompanying frustrations for mother and babies, can be avoided by working with your doctor and nurse to avoid early bottles, if possible.

Consider, too, whether continued use of pacifiers may reinforce mouth and tongue motions more related to bottlefeeding than to nursing. If overused, pacifiers, like bottles, may encourage weaning.

Also, evaluate whether substantial use of a pacifier may actually be *overly* "pacifying" babies, holding them off so they are getting fewer feedings per day than they may require. Pacifiers can be a god-send when you are trying to calm a baby who is cranky in a carseat and impatient to nurse, or to hold off a baby who must wait his or her turn at the breast while other babies are being fed. "Judicious use" of pacifiers is what lactation consultants recommend; parents, in consultation with their pediatrician, must determine what "judi-cious use" is for *their* babies.

Call a breastfeeding expert if you need suggestions to conquer nipple confusion that could not be avoided. Many nursing mothers have survived this early problem and moved on to comfortable, ef-ficient nursings.

*Alternate Feeding One Twin by Bottle While the Other Is Breast-fed.* At the next feeding, switch. Triplets and quads can also be put on such rotating schedules. Your husband and helpers can thus par-ticipate in feeding the babies. You do not have to supply the babies' entire food supply, which may enable you to breastfeed longer. If you are returning to work, this system can ease the babies' transition to being exclusively bottlefed during the day and may also enable you to continue to breastfeed at night and in the morning.

If you are returning to work as early as two months postpartum, waiting over four weeks before introducing a bottle may seem too long. Perhaps you fear that your babies will reject the bottle—making it impossible for anyone but you to give them nourishment. If possible, give yourself and your babies the four-week period to get nursing established. At four weeks of age, they are likely to be good nursers but still flexible enough to accept bottlefeeding. After four weeks, your babies' practice with bottles will help make bottlefeeding as smooth as possible for babies and their caregiver(s) during your absence—and you will still be able to nurse them when you are home.

*"I was like a mother bear in a cave. I couldn't leave! The babies didn't take bottles. But I kept thinking that one reason to hang in there was that in four or five months they would start to eat solid foods. So I could look ahead to more freedom. I also thought, why rush out of the house? These twins might be my whole family. By eight or nine months, they will breastfeed less as they eat more.*

*"Looking back on it now, it seems like a brief time. The girls were born in June. By September, caring for them was easier. By November, their grandma was letting them taste orange cheesecake!"*

When introducing a bottle, do not wait until the children are two or three months old. By then they are often so established on the breast that they adamantly reject the bottle—and you are stuck at home. By the same token, even when you give a bottle early, once a week is not enough. A week is a long time in a baby's life. Several times a week is better.

If you are able to stay home with the babies throughout their first six months or more, you may decide not to use bottles at all, but to introduce babies to the cup. You can do so as early as five months of age, depending on the babies' readiness. Use "trainer cups" whose lids have spouts. (Some Herculean babies of this age are even able to use a straw!)

Around four to six months, babies may be ready for solids. *The Breastfeeding Answer Book,* a guide for La Leche League Leaders, states:

*"Signs of readiness for solids include: the ability to sit up, a fading of the tongue-thrusting reflex so that the baby does not automatically push solids out of [the] mouth with [the] tongue, readiness to chew, the ability to pick up food and put it in [the] mouth, an increased demand to nurse that is unrelated to illness, teething pain, or a change in routine. . . .*

*"If the baby suddenly increases his demand to be fed at around six months of age and this increased demand to be fed continues for four or five days in spite of more frequent nursings, the mother can assume the time has come to start him on solids. If the baby is much younger than six months . . . this behavior may be due to other causes, such as an illness coming on, a growth spurt, or a change in routine."*[3]

For many parents, one sure sign that children are ready for solids is when they reach over and grab food from their parents' or siblings' plates and try to eat it (although some grab food just to have something to teethe on). Children who had been sleeping through the night and stop doing so may also be signaling readiness for solids.

## 🔲 Breastfeeding Positions

*"When I was pregnant, my main concern was breastfeeding. I called the Mothers of Twins Club, and a volunteer from the club talked with me a lot on the phone. She sent me materials, including a photocopy of an ad from* Twins *magazine for a U-shaped pillow for breastfeeding twins. I sent away for the pillow. It's great! I use it for the 'football hold.' "*

*"I ordered the Nurse-Mate pillow.*[4] *It gave us lots of laughs in the NICU, but I got my money's worth out of it. Even after I was finished nursing it was perfect for putting behind the babies when they were learning how to sit up—no cracked heads. When they were crawling they used it as a tunnel."*

There are several ways to breastfeed babies simultaneously. Whether you nurse in a bed, armchair, or rocker, make sure you have lots of bed pillows, cushions, or rolled-up towels or blankets to provide support during breastfeeding and burping and to protect the

[3]Nancy Mohrbacher and Julie Stock, *The Breastfeeding Answer Book* (Franklin Park, IL: La Leche League International, Inc., 1991).
[4]For information on the U-shaped Nurse-Mate pillow, contact Four Dee Products (see the Resources section in the Appendix).

babies in case they slip from your grasp while you are learning how to maneuver them.

Although handling two or more babies at a time may seem as daunting at first as learning to juggle, before too long you will exhibit a most astonishing expertise.

*"When my friends saw me breastfeeding, they almost fell off their chairs onto the floor. They couldn't believe it. First, you have to get the babies ready, and they are so hungry and anxious. Get the blouse up, the bra down. You're handling two babies singlehandedly, and one arm is stronger than the other. One baby was a stronger nurser, so I switched babies at each feeding so both breasts would be equal. It took me a good hour to nurse both babies. I changed their diapers between changing breasts to keep them awake."*

### OVERLAPPING TWINS

Position babies so that they crisscross, their bodies lying across you in opposite directions. Baby A nurses on your right breast, feet toward your left hip. Baby B nurses on your left breast, body resting against Baby A, feet toward your right hip. Their heads are supported by your arms, with your hands on their buttocks. This position is best when babies are little, since roly-poly babies don't overlap too well.

To burp them, scoop them up into sitting positions, facing each other, or rest them on your shoulders.

### FOOTBALL POSITION

Position babies so each faces a breast straight-on, with body under your arm, feet pointing behind you, with the babies' buttocks against the same back support you are using. Support their heads with your hands, or use the above-mentioned U-shaped pillow.

Burp them by easing them up against your shoulders.

### SIDEWAYS PARALLEL POSITION

Rest babies on pillows so each lies facing the same direction. Baby A's head rests on your right arm and nurses from your right breast. Baby B nurses from your left breast, head supported by your left arm. A pillow or two can help you stabilize Baby B.

*Babies overlap cozily as they breastfeed together. Strategic placing of cushions helps make babies and Mom comfortable.*

Burp babies by holding them in a sitting position or by holding them up against your shoulders.

### FRONT PARALLEL POSITION

Position babies in front of you on pillows with an arm around each, your hand on their buttocks. The babies' bodies face each other, their knees touching or nearly touching.

Burp them by bringing them into a sitting position.

### RECLINING

Lean against pillows and place babies across you, using additional pillows for support.

Burp babies by sitting them up so they are resting against your waist or chest.

*While nursing her babies in the football position, this new mother gets valuable breastfeeding hints and lots of encouragement from a member of her Mothers of Twins Club.*

## Expressing Milk

Expression of breast milk is the removal of breast milk from the mother's breasts by hand or pump. Expressed milk may be used fresh, or refrigerated or frozen and used later. Expressing milk also enables you to maintain a milk supply if you are taking certain medications or undergoing surgical procedures when you should not or cannot breastfeed.

You can also express breast milk and discard it if you want to relieve engorgement. Sometime between the second to sixth day after birth, your breasts begin producing more milk. When you first begin producing larger quantities of milk, your breasts tend to become larger, heavier, and somewhat tender. One breastfeeding book explains that this feeling of engorgement is "due to extra blood and

*In the sideways parallel position, babies nurse while lying securely
against Mom's body, well supported by pillows.*

lymph fluids in the breasts as well as the increased volume of the
milk itself."[5]

A La Leche League Leader says that "expression is one of the ways
to reduce and relieve this normal, short-lived engorgement. It makes
latch-on easier for the baby if some milk is expressed first, since some
women find that the nipple may be stretched nearly flat by the pressure of the milk and fluids within the breast."

Engorgement may also occur if you miss one or more feedings
you would normally give. Your breasts fill with milk "right on schedule"; if they are not emptied through breastfeeding or expressing,
they can feel uncomfortable or painful.

Other reasons women express breast milk:

- Expressing milk enables husbands and caregivers to bottlefeed
  while the mother rests, goes out, or works.
- Premature babies often cannot breastfeed at first, either because
  they are too weak to suck or because they are being tube-fed.

[5]Mohrbacher and Stock, *The Breastfeeding Answer Book.*

*Mom reclines and relaxes, may even doze a bit, while she nurses her twins.*

Expressing milk gets the milk supply going and provides breast milk for babies who can be bottlefed.

• Some mothers of triplets express milk so that the third baby can be bottlefed mother's milk while the others feed at the breast. Babies are alternated at each feeding so that all are both breast- and bottlefed.

Many women recommend renting a hospital-quality electric breast pump from a hospital supply house. You can also rent, purchase, or borrow other electric, battery-operated, or manual pumps. Contact La Leche League for recommendations. Avoid old-fashioned pumps with rubber bulbs, since the bulbs cannot be sterilized and may compromise the sterility of the collected milk.

You can also manually express milk:

• Wash your hands thoroughly.
• Relax and massage breasts with long, stroking motions toward the areola, the dark area around the nipple.

- With one hand, hold a sterilized baby bottle under your breast to collect the milk.
- With the other hand, gently grasp the areola between thumb (on top) and forefinger. Press inward (toward your ribs), then squeeze thumb and finger together and outward.
- Repeat evenly and rhythmically, collecting droplets, then a stream of milk, in the bottle. Hold your fingers at different places around the areola to ensure that all milk ducts have a chance to empty.
- Repeat on the other breast, or alternate breasts every few minutes until both are empty.

Due to the antibacterial properties in breast milk, just-expressed milk may stay fresh at room temperature for as long as six to ten hours, assuming that it has not touched the baby's mouth. If it has, then the milk must be refrigerated and finished within three to four hours.

Breast milk can be stored in plastic nurser bags inside the refrigerator and should be used within three to five days. Or place the nurser bags inside sturdy plastic containers and store in a Deepfreeze for up to six months. Milk can also be frozen in a well-functioning self-contained freezer unit of a refrigerator, close to the back of the freezer and away from the door, for about three to four months. When freezing milk, make sure to leave space at the top of each nurser bag for the milk to expand. Place a piece of masking tape on each bag noting the date and amount. Defrost breast milk in cold, then lukewarm running water or bowls of water, or in the refrigerator. Defrosting in the microwave can be dangerous, because the outside of the bottle may feel cool while the inside is hot enough to burn the baby's mouth. The microwave is also said to kill the immunity factors in the milk. Tightly closed milk bottles can also explode in a microwave if left in too long.

Always test any bottle before giving it to your child. Shake it to distribute heat and breast-milk contents evenly, then sprinkle a few drops of milk onto the inside of your wrist. It should feel warm but not hot. It is better to err by giving milk that is too cool than milk that is too hot.

## ⬛ Keep Milk Flowing, Yourself Healthy, and Your Outlook Positive

*"I kept thinking, there are just three words I need to remember: Rest. Eat. Drink."*

*"I drank four cups of milk every morning, three cups of juice at lunchtime, and at least one glass of water at every feeding and other times during the day. All the liquids plus eating very well enabled me to exclusively breastfeed and give no bottles for six months. I weaned them at age two."*

*Drink, Drink, Drink.* Many doctors recommend drinking eight to ten glasses of water every day, plus a couple of glasses of fruit or vegetable juice and two glasses of milk. If you cannot manage to drink this much, do "drink to thirst" and have a glass of water, juice, or milk every time you prepare to breastfeed. However, bear in mind that some babies find cow's milk hard to tolerate—even if they only get it through their mother's milk. If babies seem gassy or colicky or spit up a lot, try eliminating dairy products from your diet.

*Eat Nutritious Meals and Snacks.* Eat enough protein, fresh fruits and vegetables, and whole grains.

Evaluate whether babies are sensitive to milk produced after you have eaten such foods as onions, broccoli, cabbage, tomatoes, and spicy foods. There has been little scientific research on this subject, but some mothers do find that certain foods, such as dairy products and nuts, disagree with their babies, causing fits of crying and gas. Some women stick to a simple, bland diet—which, thankfully, is also the easiest to prepare. Although they find their diets boring, it is worth it to have peaceful babies. Yet many mothers eat hot, spicy curries and spaghetti sauces and find that these foods do not affect their babies at all. After all, children's first exposure to the foods of their culture is through breast milk. The Middle Eastern dish hummus, a pureed chick-pea dip made with prodigious amounts of garlic, was two eight-month-old babies' favorite solid food; their mother figured that they liked the garlic they had tasted indirectly through her milk.

# 140

LIFE WITH MULTIPLES

With the exception of caffeine and alcohol, there is no food that a nursing mother must give up. (Not all doctors agree with this rule: some allow a glass of beer or wine now and then. Ask your doctor what is right for you.)

*Continue Taking Prenatal Vitamins* or another vitamin supplement your obstetrician/gynecologist recommends.

*Rest As Much As You Can.* Having enough help with your home, meals, and other children is crucial. Ample rest will help keep your milk supply plentiful and has to be a priority. When guests stay too long, do not hesitate to tell them that you need to rest now.

> *"At a La Leche League meeting, someone likened breastfeeding new babies to a honeymoon. She called it a 'babymoon.' You hang out in bed with them for a whole day, drinking, eating, resting, nursing. This increases energy and builds up strength.*
> *"I remembered this one day when the twins were eight weeks old and my energy was shot. I made myself a huge turkey sandwich to eat for lunch, a peanut-butter sandwich for a snack, cut-up cubes of cheese, and put a large pitcher of water by the bed. With all my food made, I just stayed in bed all day with the babies and took it easy."*

*Are Your Babies Gaining Weight?* If you have doubts about whether your babies are getting enough to eat, weigh them. If the babies are growing and your pediatrician is satisfied with their rate of growth, they are obviously doing very well on the breast.

Also keep in mind:

- Do babies have six to eight wet diapers a day and regular bowel movements? Note that each baby has his or her own normal bowel-movement pattern. Many newborns have two to five bowel movements in a twenty-four-hour period; some have one at every feeding. Some older babies defecate substantially only once every three days. (Discuss your babies' individual patterns with your pediatrician.) Also, some disposable diapers are so absorbent that they may not *feel* "soaking wet" even though babies *have* urinated a normal amount.
- Are babies breastfeeding frequently? Most breastfeed ten to twelve times a day, while others nurse less frequently because

they are such efficient nursers or do not have as strong a need to suck. Breastfed babies usually need to eat more frequently than bottlefed babies.

Consult your pediatrician if you are concerned about your babies' rate of growth.

*Take Good Care of Your Breasts.*   The breasts naturally self-clean and moisturize. Never use soap on your nipples because it can be drying. Keep nipples soft and supple by applying a modified lanolin if you are recovering from sore nipples. Always look for, and correct, the cause of any soreness.

*"My nipples were sore from the constant barrage of little mouths.[6] The lactation consultant at the hospital sent me a really good lanolin cream and some cups with holes in them [breast shells] to put inside my bra to help air out my nipples."*

*"My sister said, 'I promise you that your nipples won't hurt in one week. Hang in there.'"*

*Do Not Take Any Prescription or Over-the-Counter Drugs*   without first checking with your pediatrician about whether they might adversely affect your baby through breast milk.

*Do Not Take "Street Drugs."*

*Give Yourself Time to Get Used to Breastfeeding.*   For both you and your babies, breastfeeding is a new skill; like any new skill it demands patience and practice.

*"I felt like a little factory. I was sure at the beginning that my breasts would fall off! Nobody told me that nursing can hurt. But I stayed with it. After the first few weeks, my breasts were used to nursing, and I felt comfortable.*
*    "I nursed every two hours until the twins were three months old, then for the next two months, every three hours. For the first four or five months, I nursed simultaneously. It's like climbing a mountain. You don't look up. You just keep going."*

[6]NOTE: Proper positioning and latch-on should alleviate this type of soreness.

*"I had planned to breastfeed for only three months, to give the babies my antibodies. But at three months, nursing was working so well that I continued."*

*"One day, when the girls were two-and-a-half months old, they were both crying and fussy and I couldn't satisfy them. I felt like I had no milk left, it was a nightmare. My friend advised, 'Just let go. Maybe they are having a growth spurt. Get some rest. Things will be better tomorrow.' And they were."*

## ▧ When Babies Nurse Differently

Two breasts, two babies at a time: It seems a perfect symmetry. Yet two babies have two separate personalities and may have different appetites or reactions to breastfeeding. Sometimes babies develop a preference for one breast over another. One baby might latch on to the breast with firmness and determination, sucking with a steady rhythm, while the other is a distracted "snacker." A smaller or weaker baby may take longer to get the knack of breastfeeding, while the twin chows down with nonchalant ease.

Multiples' differences can be confounding. One woman had enjoyed breastfeeding her older child and looked forward to nursing her twins. But her boy nursed so vigorously and copiously that she felt she "had nothing left" for her girl, who was a "sipper." The experience was so fraught with anxiety that she stopped after four weeks.

It might have helped this mother to realize that babies have different nursing styles, and that a "sipper baby" can still get a good feeding if provided the opportunity. Perhaps she was overwhelmed with twins and felt emotionally that she had nothing left. Since the boy nursed more vigorously, she may have found it helpful to ask a lactation consultant for ways to make sure her daughter could also feed successfully.

When one child refuses to nurse and the other(s) thrive on it, what do you do? One woman nursed one twin two months longer than the other, who refused to nurse after two weeks, perhaps confused because breast and bottle had been alternated. Another mother faced the same situation—but weaned the twin who was willing to breastfeed because she did not want the twins to be "unequal."

La Leche League and other breastfeeding educators can help you adapt to varied nursing styles and encourage reluctant nursers. There are many possible solutions to a wide array of breastfeeding challenges. For example, you may find simultaneous feeding of dissimilar babies disconcerting, while feeding one at a time allows you to relax and appreciate each child's special ways.

*"One day when my girls were only two weeks old, I was having such a hard time that I packed them up and we all went to a La Leche meeting. I think they were surprised to see me; my babies were so little. But I needed support. And I got it."*

But logistics are only one side of the story. Breastfeeding differences between twins highlight essential values issues. How equally do you feel you must treat your multiples? How okay is it for them to be different? Even after a successful start of nursing, if one twin continues to nurse well, should he or she be penalized if the other prefers the supplemental bottle? If one triplet prefers the bottle, will you feel personally rejected, or will you accept that child's "choice"? If one baby is a "no-nonsense," focused speed-eater, and the other is a casual, more leisurely diner who spends more time at the breast, will you feel it necessary to make the feedings equal, or will you feel that their difference should be respected?

During the babies' first months of life, you spend a great deal of your time feeding them, getting to know them while nursing or when giving a bottle. Breastfeeding is a wonderful gift you alone can provide, but neither method has exclusive claim to better mother-child bonding. Rather, it is your acceptance and love of your children as individuals that is the key to your blossoming relationship—both now, when they drink breast milk or formula, and later in life, when they'll prefer milk shakes.

# ⌘ *Chapter 10*

# ℬOTTLEFEEDING

⌘    Many parents choose to bottlefeed their multiples, either exclusively, or to supplement breastfeeding, or because breastfeeding was unsuccessful or not recommended. (For information on breastfeeding multiples, see Chapter 9. Even if you prefer to bottlefeed, just a few breastfeedings can benefit your babies. And some women decide to bottlefeed because they are not familiar with how very possible and positive an experience breastfeeding multiples can be.)

Whether babies are breastfed or bottlefed, feeding time is important not only to fill their bodies, but also to fuel your shared love. Cuddled bottlefed babies flourish on the warmth of your body, the gaze of your eyes, the affection of your touch. A parent's face is a baby's mirror. Your loving smile makes the baby feel: I am worthy of love. It is this interaction that is most crucial to your relationship—not the choice of bottle or breast.

## ⌘ *Advantages of Bottlefeeding*

***Many Nutritious Infant Formulas Are Available.***   No one would claim that formula is breast milk's nutritional equal. Yet millions of babies thrive on it and grow to be healthy and strong.

Most formulas are based on cow's milk. Allergic babies may require soy formula or "protein hydrolysate" or "elemental" formulas that are specially designed for babies who are allergic to cow milk proteins. Your pediatrician will recommend the formula that is best for your babies. Sometimes several brands must be tried to determine which are best suited to your children's needs. Some multiples require a different formula from their siblings because of allergic reactions or variations in their digestive systems.

*Bottlefeeding Enables Both Parents to Feed the Babies.* Mealtimes are such important times in babies' lives. Fathers of bottlefed babies treasure their ability to participate. Bottlefeeding frees the mother from the responsibility of being the babies' only source of food. Also, she may be able to get more rest when other people can feed the babies. Exclusive or supplemental bottlefeeding is essential for mothers who work outside the home. (However, some women with part-time jobs, job sharing, flex-time, or an on-site child care facility may be able to supplement less and breastfeed more than those who must keep to a more rigid work schedule.)

*Since Baby-Sitters Can Bottlefeed, Too, Both Parents Can Get a Break.* Teach baby-sitters the bottlefeeding positions described in this chapter.

*Bottlefed Babies Can—and Should—Be Held During Feeding, Creating Intimate Moments Between Parent and Children.* Whether fed by breast or bottle, babies need the comfort and nurturing of contact with your body. Whenever possible, hold babies when you feed them. Overwhelmed parents often feel the need to prop babies' bottles, either with bottle holders or by holding bottles in place between cushions or rolled-up blankets. Only prop bottles if you are right next to the babies to supervise and make sure they do not choke. Never leave babies alone with propped bottles. See page 146 for positions that enable you to hold and bottlefeed two babies simultaneously.

*Bottlefed Babies Often Do Not Get Hungry As Quickly As Breastfed Babies Because It Takes Them Longer to Digest Formula.* Longer intervals between feedings give parents some relief from being constantly "on call."

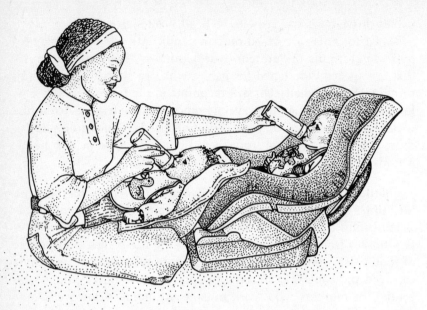

*Having both babies face her lets Mom easily maintain eye contact with each child.*

Ask your pediatrician how much formula each baby needs. Even some identical twins may not have identical appetites or needs.

***Bottlefeeding Is Convenient.*** You can buy ready-to-pour formula (the most expensive), liquid formula concentrate (less expensive), or powdered formula (least expensive). Mix the concentrate or powder with boiled water. Directions on the can give you amounts to use when preparing one bottle or more. Pour the formula into bottles, cover them, and store them in the refrigerator for up to forty-eight hours. Warm the bottles in bowls of hot tap water. Do not heat bottles in the microwave, since a bottle that feels warm to the touch may have a scalding-hot internal temperature. Always test bottles before giving them to babies by sprinkling a few drops of formula on the inside of your wrist to make sure it is warm, never hot.

Disposable plastic nurser bags that fit into hard plastic holders are a boon for parents of multiples. They eliminate the need for more time-consuming sterilizing of glass or plastic bottles.

Use bottles of different colors, styles, or brands to help you, and later the babies, distinguish each child's bottle from the others. This

*As Dad holds a bottle in each hand, his babies lie sideways on his lap,
their heads resting on his right arm.*

is especially important when babies require different formulas.

In one family, one twin needed to take smaller amounts of formula more frequently, while the other had no such restrictions. So the parents gave a four-ounce bottle to the first twin and an eight-ounce bottle to the second. Bottles of different sizes could be told apart at a glance, and both girls got a full bottle at each feeding.

Buy color-coded nipples that are specifically made for formula, juice, and water. Ask your pediatrician to recommend nipples whose shapes enable the baby to more closely duplicate the breastfeeding experience.

***Babies Can Be Bottlefed Easily When Parents Take Them Out.*** This is in contrast to breastfed babies, whose mothers must consider how to breastfeed discreetly. Tote bottles in insulated bottle bags to keep them fresh. If you plan to be out long, consider splurging on ready-to-feed cans of formula. Most require no can opener. Some are packaged as bottles that can be fitted with a nipple and ring for on-the-spot feeding.

*Babies bottlefeed while positioned face forward on Dad's lap, nestled against his chest.*

**Parents Can Keep Track of How Much Babies Eat.**   While this is not important for all babies, it can be useful for those who are having feeding problems or not gaining weight. Keep a chart on the refrigerator door listing the time and amount each baby ate that day. Show baby-sitters how to fill in the chart, too. Share the chart with your pediatrician.

## ⊠ Bottlefeeding Positions for Multiples

*"It would take each infant a full hour to finish a bottle, and they ate every three hours. So I'd feed one, then that one would sleep for three hours. During the first hour, I'd feed the other twin. If she wasn't up, I awakened her so that I would not have my own sparse sleep interrupted. I was exhausted all winter. I didn't even leave the house for the first six weeks."*

*"My twins take a bottle every four hours. One week I counted how many bottles this was per week: eighty-four!"*

*Dad bottlefeeds the babies in their seats while Mom catches up on some long-overdue phone calls.*

*"It was the biggest relief in my life when the twins could hold their own bottles when they were four months old. It was heaven."*

New parents often struggle to find ways to feed babies simultaneously. It is a time to envy the rubbery-armed, many-limbed octopus. How can you hold two babies and two bottles without dropping anybody or anything? Life will be much easier when the babies are older and can hold their own bottles. Then they can easily sit on your lap at the same time. (Unless one starts kicking—but that's another story.) But for now, try the following:

## TWO SIDEWAYS ON A LAP

One couple was astonished at their baby nurse's feeding facility. A broad, cushiony woman, she placed both babies on her lap, their heads supported by her right arm. With her left arm she held a bottle for the baby closest to her body. In her right arm, she held the other baby's bottle. The contented babies fed side by side.

The parents doubted their ability to duplicate this feat, since they

*It's good to try a variety of feeding positions to see which suit you and your babies best. Here Mom feeds one baby in a seat and the other on her lap.*

were both small and rather bony. Their forearms combined could not equal the nurse's single ample one. But lo and behold, with the aid of some pillows they found that they could approximate this comfy, efficient trick.

### Two Facing Forward on a Lap

Sit both babies on your lap, facing forward, their heads resting on your chest. Use cushions for support. Hold a bottle in each hand.

### Two in Seats

Infant seats are essential equipment for parents of two or more. Sit on a couch or on the floor in front of the couch. Have each baby in an infant seat on either side of you. Rest your back and arms on the couch for support while giving each a bottle. If the infant seats are on the couch, make sure they are stable so they don't tip over or fall on the floor.

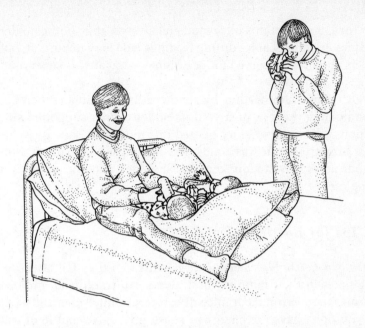

*Mom bottlefeeds in the V position: Babies snuggle against pillows, framed by the V of her legs.*

### Lap One, Seat One

Bottlefeed one baby in your lap, the other in the infant seat next to you. Use pillows to support your arms, if necessary.

### Feeding in the V

Sit on a bed with your legs open to form a V. Lay both babies in front of you inside the V. Support their bodies with your legs while you give each a bottle.

### Each Parent Takes a Baby

This is easiest of all. When both parents (or one parent and a helper) are available, each of you can have one baby all to yourself.

Parents of triplets and quads can use these positions, too, rotating babies. Use pacifiers or, later, toys to calm babies who are waiting their turn. Some parents like commercially available "bottle holders." But since cuddling babies during feedings is so very important, bottle holders should be reserved for occasional—and always supervised—use.

Burp babies after feeding by gently patting or rubbing their backs while holding them against your shoulder or in a supported sitting position. A newspaper story quoted one mother as saying, "When I burped my triplets, it was almost like playing a bongo drum. I often had one across my lap, one over my shoulder, and one on the couch beside me."[1]

## 🔹 Tips for Bottlefeeding

*Do Not Let Babies Sleep with a Bottle.*   If they fall asleep with the nipples in their mouths, tooth decay can result from prolonged exposure to the formula or juice. If babies absolutely demand a bottle and you don't have the energy to resist, give only a bottle of water. Pacifiers are better. (Never allow children to wear pacifiers on a string or ribbon around their necks, since they could strangle if it gets caught or twisted.)

*Do Not Add Sugar, Honey, or Other Sweeteners to Bottles of Water, Juice, or Formula.*   Also, do not daub pacifiers with sweeteners. Giving sweeteners to babies promotes tooth decay. Because honey can contain spores that can cause botulism in babies, do not give it to children under a year old.

*Buy Colorful Cups and Lids with Built-In "Sippers" to Encourage Weaning from Bottle to Cup.*   (Ask your pediatrician about the best time to wean.) Consider whether you want to buy cups of the same or different colors. One pair of twins waged a bitter battle over who would get the orange cup instead of the green. Their ingenious dad finally found a solution. He put the orange lid on the green cup and the green lid on the orange cup. This so confused the twins that they surrendered the battle, unsure now about which cup was more worth fighting for.

[1]Popsy Sadock, "Three Babies at a Time? Wombmates," *Tribune-Review* (Greensburg, PA), November 26, 1992.

# ❧ *Chapter 11*

# $\mathcal{E}$QUIPMENT, CLOTHING, AND SUPPLIES

❧ Stuff. So much stuff! A milelong stroller, countless stacks of baby clothes and diapers, a fleet of infant swings, infant seats, and high chairs, a passel of pacifiers, and the entire cast of *Sesame Street* (stuffed versions, that is). Just *thinking* about all the things your children will need can make your wallet seem anemic and your home too cramped.

When money and space are limited, separate the nice from the necessary. As with airplane travel, either first class or coach gets you there. For a sturdy stroller, you may be willing to "go first class" and spend more; on clothes, you might splurge on a few special-occasion outfits but choose lower-priced alternatives for everyday messing up and messing around. Little ones look darling in designer outfits, but let's face it, they look darling in discount-store clothes, too—and you suffer fewer pangs when they outgrow or irrevocably stain them.

Let your particular needs and values guide your budget. One couple who prized running in the park felt that a twin jogging buggy was essential. One woman always promised herself that when she had children, she would invest in a big antique rocking chair. A third family bought very little new clothing or equipment but did set aside money for baby-sitters to help tide them over the stress of the first months of parenthood.

> *"When you have twins, it's a lot of mileage. They should have Frequent Children Miles! The first year was 'The Year of Discovery.' My wife and I learned to take fewer steps, be more precise. We kept a changing table on the first floor and the second floor to reduce the number of times we had to go up and down steps. We kept bassinets on the first floor for naps. We put a small refrigerator in our bedroom and an electric bottle warmer in our upstairs bathroom for nighttime feedings."*

Using secondhand items can save you a fortune. Many Mothers of Twins Clubs newsletters feature lists of equipment and clothing members want to sell or buy. Accept relatives' and friends' hand-me-downs. Scan obstetricians' and pediatricians' office bulletin boards, neighborhood flyers, and yard sales for bargains. One mother frequents thrift shops for exclusive charities or rummage sales at private schools, finding that she gets higher-quality items at unbelievably low prices. Launder all used clothing and bedding before using them.

As terrific as it is to save money on secondhand things, do familiarize yourself with what local baby stores carry. Patronize stores with helpful sales clerks who can explain the features of different types and brands of equipment. Advances in product design may make it worthwhile to buy certain items new, if you can afford them. And you never know what nifty gadgets you may discover.

> *"One of the best things we ever bought were gadgets from a baby-supply store that keep bottles attached to the stroller. A strap fastens around the stroller and a ring fastens around the bottle. So when the babies start throwing their bottles out of the stroller a thousand times, you don't have to stop and pick up all those thrown bottles because the bottles never really leave! After a while, the babies learn to retrieve the bottles themselves."*

(Note: Do not make your own version of this gadget. If the strap is too long it could present a safety hazard, as a child could become tangled in it or choke on it.)

Make sure any new or secondhand cribs, playpens, carrier seats, gates, high chairs, strollers, toy chests, and other equipment have no sharp edges, are in good working order, and meet current safety standards. *To request free nursery and play equipment safety checklists, write to the U.S. Consumer Product Safety Commission, Washington, D.C. 20207.*

## ▣ *Befriend Your Local Market*

You may be able to arrange discount prices at a local store for items you buy by the case, such as infant formula or diapers. Make the deal especially enticing by forming your own informal "buyers club" with other parents of multiples.

If you live in a city where prices are higher than the surrounding suburbs or rural area, ask a friend or a commuting spouse to buy diapers and other supplies for you at the lower prices. Buying in bulk can save you a great deal of money. However, consider whether a higher-priced local store may offer service, convenience, or delivery that offsets the additional cost.

## ▣ *Shopping by Phone*

To save money and/or time, or to locate hard-to-find items, consider ordering from catalogs. If you're unfamiliar with this kind of shopping, ask friends to recommend catalog companies they like. Also check out mail-order companies that advertise in *Twins* magazine and other parenting magazines and publications for parents of multiples (see the Resources section in the Appendix). Some companies specialize in products for multiples (and in some cases were founded by parents of multiples) and offer such items as twin/triplet strollers and baby carriers, pillows that help you to breastfeed twins comfortably, and books, stationery, jewelry, novelty items, and gifts with a twins/multiples theme. Some catalogs even have gift registries. (For a list of catalogs, see the Resources section in the Appendix.)

Before you buy:

- ask whether the catalog accepts returns.
- ask if the catalog offers a discount for multiples or large purchases.

• assess whether the cost of shipping and handling makes items unacceptably more expensive than buying from a local store.

But also remember that your time is a valuable and scarce commodity! If a catalog costs you a bit more but repays you in time saved, you may come out ahead.

## 🎴 *Shop Early*

Some parents-to-be set up nurseries before the babies arrive. Others prefer to wait, whether from superstition or caution or religious beliefs. They feel that if anything goes wrong, they would rather cancel a baby-furniture order than dismantle the nursery. (For the same reason, they prefer that baby showers be held after the births rather than during pregnancy.) However, do shop during pregnancy since afterward you will have little time. Most stores honor customers' requests to delay delivery and billing until babies are born. Some stores also have "baby registries," similar to bridal registries, to help friends and family choose baby gifts you can really use. When you shop, consider taking along a friend or relative who has multiples and can advise you on how to choose wisely. Leave tags on clothing until the babies are born since you don't know what baby gifts you will receive. You do not want to be stuck with nonreturnable items.

## 🎴 *Desperately Seeking Freebies*

*"The hospital suggested I send copies of the twins' birth certificates to companies and request samples and coupons. I got three free cases of formula, coupons for diapers and baby food, and little samples of powder, soap, shampoo, and diaper wipes."*

When there were fewer twins, triplets, and quads, many manufacturers supplied infant formula, baby food, diapers, and other supplies to parents of multiples free or at a discount. Today, this is less common, but some companies provide free samples or discount coupons, either through obstetricians' or pediatricians' offices or directly upon customer request. Contact companies by writing their customer service departments or calling their toll-free 800 numbers (found on product packages or in parenting magazine ads). If you have no time to write or call, enlist a friend's help. Here are two examples of complimentary product offers:

Procter & Gamble offers a free bag of Pampers or Luvs diapers to parents of triplets or more, upon receipt of (a) a note from your doctor on hospital stationery verifying that you had triplets or more; (b) a photocopy of each birth certificate; and (c) a note from you giving the babies' gender(s) and stating which size diaper you want for each baby. Write to:

> Procter & Gamble Triplets Diaper Offer
> P.O. Box 599
> Cincinnati OH 45201
> (1-800-543-0480)

Ross Laboratories provides membership cards for its free "Welcome Addition Club" to obstetricians and pediatricians; send in the card for coupons and a free starter supply of formula. In addition, the company provides a free gift pack for twins, triplets, or more upon request. Call 1-800-227-5767, or write:

> Consumer Relations Department
> Ross Laboratories
> Columbus OH 43260

## ✿ *What Do You Really Need?*

Here, in alphabetical order, are equipment, clothing, and supplies for multiples, some essential, others helpful but optional. Stores and Mothers of Twins Club "swaps" may have additional products you will find helpful.

### ANSWERING MACHINE

Barring a butler, nothing is handier for managing untimely phone calls than an answering machine. When you are feeding, napping, or just playing with your babies, you may not wish to be interrupted. And when it is dangerous to leave babies unattended (for example, when they are in a bath, infant swing, or walker, or drinking from a propped bottle), you simply cannot answer the phone. The answering machine puts you in control, lets you screen calls, and eliminates the need to take the phone off the hook or let it ring. You can get an effective, no-frills answering machine for a fairly low price, or suggest it as a gift.

### BABY BATHTUB

Baby bathtubs can be used on a table or positioned in a sink or bathtub. Most are lined with foam to cushion the baby and have a tilted back to help you keep the baby's head elevated and out of the water. You need only one baby bathtub. When babies are little, you will probably bathe only one at a time, unless your mate or another adult helper is there to hold a second baby in the tub while you are in charge of the first. When babies are older and able to sit by themselves, you can bathe them together in a regular tub that has been lined with a nonslip mat, or use bath seats that have suction cups on the bottom. (See "Bathing Babies" in Chapter 12.)

### BASSINETS OR PORTABLE CRIBS

When money is tight, you can postpone purchasing cribs and start your babies off in bassinets or portable cribs.

Bassinets, often made in pretty wicker, can be passed from friend to friend. Even if you have cribs, bassinets are useful in the first months. Because they are small and portable, bassinets can be wheeled easily from one room to another so you can have the babies near you, even in the kitchen if it is big enough. Some parents like to keep bassinets on the first floor for naps. You do not need to buy special bassinet sheets; just pop a pillowcase onto the bassinet mattress.

Bassinets should not be used when babies start moving around a lot or getting up on their hands and knees. At that point, lend the bassinets to someone else.

Portable cribs give you more months, even years, of service than a bassinet. They can be used much longer than the first three months, can fold for travel, can be stored compactly when the babies outgrow them and be set up quickly for guest babies in the future. Some parents find their babies are not happy in bassinets; their babies prefer the portable crib, perhaps because it is roomier or because it offers greater visual stimulation. (One family whose children have out-grown their portable crib now uses it as a toybox.)

Another option is to put babies on blankets in a playpen for an extra sleep-site. This gets babies used to a playpen early, if you are planning to use one later on.

## BOTTLES

The number and type of bottles you need depends, of course, on whether you will use them exclusively or to supplement breastfeeding. (See Chapters 9 and 10.)

Disposable bottles may be helpful for breastfed babies since breast milk can be frozen in the plastic bottles. For exclusively bottlefed babies, you need enough regular or disposable bottles (at least six to eight per child) so you can make a quart or so of formula and fill and refrigerate bottles for use later. (Check the instructions on the formula label.) You may want to purchase an electric bottle warmer, some of which are thermostatically controlled. Ask your pediatrician whether you need a bottle sterilizer.

You can choose latex or silicone bottle nipples. Silicone nipples last longer. Old and worn latex nipples can be hazardous, since children can bite off and swallow pieces of latex.

You can also choose a traditional nipple shape or an orthodontic shape that is said to more closely mimic the experience of breast feeding.

After a bottle comes a cup. There are many different types of training cups. Some have a spout or a straw, a weighted bottom, one or two handles, or no handles at all. You may need to experiment to see which cups you and your children like best.

## BREAST PUMP

If you plan to breastfeed, you may have regular or occasional need for a breast pump. Some women get the hang of breast pumps, while others hate pumps and use their hands to express milk or avoid pumping altogether. If you do need to pump often, consider renting a hospital-quality pump from a hospital supply house or buy one. However, these are very expensive. There are also other electric, battery-operated, or manual pumps to choose from that cost less and work well. Contact La Leche League or a local Mothers of Twins Club for advice.

## CARS AND VANS

Compact cars look neat, slide neatly into tiny parking spaces, and neatly reduce gasoline bills. But for couples with multiples, they may be as impractical as a coach fashioned out of a pumpkin. The first thing one couple did when they discovered they would have triplets was to trade in their small car for a van. They say it is the best decision they ever made.

When deciding what car or van to purchase, or whether to replace the one you have, consider how many car seats it must accommodate, ease of entrance and exit (four-door cars are more convenient than two-doors—but make sure rear doors have safety locks), how many people it can hold (in addition to parents and babies, will the car be needed for visiting in-laws, baby-sitters, friends?), and the trunk's or backseat's capacity for folded-up strollers, overstuffed diaper bags, and packages.

## CAR SEATS

Babies and toddlers must ride in car seats; older children must use booster seats or wear seat belts (check your state's law to determine by what age or weight children are no longer required to sit in car seats or booster seats). Some late-model cars and vans have built-in car seats.

When buying car seats, measure your car to make sure they will all fit and consider whether any special hardware or attachments will work in your car. Some parents like using infant car seats instead of those that can be converted for different ages, since infant car seats permit babies to lie down in a natural position instead of reclining in a semi-sitting, "scrunched-down" position in which their heads can roll forward. Many infant car seats are relatively light and have handles, so if the babies fall asleep, you can carry them inside, letting the babies continue their naps.

Any car seat in a position that uses a shoulder belt requires a locking clip. It looks like a metal *H* and enables you to ensure that the seat belt will maintain the proper tension. The most secure car seats have a five-point harness: a strap over each shoulder, and one across each side of the waist feeding into a crotch strap. Some car seats have a reclining lever that lets you recline the seat without disconnecting the seat belts, a valuable feature when adjusting sleeping children.

Also buy washable fabric covers for car seats. They help keep car seats clean, are cushiony and comfortable, and protect babies from getting burned if car seats get hot in the summer sun.

### CARRIAGE

Carriages are wonderful when babies are young, but they also are cumbersome and expensive, especially because they are in use for a relatively short period of time. If possible, borrow one, or buy a carriage that converts into a stroller. (See the section on Strollers, page 170.)

### CHANGING TABLE

A changing table is not an absolute necessity. A pad or mat on the floor, couch, or bed plus a basket stocked with supplies works perfectly fine in the early months. But once the babies start rolling over, do not use a bed or other surface with no guardrail.

A changing table can be a worthwhile addition to the nursery if you have room for it. (Some people even buy two, one for the nursery, the other located elsewhere in the house.)

A changing table offers additional storage space for diapers, wipes, ointment, and clothing. The table's height can spare you backaches and eliminates the need to bend. It also lifts the babies away from a jealous older sibling. One mother felt that the changing table allowed her special time with each infant. Her older child normally interfered when she tried to focus on the babies. But he understood that diaper changes were necessary, not optional. She took full advantage of this perception and sometimes spent ten minutes per infant on diaper changes. One of her six-month-old twins liked the changing table because he was enthralled by the yellow venetian blinds over the window by the table. His twin, interestingly, could not have cared less about the blinds, and instead enjoyed a rattle that resided on the table just for him.

However, the height can also result in a nasty tumble should a baby roll off. Use the straps to keep the baby centered, and never leave a baby unattended on a changing table, even for a second. While changing one baby, keep the other(s) in a crib or playpen or perhaps on a quilt on the floor.

## Cloth Carriers, Slings, and Backpacks

Snuglis and other cloth carriers are cozy pouches that strap onto your front or back and let you carry one or more babies around like a kangaroo, hands free. Babies love being close to your skin and smell and motion; in a way, these carriers mimic the coziness of the womb and can calm a cranky baby. And many parents enjoy having the babies so close.

However, some parents find it awkward or uncomfortable to carry more than one baby at a time. You can alternate pushing one twin or two triplets in the stroller, while carrying another baby on your body. Some parents find carriers annoying and claustrophobic but put up with them because they calm fretful babies so effectively. The parents gladly sacrifice physical comfort for peace and quiet.

Older babies who can support their backs and heads qualify for rides on your hip in sling carriers such as "Sara's Ride," a miniature hammock that straps on across your body (sold in baby supply stores). Babies enjoy getting a nearly adult's-height view of the world while still being right up against you.

Backpacks can be used for babies who can sit up easily. Choose backpacks that stand alone for easier on and off. If your back is strong, these can be great for hikes or errands. Again, one baby can ride with you, the other(s) in a stroller. Use caution in a crowded bus or subway, where you will not be able to see your baby pulling someone's hair—or having his or her nose tweaked by a stranger. And never bend over to tie your shoe while wearing a backpack— the baby could fall out!

## Clothing

Babies outgrow clothing very quickly. Borrow as much as you can to avoid spending the money for new clothes that won't fit within months or weeks.

The amount of clothing you need depends in large part on how often you will do laundry. Many parents of multiples do laundry every day, so they can make do with fewer articles of clothing. If you have no washer and dryer, more clothes means fewer trips to the Laundromat. Also consider whether children have medical problems that will increase their number of clothing changes. One mother figured that her infant daughter with short bowel syndrome went through ten to fifteen premie-size outfits a day.

One disadvantage of dressing multiples alike is that you may need more clothes, since if one baby soils or spits up on an outfit, you may feel the need to change all of the babies. You will save time if you are willing to let the children dress differently. (See Chapter 16, "Same Genes, Same Jeans?".)

When choosing clothes, buy warm comfortable outfits that are easy to put on and take off. Many parents like the softness and breathability of cotton. Front zippers and snaps that extend down the leg of a stretchie are easier than those that fasten in the back. Some stretchies have unbelievably complicated snap arrangements that sorely test the patience and self-esteem of a parent changing a child by the dim glow of a night-light.

Clothing should be easy-care wash-and-wear. Forget about ironing. And avoid clothing that needs special care, such as cold-water washing and drying flat. Who has time for that?

Buy larger clothing children can grow into. When your children are wearing size six months, an eighteen-month size may look huge—yet they may fit into it sooner than you think possible.

If you buy all-cotton clothing, buy it in a larger size than you will need, and immediately wash it in warm water and put it in the dryer. This will shrink it—and you will learn what size the clothing really is. It may be marked size 4, but once shrunk, it becomes size 2. Once shrunk, it is unlikely to shrink more. And you do not want to have to wash any baby clothes in cold water to avoid shrinkage. The need to take shrinkage into account with all-cotton clothing is worth any hassle, because these are probably the clothes you will most enjoy dressing your babies in. All-cotton clothes are the softest and most cuddly next to your babies' skin. However, pajamas are made of synthetic fabrics, since by law sleepwear must be nonflammable.

As a general guide, consider the following list. For *each* child, have on hand:

- *8 to 12 one-piece Stretchees or gowns* (Some parents like gowns that resemble bags with neckline and sleeves, since they keep babies' feet warm even if they kick off the covers.)

- *8 to 12 undershirts*
- *2 sweaters*
- *2 hats* (summer sun hats; warm winter hats; medium-weight hats or bonnets for mild fall and spring weather)
- *1 bunting,* a cozy bag that keeps babies warm out-of-doors
- *1 washable snowsuit with mittens and feet* (Try to find snowsuits with detachable feet that can be replaced with warm booties as babies grow. Buy oversized snowsuits so that during the coldest of winter, when babies are not walking yet, you can sew closed the bottoms of the feet and arms to eliminate the need for mittens and booties. This will save you not only a great deal of time but also aggravation if you have babies who love to bite off their mittens. When spring comes, just remove the stitching. Snowsuits that are like bags and have no legs may be difficult to fit into a Snugli, car seat, or stroller.)
- *3 to 4 receiving blankets*
- *2 to 3 crib blankets*
- *4 crib sheets and rubber-lined flannel "puddle pads"*
- *4 bibs* (Cloth bibs are soft and attractive, but they stain. Wipe-clean plastic bibs are usually larger, so they protect babies' clothing better, and many have pockets that catch crumbs.)
- *cloth diapers* (Even if you plan to use disposables, buy a dozen cloth diapers per child for wiping and for keeping on your shoulder to catch drool and spit-up while carrying or burping the babies.)

## CORDLESS PHONE

This gadget is indispensable. You can keep talking through diaper changes, toddler chases, dishwashing late at night, and other opportunities to do two things instead of one. A speaker phone enables you to talk while you take care of children, cook, or do dishes.

## CRIB(S)

So close in the womb, so far away afterward, is how some infants feel when started off in separate cribs. Fretful sleepers often calm down when allowed to sleep together in the same crib. When they are older, babies are more ready to have their own space and move into separate cribs.

Buy soft "bumpers" to protect babies from the hard walls of the crib. Remove bumpers by the time babies can pull themselves up since they may use the bumpers as steps to escape from the crib.

### CRIB MOBILES

Great baby gifts, these nifty spinning toys can entertain babies long enough for you to toss clothes in the washer, write a few thank-you notes, or even, on a rare day, read a few pages of a novel. Some mobiles play music and revolve for as long as twenty minutes. Best are those you can turn off as well as on (rather than being at the mercy of the built-in timer). But even nonmechanical mobiles capture children's attention and curiosity.

### DIAPER BAG

A shoulder strap or backpack style is a must; several compartments will keep you organized; a built-in changing pad is helpful. You will be toting so many things that the bigger the diaper bag, the better. Choose one that can fit onto your stroller. Keep your wallet, keys, comb, etc., in a small handbag that you can tuck into the diaper bag. If possible, buy a machine-washable diaper bag since they can get very grungy very fast.

### DIAPERS

You have four choices: disposable diapers, cloth diapers you launder yourself, cloth diapers obtained through a diaper service, or a combination of the above. Cloth diapers may be better for the environment and soft against babies' skin but may not be as convenient as disposables. However, many parents say that using a diaper service proves to be easier and more economical than they had expected, and there is no extra delivery charge when you have multiples. In fact, many diaper services give a discount for twins, and even greater discounts for triplets and more.

If you use cloth, try to find pre-folded diapers. Diaper services often provide approximately seventy pre-folded cloth diapers per newborn per week. If you launder your own cloth diapers, you will not need so many.

You will also need rubber pants or waterproof cloth diaper covers with Velcro closures that eliminate the need for diaper pins. Most diaper services provide both diapers and diaper covers. You can also buy diaper covers in baby supply stores or through catalogs.

The Biobottoms catalog (see the Resources section in the Appendix) sells diapers, liners, and cotton or wool diaper covers in several styles and colors, in infant and toddler sizes, as well as other diapering products. Biobottoms gives a 10 percent discount for multiples. You can also request Biobottoms' free handbook, *All About Diapering,* and copies of articles on health and environmental issues pertaining to diapers, or call for advice on how to handle diapering problems.

The Seventh Generation catalog (see the Resources section in the Appendix) also sells cloth diapers, diaper covers, and other diapering products.

Some parents use cloth diapers at home and disposable when they go out or take babies to day care; some day-care centers permit only disposable diapers.

To save money on disposables, buy by the case, search out stores that charge less, and take advantage of special sales.

If you need premie-size disposable diapers, you can order them wholesale by the case through Commonwealth Premature Pampers (see the Resources section in the Appendix). This company estimates that one case (six boxes of thirty diapers each) lasts one-and-a-half weeks for twins, one week for triplets.

## DIAPER PAIL

The diaper pail you buy should have a snug-fitting lid with a deodorizer holder and a toddler-proof closure. Pails with foot pedals are handy. Some diaper services also provide or sell the pail.

*"Our pails are too big and the odor becomes lethal! I tell my friends to buy a small pail. Small bags mean more frequent changing so the room smells fresher."*

## GATES

Gates are crucial at the top and bottom of stairs, unless you have doors that can cut off access to stairs. Even when babies have learned how to climb up and down stairs, you cannot necessarily trust that their climbing skills will prevent them from falling when no one is behind them. Gates can also be used to restrict access to certain rooms, such as the kitchen, in order to reduce accidents and mischievous pranks. Some parents transform an entire room into a play area for their multiples and use a gate to keep them in it. Even so, children always need to be supervised: They can learn to climb a gate, and ingenious youngsters can concoct mischief even the most painstaking parents cannot predict. Make sure gates at the top of stairs are hardware-mounted rather than pressure gates that may be released if pushed too hard.

## HARNESSES / HAND-HOLDERS

Until one has children, it is hard to imagine that a hand-holder (similar to a leash) or harness can be humane. One strollerless trip with active toddlers going in opposite directions can point out their merits.

In other countries, hand-holders (a cord with a Velcro strap at each end for adult and child) are used more commonly than in the United States, where you may get a glare or two from people who simply do not understand the challenges of keeping track of active toddlers. One mother said that her children actually enjoyed their "leashes" and handed them to her to let her know they wanted to go for a walk. Her children far preferred the freedom the hand-holder gave them to having to hold on to their mother's hand.

A downside is that these items can get tangled and cause frustration for children and parents alike.

Many babies become very good at maneuvering out of their strollers by the age of one. They squirm out of even the snuggest seat belt like little Houdinis. The minute you stop strolling, your babies are bopping around you. However, if they are harnessed into the stroller, they quickly get used to the idea that they *cannot* crawl out and are quite content to stay in. If possible, start using harnesses at the first sign that your babies are getting the idea that they can crawl out of the stroller. Although harnessing the babies may seem like added work, it is much worse to reach a point when you can no longer enjoy taking the babies out in the stroller because you must constantly monitor their Houdini-like skills.

Harnesses are also helpful in high chairs, since they keep babies from trying to stand on the seat or otherwise disrupt mealtime. But make sure to read the instructions for the harness carefully. The harness must be snug (though not tight) so the child has no room to stand or lean far out, which could leave the child suspended and perhaps in danger.

## HIGH CHAIRS

High chairs should be sturdy and stable, have a seat belt, be easy to clean, and have a tray that slides on and off easily but fastens securely. It's nice to have a large tray to accommodate suction cup rattles and other toys. Wooden high chairs are often harder to clean and so roomy that they are suitable only for big, older babies.

*"After one of my twins had the breath knocked out of her when she fell from the high chair, I always used harnesses until the girls could move into regular chairs."*

## INFANT SEATS

You need an infant seat for each child. If you can find some at a yard sale, have some upstairs *and* downstairs. You will find infant seats virtually indispensable at many points during the day. Choose infant seats that you can easily rock with your foot, keeping one baby content while you hold or feed another one. At bathtime an infant seat can hold a freshly scrubbed baby while you bathe the other. Some infant seats bounce so appealingly that one dad said he would buy one for himself if it came in his size. A drummer, he praised the way bouncing seats help develop children's sense of rhythm, timing, and coordination.

## INFANT SWINGS

Novice parents who invest in Rolls-Royce–level infant swings moan when they belatedly discover the truth about infant swings. There are two types of babies in this world: babies who allow the swing to lull them into a blissful trance and those who are so insulted by the idea that they scream with horror at the very sight of the thing. Far better, if possible, to test your babies on a borrowed infant swing before laying out the cash.

Some infant swings include a cradle for infants that converts into a seat for older babies. In either case, be aware that while newer infant swings have reasonable start-up gadgets, some older ones have a crank that emits a hideous ratcheting noise that challenges the good-will of the trance-loving baby and does nothing to win over the reluctant one. Also, some older cradle swings were found unsafe and removed from the market. New ones rock infants safely from side to side.

## INTERCOM

Intercom systems enable you to hear, and in some cases, see, what is going on in the babies' room when you are elsewhere in the home. Intercoms assure that you are spared the distressing discovery that your babies have been awake and screaming while you, doing laundry and unable to hear them, assumed they were still napping. On the other hand, intercoms can feed into the worries of jumpy parents, who, hearing either nothing or something, run to the babies to check them out. Some parents adjust the volume of the intercom so they hear only genuine crying, rather than every whimper.

## PLAYPEN

*"My eighteen-month-old twins love their playpens. We have two, to give each child a lot of space, and we put them close together. The boys enjoy chattering together and throwing toys into each other's playpen. Plus, having two playpens downstairs means they can go in for a nap either downstairs in the playpens or upstairs in the cribs."*

A playpen and a crib are "safe havens" for babies and a relief for the adults who must watch over them. They also offer separation from older siblings and pets. Although to some adults a playpen resembles a jail cell, if the playpen is not overused it can be a merry place stocked with entertaining toys and a playful twin.

Then again, expect some playpen battles as the children play tug-of-war with a stuffed bunny—even when the bunny's own twin is right there, watching the scene. (Why is that bunny ignored? It lost the shiny satin tag that used to decorate the back seam.)

Some parents have a playpen for each child, placed close enough that they can toss soft toys back and forth.

Do be aware that if you wait to introduce the playpen until children are six months or older, they may resist it. Put babies into the playpen for naps so they will get used to it.

## ROCKING CHAIR

The motion of a rocking chair soothes parents and babies alike. A good rocking chair is used throughout childhood and beyond; it creates good times and seems to store memories that flood over you years later. Choose a wide, sturdy, well-made rocker, new or old, wood or upholstered or wicker. Glider rockers, like old porch swings, are popular because of their gentle motion.

## STROLLER

The stroller may be your most important purchase. A thoughtfully designed, well-made, comfortable, smooth-rolling stroller makes outings—and your life—easier. Select a sturdy stroller that will last three or four years; multiples often use a stroller longer than single children because taking two or more toddlers or preschoolers for a walk is so challenging.

Ask Mothers of Twins Club members and other parents of multiples, both friends and strangers, how they like their strollers and what they recommend. If possible, visit at least two stores to compare prices and how salespeople describe the relative merits of the merchandise. Ask whether the store services and repairs strollers, or assists in returning them to the manufacturer for warranty service. If a store must special-order your double, triple, or quadruple stroller, check on whether it is returnable if you are not happy with it. You may be able to get a good deal or a special stroller through a mail-order catalog that features products for multiples.

Decide whether you want a double (side-by-side) or a "limousine" or "tandem" single-file stroller, in which babies face forward or face each other. Although many double strollers fit fairly easily through doorways or store aisles, others are wide-bodies that effectively prevent you or your baby-sitter from combining strolls with errands. (If a stroller does not fit in a store, make sure your baby-sitter knows to abandon the store and never to leave the stroller, with or without babies in it, on the sidewalk outside the store.)

Limousine strollers are more maneuverable and recommended if you plan to use them for a lot of shopping. Many stores are set up

with narrow security gates and narrow aisles to ensure that the customer focuses on the merchandise—and that the store can focus on
the customer. The limousine stroller can let you navigate these stores
more readily. The downside is that long, weighty strollers may be
more difficult to fold, carry, and fit into a standard car.

Some single-file strollers made for an older child and a baby have
only one reclining seat but are less expensive. These may be useful
for older twins; they can take turns on the reclining seat.

Some parents fasten two single strollers together to make their
own double stroller. Do-it-yourselfers are most successful with lightweight umbrella strollers, which generally do not recline but are fine
for older children who need less back support. Home-fashioned double strollers are ingenious money-savers or precarious experiments,
depending on the skill with which they are contrived. *Continually
assess yours for safety.* Before putting your children in it, load it with
packages similar to your babies' weights and test it.

*With the twins strapped into their stroller and the stuffed bunnies along
for the ride, this mom is ready to roll.*

## *Stroller Checklist*

Following are some things to keep in mind when deciding which stroller to buy:

- *Is the stroller safe?* Whether it is new or used, make sure it meets current safety standards.
- *Are all parts in good working order?* Check seat belts, crotch straps, brakes, and the folding mechanism.
- *Is the stroller sturdy?* It should have a wide wheel base for stability.
- *Is the stroller easily folded?* How compact is it when folded? Does it fit in the trunk or backseat of your car? (Measure.)
- *Is the stroller adaptable to your children's changing sizes and needs?* Is each seat adjustable so babies can recline or sit up? Does each seat have a footrest? Are seats roomy enough to accommodate children as they grow? Are there canopies or hoods for protection from sun, wind, rain, and snow?
- *Is the stroller comfortable for you?* Are the handles at a good height? Are they adjustable to be user-friendly to both tall and shorter parents and baby-sitters? Wheel different strollers around the store and see how they feel. Umbrella strollers are generally easier to tilt on curbs, and some recline. Check with your pediatrician about when your babies are ready to use them.
- *Are there special features you want?* Is there a good-sized basket for packages? Does the stroller have strong individual handles on which you can hang shopping or diaper bags without tipping the stroller backward? Are seat pads washable? (If not, you can buy or make seat covers.)
- *Is the stroller fairly easy to lift?* Some parents advise getting as lightweight a stroller as possible.

### SINGLE STROLLER(S)

In addition to a stroller that can accommodate twins, triplets, quads, or more, many parents like to have at least one single stroller as well. They use it for helping a fretful baby calm down or go to sleep—right in the house! It is also convenient if you take one child for a walk. One couple with twins had a double stroller as well as two single strollers that they used for taking the children on separate errand runs from time to time.

Of course, you can also use a twin stroller on outings with one child; the empty seat can hold packages.

## WALKERS

Walkers give pre-walking babies a taste of how walking feels and allow them to rove and explore. Unfortunately, walkers have been implicated in many accidents, especially when used near stairs where gates were missing or accidentally left open, or in kitchens where children pulled hot pots off the stove.

And walkers can actually *delay* walking for some babies. Check with your pediatrician before buying walkers. If your doctor says one child should not use one, it is probably better not to buy one for the other twin. The non-walker baby may feel frustrated by the ban on using this intriguing apparatus—and could get knocked over by the baby on wheels.

# Chapter 12

# MULTIPLE FEATS: THE LOGISTICS OF CARING FOR MULTIPLES

## Going Out

Figuring out the logistics of caring for twins or triplets sharpens your ingenuity. Just getting out of the house can feel like an accomplishment. People with one child do not always understand this. They say, "Just pack the kids up and leave!" It's not so easy.

Often, you get one twin all set to go out, then the other, and by that time the first one is wet, and you change her, and then the other one is hungry, and you nurse him, and then you nurse the other one, and now both need diaper changes, and the nice sunny weather has given way to clouds and you wonder where the time went and when you can get some fresh air. All of a sudden, it is their naptime and your lunchtime. You discover there is no tuna left, because it is so hard to grocery-shop with twins, and you and your spouse have been feeling overwhelmed. But tonight, for sure, you *must* get around to bathing these babies.

Getting out and about with multiples is complicated but necessary. "Cabin fever," the feeling of being cooped up and fed up, can lead to irritability, crying jags, harsh words, and even a disoriented feeling that the world at large doesn't include you. *Sometimes just stepping out the front door feels like a journey achieved, a revelation seen.* Once outside, it seems so natural to be there; when you are inside, surrounded by crying children, unwashed dishes, rumpled beds, and strewn-about toys, the other side of the front door might as well be Oz.

After the children go to bed at night, do the dishes and pick up a toy or two, but while the sun shines, let it shine on you. You and your children need the fresh air and fresh outlook outings provide. Keep the diaper bag ready and the resolve firm. Occasionally, you may just have to scoop up your fretful babies and change and feed them in the backyard or the park.

One active mother of triplets worried that her friend, who had twins, was not getting out enough. She offered to come over a couple of times a week so they could walk together. The sight of her friend sauntering down the block with *three* babies energized the mother of two.

## TIPS FOR SUCCESSFUL EXPEDITIONS

*Check Out the Territory.* When heading somewhere new with your stroller, call ahead to determine whether places you plan to go are accessible to the disabled. If they are, you will be able to wheel the stroller up ramps and get it through wide doorways and elevators, and will not need to worry about negotiating steps.

*Pair Up with Friends and Their Children.* You can lend each other moral support and reinforce the crazy humor of keeping track of everybody.

*Do Advance Preparations the Night Before.* Choose the children's outfits and your own. Pack up snacks, prepare bottles, check that your purse and diaper bag are ready to go. None of these tasks individually is so time-consuming—unless you try to do them at the same time you are keeping an eye on your children. Getting them done when the children are asleep paves the way for a smoother morning.

***Keep the Diaper Bag Stocked and Ready to Go.*** After each outing, replenish supplies right away to ease your next departure. Tuck a checklist inside the bag so you do not have to think about what you need. (Never bother remembering anything a piece of paper can remember for you.)

---

### A Diaper-Bag List for Ten-Month-Olds

- ☐ 1 bottle of formula *each*
- ☐ baby food and spoons
- ☐ 3 diapers *each*, wipes, ointment or lotion (if needed)
- ☐ 1 receiving blanket *each*
- ☐ 1 cloth diaper *each*
- ☐ 1 plastic bib *each*
- ☐ plastic bags for dirty clothes, used diapers, leaky bottles (Keep the bags away from the children.)
- ☐ 1 small bag Cheerios, crackers, unsalted pretzels, breadsticks, or other finger food *each*
- ☐ changing pad
- ☐ tissues
- ☐ 1 change of clothing *each*
- ☐ toys, rattles, teething rings
- ☐ 1 large waterproof flannel pad for your lap

---

***Tell the Children What the Day Holds in Store.*** Babies mentally prepare to go out when they hear you zipping up the diaper bag and see you unfolding the stroller. Even when babies are tiny, talk to them about the day's itinerary. Before long, they will be able to understand your words. Telling children the day's plans is not only pleasant conversation and a courtesy; it orients them and gives them a feeling of confidence. Children like knowing what to expect.

### IN THE CAR

***To Keep Car Rides Safe, Never Compromise on Car Seats and Seat Belts.*** Let children know that *this* car does not—will not—work until everyone is belted in and the doors locked.

***Make Your Car a "Home Away from Home."*** It is horrible to be stuck in a traffic jam with nary a cracker in sight. Sometimes children act out because they are hungry. Stash snacks and juice boxes in the glove compartment or in a box under the seat. (And how about a letter-writing campaign to car manufacturers requesting roomier "snack compartments"?) Keep some toys in the car and a blanket or two in the trunk in case it gets chilly.

*Tame the "Kings of All Wild Things."* When the backseat becomes *Where the Wild Things Are,*[1] with toddlers squirming out of their car seats, hurling toys, and whooping, "Let the wild rumpus start!" pull over to the side of the road to help them calm down. (When they are older, pull over and read a book until they calm themselves down.) Have children switch places, sing songs with you, or take a vow of silence until you reach your destination. To help them keep that vow, promise to tell them a story in which they are the heroes. If (and only if) your nerves can stand it, suspend the vow of silence and channel their high spirits into making sound effects for your story. ("So the bumblebees *buzzed,* and the hummingbirds *hummed,* and the brave twins pounded on their little bongo *drums.*")

Later, at home, read them Maurice Sendak's book and let them act it out in the nonmoving vehicle of your living room. There is a time and a place for roaring "terrible roars," gnashing "terrible teeth," rolling "terrible eyes," and showing "terrible claws!"

*Play Games to Keep Children Entertained.* The Alphabet Game sustained one family's nursery-school students for two years: Taking turns, everybody names a word that begins with a certain letter, beginning with *A.* Variation: Start the game with *Z* and work backward. Advanced: Restrict the words to categories (foods, animals, names, silly made-up words).

In *Growing Up Creative,* Teresa M. Amabile suggests the "Opposites Game," a deceptively simple game that teaches children "a most important creativity skill: *There is often no such thing as a right answer.*" Players take turns saying a word and having one another suggest the opposite. With young children, use words with simple opposites (hot/cold, in/out). "The game really becomes interesting—and creative—when the words become more complex, when they don't have clear opposites. Often the players will discuss different possible answers, explaining one or the other, and mull-

---

[1] Maurice Sendak, *Where the Wild Things Are* (New York: Harper & Row, 1963).

ing over which answer might be 'better' than another."

For example, Amabile describes how one child pondered the opposite of *flower*: "Maybe *seed*? Because a flower is all grown, and a seed isn't grown at all . . . [or] *Rock*! It's not living at all, and a flower is living. . . . Now, here's a toughie. What's the opposite of *outer space*?"[2]

Creative games that feature open-ended rather than right-or-wrong questions are particularly valuable for multiples since they downplay competition and encourage appreciation for one another's ideas.

**Recite Nursery Rhymes and Poems.**   One dad, unable to remember any, started driving lessons early, teaching his toddlers to chant, "When you want to go fast, step on the gas/When you want to go slow, the brake gets your toe."

**Reading-on-the-Road.**   Prior to every outing, get into the routine of asking your children two questions: Do you need to use the bathroom? What book are you going to take with you to read in the car (bus/subway/plane)? Although some children find reading in a moving vehicle uncomfortable, for most it is a delightful way to make travel time pass more quickly. Even if children prefer to gaze out the window and daydream (which is also a highly worthwhile activity), having a book along gives them an option whenever they are ready for it.

Getting children into the habit of taking books around with them—and doing so yourself—shows them that you value reading and helps establish reading as an important and pleasurable part of daily life. Start early by buying cloth, plastic, or "board" books for babies. (For a list of books for different ages featuring twins or triplets, see the Bibliography.)

**Portable Fun.**   Children engrossed in a book, game, craft, or drawing are less likely to fall into backseat quarrels than those who have nothing to do. When possible, buy toys that travel well. "Manipulatives"—toys children can move—entertain children longer than toys they only hold. Find "activity centers" that fasten onto babies'

[2]Teresa M. Amabile, Ph.D., *Growing Up Creative: Nurturing a Lifetime of Creativity* (New York: Crown Publishers, 1989).

car seats. Depending on their age, children enjoy movable action figures, color-forms, hand puppets, Duplo blocks and other "fit-together" toys, Etch-a-Sketch, toy looms, magnetized checkers and Scrabble, dolls they can dress by themselves, books of mazes or cross-word puzzles, and sketchbooks. The "Anti-Coloring Books," a series by Susan Striker[3] that encourages children to create original artwork, are worthy alternatives to standard coloring books.

*Activity Bags.* Give each child a sturdy backpack to serve as his/her "activity bag" on trips. Deciding what books, toys, and dolls or stuffed animals to include gives children a sense of responsibility and control and helps them develop the skill of planning ahead for what they will need.

## WALKING TOURS

*Acknowledge the Importance of Fresh Air and Exercise.* Unless it is raining or icy cold, try to make a daily walk an integral part of your life. Even a walk in a fine drizzle (use a rain hood on the stroller) can be nice.

*Vary the Route on Daily Walks to Stave Off Boredom.* Take along a quilt to spread out on the grass at the park so your babies can lie under the open sky and gaze up at the leafy trees. Make walking dates with other parents. With toddlers, use "hand-holders" made for children to keep them from running off (see page 167).

*Scale Back Ambitions for Accomplishing Errands.* Prioritizing is key for busy parents of multiples. Yes, errands must get done. But children have limited tolerance for them. If you set out to do only one or two things, you are more likely to keep children calm.

---

[3]Susan Striker, Anti-Coloring Books Series (New York: Henry Holt & Co., 1978–86).

## One Couple's Exit Plan

Allow at least two hours to go out.

Prepare yourself, eat.

Next get five-year-old ready, dressed, and involved with a temporary activity.

Wash, dress, change the twins.

Pack a small bag (with a big bag we take too much stuff): diapers, bottles, old cloth diapers for wiping, extra outfits.

While Dad amuses the kids, Mom (always the last to be ready) finishes getting ready to go out.

One parent takes stroller to van.

Cart the two babies out, put in car seats. One parent stays.

Other parent gets five-year-old mentally prepared to go into van, and then physically *in* the van.

TIP: Never give people an exact arrival time. If the babies nap between nine and ten in the morning, tell people, "We'll be there mid-morning, sometime around ten-thirty or eleven." It usually works out, but if you're running late, feed the kids in the van on the way. Allow more time than you think you need for getting places—that gives you a shot at being on time.

## Bathing Babies

*"I do all the bathing and nail-clipping right now. My husband dresses the babies. He doesn't feel comfortable bathing them, so I do it."*

Bathtime can be highly enjoyable for both parents and children. You can really concentrate on the child you are bathing—singing, chatting, making eye contact, stroking and cuddling each child in turn. To enable you to focus undistractedly and *safely* on one baby at a time, bathing multiples is best done as a two-person job. Many parents schedule this "assembly-line" activity for early evening, when both are available. A single parent might invite a friend over to help.

Safety is the paramount concern because of the potential for accidents. A child can drown in only an inch of water. *Never leave a child unsupervised even for a second.* Let the phone ring or have the answering machine pick up. If you forgot a towel, carry the bare baby with you to get it. The child who is not being bathed at the moment should be in an adult's arms, a crib, or a playpen, or strapped into an infant seat on the floor right next to you.

> *"I keep one baby on the floor in the infant seat so she can see me. They don't like being in a room by themselves. They are used to being near someone all the time."*

Begin bathtime by laying out everything you need: clothes, diapers, wipes, washcloths, shampoo, soap, towels (those with hoods are cozy for infants). Place a baby bathtub in the tub or in the kitchen sink so you do not have to bend. If you bathe babies in the kitchen, lay a quilt on the cleared kitchen table for drying and dressing babies, but of course do not leave a child unattended as he or she could roll off the table.

Sometimes one parent bathes each child, while the other parent is in charge of drying, diapering, and dressing. Or each parent bathes and dresses one child apiece. With triplets or more, parents may need to have one child or more in an infant seat awaiting a turn while the others are being cared for.

Always bathe young babies individually. When babies are old enough to sit up in a tub, they can be bathed together. Bath seats with suction cups on the bottom keep kids sitting upright. Some bath seats even swivel, which is fun for kids and convenient for you. Faucet covers protect children from painful bumps on the head. Bath cushions and nonslip bath mats limit potentially dangerous sliding. Again, bathing is best done by both parents or by one parent with a helper. A school-age sibling can be a terrific assistant with toddlers, but at least one parent should be in the bathroom at all times. Splashing, slipping and sliding, and sinking toy boats are jolly commotions but could result in a child falling over and drowning if not adequately supervised.

Since bathtime with multiples can be such a production, many, *many* parents do not bathe babies every day, but only once or twice a week. Every day, do change their clothes and wash each baby's face, neck (clean between the folds), hands, and diaper area.

### ◪ Mealtime

*"I tried to get the children on the same schedule. When nursing or bottlefeeding, I woke one baby after feeding the other. I never let the children go four hours in the daytime without eating. For example, I would not let them sleep six hours and miss a feeding. I set up mealtimes so that I fed them solids at the same time."*

Introducing solids is a milestone in children's lives. The transition from a liquid diet is very exciting for them, as they discover new sensations of taste and texture and learn new ways to use their gums, teeth, and tongue. Mealtime is also a social occasion, with children arranged in a circle around you. Whereas single-born children have Mom, Dad, or baby-sitter to themselves, multiples have no choice but to accept the other children's needs for a turn, too. Thus, mealtime also becomes an experience of cooperation, sharing, and learning patience.

*"I know it's probably unsanitary, but one of the best things I did was to feed the twins from the same spoon and bowl unless one was ill. It saved me so much time. I did give them separate bottles, though."*

When you consider that your children are constantly playing together, mouthing the same toys, and sharing the same space, sharing a spoon may not be so bad, unless one child has a health problem that warrants separate utensils. Ask your pediatrician for advice.

Arrange the children's infant seats or high chairs in front of you, with a plastic tarp underneath to catch spills. If children have different food preferences, use a divided dish so you do not have to juggle separate bowls. Use commercial baby foods or make your own by pureeing steamed vegetables, fruit, etc., in a blender or food processor. Freeze meal-size portions or make "food cubes" by freezing purees in ice-cube trays. You can save lots of money and assure that babies are getting simple, unprocessed food with no added salt or sugar. Many parents use both homemade and commercial baby foods, depending on what is most convenient at a given time.

When feeding triplets or more, sitting on a chair with wheels helps you shuttle among the high chairs. However, one mother of triplets preferred to use walkers instead of high chairs:

*"I fed the babies in their walkers, which had feeding trays. I could get the kids in and out easily, and they couldn't hurt themselves if they climbed out. I felt that high chairs were too dangerous, too high up. Besides, my kids liked scooting around in the walkers on the first floor. We didn't have a basement, so we didn't have to worry about them falling down stairs. And I always kept close watch on them."*

Toddlers enjoy sitting together around a low, easy-to-clean plastic or wooden children's table. To enhance family closeness, have siblings eat with the multiples or help feed them. However, respect their right to bow out on occasion if they express a desire for a quieter, more peaceful dining experience!

Serve finger foods—small chunks of steamed vegetables, toast, Cheerios, cheese, bananas, melon. Introduce spoons as soon as the children show interest in them. The sooner children can feed themselves, the more independent they feel, and the easier mealtimes are for you. Although you may long for a "wall tarp" to catch flung yogurt, eventually the children will learn how to move food less messily from bowl to mouth.

As soon as children are out of high chairs, they are old enough to help set and clear the table. Start with small things: One twin is in charge of folding napkins, the other sets out spoons. The responsibility pleases them, and you are establishing habits that eventually will help the whole family.

## Laundry, Laundry, Laundry

*"I'm never caught up. No matter how much I accomplish in every other way—with the kids, at work—I'm always behind with the kids' laundry. It haunts me!"*

Multiples' laundry, that self-replenishing, bottomless heap, is a Sisyphean task: impossible ever to say, "Done!" Laundry can undo you if you don't do it often enough.

The first coping tip: Buy only easy-care, machine-washable and dryable, no-iron clothes. If somebody gives you baby gifts of must-iron pleated dresses, think about all the time you do not have for ironing and consider exchanging them for something more practical and parent-friendly.

Buy only one type of socks so you do not have to match any. If buying colors, buy at least two or three pairs that are the same. Keep a box of single socks; the other one turns up eventually, or the lone sock can become a hand puppet.

Sort laundry on a table as soon as you take it out of the dryer, or dump it all in a basket and sort and fold while you take a TV break or talk on the phone later on. If a friend is visiting, ask him or her to fold laundry while you prepare dinner. (Visitors to homes of multiples must be prepared to pitch in!)

Only fold what really must be folded. While neatness standards vary, consider that some parents do not bother folding diapers, stretchies, towels, washcloths, sheets, receiving blankets, undershirts, and more. *Every five minutes you spend folding is five minutes you are not doing something more important, such as napping.*

> *"I sort laundry and never fold it. But when my mother visits, I'll come home from work and find all the laundry neatly folded and put away. She never says a word about it. And the next time she comes to visit, the drawers are filled with unfolded laundry—and once again, she folds it!"*

If you do not have a washer and dryer, try to find a Laundromat that offers free pickup and delivery. One set of grandparents offered to pick up, launder, and drop off their twin grandsons' laundry every week.

As soon as children are old enough, enlist their help. If space permits, have two or three laundry hampers: for dark clothes, lights, and whites. Even preschoolers can learn to mate socks and toss dirty clothes into the right hampers. It's not just for your benefit, it's educational! Sorting is a pre-math skill. It teaches children to recognize colors, become organized, and develop neat habits. They also learn that they can be good helpers for Mom and Dad.

Once her children learned to read, one mother posted a poetic reminder on the inside of the hamper about their laundry responsibilities (the last line refers to a stain-remover stick):

> *My pretty girl, my handsome boy,*
> *You like to look your best.*

*I wash your laundry every week*
*So you can be well-dressed.*

*Please empty all your pockets*
*And turn clothes right-side-out,*
*Let me know if clothes are torn,*
*And rub the stains with Shout.*

## ▣ Shopping

***Shop Alone or with Just One Baby, if Possible.*** One mother of triplets does all of the family's grocery shopping Sunday mornings while her husband stays with the children. Bright and early, she tours several stores—and enjoys the time alone.

Another couple splits up the twins for the occasion. On alternating Saturday mornings, one twin goes shopping with one parent, while the other parent and twin go for a stroll or to the park.

***Seek Alternatives.*** Use phone-in delivery services for groceries, pharmacy items, dry cleaning, laundry. Or have a friend shop for you, hire a teenager to shop, or buy through catalogs.

***To Manage at the Supermarket,*** try to take a helper along. Carry one baby in an infant carrier on your chest or back, and buckle the other in an infant seat in the shopping cart.

But such arrangements only work when babies are little and still. Once they start sitting, standing, and generally moving around, they can throw the cart off balance, leading to accidents. When shopping with older babies and toddlers, use a harness to keep one in the grocery-cart seat; use a "leash" to keep each other child with you. If both parents go shopping together, each can harness a twin into a separate cart; with triplets, do the same with two and rotate the privilege of allowing one triplet to trot alongside you.

## ▣ Childproofing and Play-Enhancing Your Home

*"I collected porcelain figurines for ten years. When I was pregnant, my mother said, 'Listen, honey, I've raised six kids. I suggest you pack up your porcelain and put it away.'*

*" 'Oh, no, my kids will be different,' I said. 'I'll teach them not to touch.' Sure enough, when the quadruplets were two years old, they knocked over the entire shelf unit and destroyed my whole collection.*

*"The 'Quad Squad,' as we call them, also knocked over our television set—twice. Now we have it bolted to the wall.*

*"They also learned how to open the screen door, so we installed a hook and eye high up, near the top of the door, so they couldn't open it.*

*"Now that they are almost four, life's a little easier. I don't have to worry that they'll try to put their heads in the toilet. Now I have other things to watch out for!"*

It is only logical: Two or three babies or toddlers together can make more mischief than one child. By putting their heads together, multiples can move your armchair across the floor, figure out how to open the china closet, or make little hills of breakfast cereal all over the kitchen floor. If you are distracted with one child, the other(s) can get into trouble behind you in the same room or elsewhere in the house.

Making the home safe is one of parents' most important responsibilities—not only to keep children out of danger, but also to free them to play and explore the space around them. *Childproofing reduces the number of times you need to say "no"—and the number of times children need to hear it. The more you can fill your children's day with "yes," the calmer everybody feels.*

A first step in childproofing is to get down to your children's level—literally. If your children are crawling or about to start, sprawl on the floor and take a look around. What do you see? Electrical cords that seem to say "Yank me"? Electrical outlets that say "Poke me"? Cabinet doors that say "Open me"? Sharp glass coffee-table corners that say "Grab me"? A paper clip under the couch that says "Taste me"? The forbidden is actually very inviting, from a child's point of view.

So make liberal use of childproofing gadgets—cabinet and drawer latches, various types of electrical-outlet covers, electrical and telephone cord shorteners, table corner guards (or substitute a wooden table with rounded corners for the glass table). Although safety gadgets require a small investment of money, they are a bargain if they prevent injury or save a life.

Look at your furniture arrangements not with a decorator's eye, but with an eye for safety. Move the standing lamp between the couch and the wall so children can't knock it down. Pull furniture away from windows so children can't climb onto the windowsills. Install window guards. Consider buying an "entertainment center" that keeps your television, VCR, radio, stereo, CD player, records, CDs, and tapes behind doors. Remove knickknacks and plants from table-tops. Plants can be poisonous. Vacuum under and around the furniture.

Use gates to control the flow of traffic. Situate them at stairs (including basement stairs) and at the entrances to the kitchen and bathroom(s). Lock doors (including bathroom and screen doors) with a hook and eye installed at adult shoulder height.

Remove cleaning supplies and other dangerous substances from low cabinets. Relocate them to high cabinets—and lock them to make sure climbing children cannot get into them. Keep one or two low cabinets accessible to children and stock them with the musical instruments we call pots and pans and wooden spoons.

Get into the habit of using back burners and turning pot handles away from little reaching hands. Buy burner guards or a stove guard-rail.

Install night-lights in hallways, bedrooms, and bathrooms. Those with light sensors go on automatically; some have dimmers. You can also buy lights that attach to the side of the crib so you can check on children at night.

Place safety locks on appliances and toilets. Lock away not only medicines, but also any toiletry items that children should not have, including toothpaste, cosmetics, perfumes, and the like. Keep syrup of ipecac in the house, but use it only when directed by the label on the package of the substance your child ingested, or by the poison-control line (keep the number by each phone) or your doctor.

Empty mop buckets completely and put them away so curious children don't fall in.

Consider making one room into a room-sized playpen filled with soft furniture, toys, and climbing equipment on a well-padded rug. Gate the entrance. But remember that even the most childproofed room is not necessarily multiples-proofed if you are not in it with them.

Teach children safety through games as well as warnings. Sing "Ten little monkeys jumping on the bed/One fell off and bumped his head" to remind children not to jump on *their* beds.

Preschoolers love this challenging game: Make up a story about a child who sometimes does safe things and sometimes does *unsafe* things. Have children bang on a pot every time the child in the story does something unsafe to "warn" him or her. ("And *then* Henrietta heard a knock on the door and went to open it." BANG! "What *should* Henrietta do?" Children: "Tell Mommy or Daddy that someone is at the door so *they* can open it.") Give "Henrietta" a twin, and make sure that both twins in the story do safe and unsafe things; don't make one the "right" twin and the other the "wrong" twin. Let children have a turn being the storyteller, too.

Making your home safe opens the doors to youthful exploration. Crawling, climbing, touching, and tasting are essential ways that children learn. Close the doors that need to be closed; open all the rest.

All of the logistics connected with the daily care of multiples can seem overwhelming. But as you get organized, you will find you are able to take your children out more often. Baths get easier, shopping and laundry do get done, the children are getting older, and you all manage far better than you ever could have imagined.

## Scheduling and Routines

*"When I started walking into walls in the middle of the night, I knew this had to stop. I couldn't function! I had to get the children on a schedule."*

Many parents of multiples say that if they'd had only one child, they would shun a schedule and have the child eat and sleep on demand. But with multiples, said one father, "Keeping children on the same timetable is key to being able to enjoy them." He coined what may be the definitive motto for parents who schedule: *"Discipline is sanity."*

*Parents schedule in order to minimize chaos and enable themselves to get desperately needed rest.* But sensitive scheduling also accommodates children's needs for routine and for relatively serene parents. Scheduling does not guarantee parents eight hours of shut-eye and a tranquil disposition. But it may decrease fatigue-related irritability and help parents feel less overwhelmed.

*Three Paradoxical Facts About*
*Successful Scheduling*

1. Babies and children seem to want to do *what* they want to do *when* they want to do it. Yet they often function better and are happier when there is a routine and they know what to expect.
2. A "fixed" schedule must also be flexible. As children grow and change, parents must be willing to adapt schedules accordingly. The best schedules are not arbitrarily imposed but "grow out of" what children are doing anyway.
3. Schedules benefit parents by giving them increased rest and a sense of control; children benefit from having more rested, calm, and confident parents.

## IS SCHEDULING FAIR TO CHILDREN?

Some exhausted, frazzled parents yearn for some predictability in their lives and envy those parents who are able to achieve a schedule. Yet they are ambivalent over whether they have the "right" to schedule. Is it fair to interfere with children's natural body clocks? Ideally, shouldn't children be allowed spontaneous expression and fulfillment of needs? This "ideal" allows each child to follow his or her own drummer, so to speak, and encourages each child's individuality from the very beginning; children are not urged to conform as a group to a single schedule.

Yet your little "different drummers" may be on such diverse timetables that you are literally on call around the clock. If you have sufficient equanimity and stamina, adequate help, and a lack of other obligations, you may indeed find it satisfying to give over your time and body to the flow of your babies' disparate patterns.

Yet the realities of your life may preclude such an approach. Perhaps you work. You certainly have errands to run, things to do. You may have other children to tend to. You need some time for yourself and your partner. And you probably have limited tolerance for inadequate sleep and complete unpredictability, which is far greater with multiples than with single-borns.

So you need to consider whether laissez-faire is fair to *you*. The notion of body-clock autonomy for babies may be far outweighed by your need—perhaps desperate—to feel less overwhelmed. And when you get more rest, you have more energy to be an attentive, loving parent.

Scheduling might be compared to gardening. Left unattended, the branches of a rosebush will spread any which way. Pruning the rosebush does not negate the essence of the plant; it enhances its ability to flower by making more energy available to each rosebud. When multiples sleep and eat any time at all, parents are pulled any which way. Sensitive scheduling of children shapes their time, assuring that everyone in the family gets the rest and calm that can help them flourish.

## SLEEP EDUCATION

Many parents feel that the single most difficult task of early parenthood is getting children to sleep. For many parents, just letting sleep happen when it happens is too frazzling, especially with multiples whose naps may seldom coincide. The goal in scheduling is to identify a reasonable sleep pattern for your children, and to help them learn how to go to sleep relatively peacefully.

*Before beginning any sleep scheduling, consult your pediatrician, who will help you gauge your babies' readiness.* Do not even attempt to encourage the babies to sleep through the night in the first few months of life, or longer if they were born prematurely. Richard Ferber, M.D., author of *Solve Your Child's Sleep Problems,* wrote that "by about three months of age most full-term healthy infants are, or could be, sleeping through the majority of the night. If your baby hasn't settled by five or six months, then you should take a close look at his bedtime routines. If your child is always nursed or rocked to sleep he may have difficulty going back to sleep alone after normal nighttime arousals."

The key to sleep education, according to Ferber, is that "for your child to sleep well at night he must learn to fall asleep alone in his crib or bed *and* he must fall asleep under conditions that he can reestablish for himself after waking at night."

Ferber explains that "if you are in the habit of rocking your child to sleep for twenty to thirty minutes each night and getting up once or twice to rock him back to sleep in the middle of the night, you actually may be interfering with his sleep and postponing the start of his sleeping through the night. Even if you 'don't mind' getting up, I suspect you would be happier if you could simply put him down at bedtime without rocking and have him sleep through the night as well. Whether this is true or not, you should still be aware that it is in your child's best interests to have uninterrupted sleep."

Ferber acknowledges that "there is no way to treat this problem without having to listen to *some* crying, but you can keep it to a minimum."[4]

It is distressing to parents to hear their children cry, let alone to "let" them cry. Yet Ferber's method is *not* to let children cry unendingly, but to use a progressive approach in which parents reassure children at frequent, regular intervals (from every couple of minutes to every fifteen minutes, depending on the children's age and readiness) that they are close by. Thus the fundamental insecurity of independent sleeping—the separation from parents—is eased, and children feel safe enough to yield to their fatigue and to go sleep.

*Babies should not be crying alone in their cribs for long periods every day.* If that is your experience, contact your pediatrician immediately for assistance.

It is easier to sleep-train six-month old babies than twelve- or eighteen-month-old children (especially after they have learned how to pitifully cry out, "Mama, Mama!"), but it is still not overwhelmingly difficult.

*"It helped me to keep in mind that I was not doing my children any service to let them feel anxious and worn out and fretful; I helped them more by understanding that most babies need lots of sleep, and need to learn how to go to sleep when tired."*

*"Our pediatrician said that once the babies weighed eleven pounds, they could make it six, maybe even eight, hours without a bottle. So we started trying to stretch out the times between feedings. One night, my son slept through the night, and another night, he took only two ounces when he woke up. I knew then that I could start training both twins to sleep through the night, especially with Richard Ferber's book."*

[4]Richard Ferber, M.D., *Solve Your Child's Sleep Problems* (New York: Simon & Schuster, 1985).

## *The Turning Point for a Mother of Three*

"I never knew when my first child, Clark, would nap. Fortunately, he slept okay at night. But during the day, forget it! He would only sleep when he was moving—in the car seat, the stroller, or the infant swing. My whole day seemed to be dedicated to getting him to nap. When he did, we were usually out, so I never got anything done! On top of that, when he wasn't sleeping, he wanted to be held all the time. If I put him down he screamed, and if I put him in the crib, he screamed louder. I carried him for hours a day. This went on for almost a whole year!

"When Clark was almost four, Trevor and Ben were born. I assumed that because I was an experienced mom now, the babies would be pretty mellow (unlike Clark). I figured that the good thing about having twins was that they would keep each other company and be happy most of the time.

"Ha! It was the same scene all over again. It was like having Clark the second and Clark the third, but this time I also had Clark the first, and he needed attention, too!

"When the twins were three months old, something small happened that I feel literally changed my life. Just before dinner, I finished feeding and changing Trevor and Ben and put them in their infant seats. Just as my husband, Lenny, and Clark and I sat down to eat, the babies started screaming in unison! Lenny and I each took a baby and started walking them to calm them down. Eventually they calmed down to steady, anxious whimpers. I looked over at the dinner table and saw Clark eating alone.

"My patience broke. These babies had eaten, now it was our turn. I was so worn out and hungry and feeling so guilty about Clark that I decided to let the babies cry in their cribs for fifteen minutes so that Lenny, Clark, and I could finish our meal.

"Of course, Ben and Trevor started screaming again as soon as we put them in the cribs, and this made me feel even more guilty. But in less than ten minutes they stopped crying and slept for almost three hours! Clark and Lenny and I sat at the dinner table for an hour!

"After that night, I did things totally differently. Whenever the babies grew fretful and nothing seemed to help, I put them in their cribs and within a few minutes they'd be asleep. Soon they were taking two two-hour naps a day, incredible time that I had alone or with Clark. On top of that, the babies got to the point that when they were tired and I put them in their cribs, they would fall asleep without crying at all. It was as if they had learned that their cribs meant sleep, which meant relief. Sometimes they almost seemed to dive into their cribs, as if they couldn't wait to snuggle under their covers and go to sleep.

"The more I think about it, the more I think that a lot of Clark's crankiness as a baby was sleep deprivation."

## TIPS FOR SLEEP SCHEDULING

**Babies Should Sleep More at Night Than During the Day. Set Up Different Routines for Naps and Bedtime.**

*"To help our twins distinguish between day and night, we have them take their daytime naps in bassinets with low lights on. At night they sleep in their cribs in a very dark room.*

*"For a while, we played cassette tapes of lullabies at night, but we stopped after a few months because we did not want the children to become dependent on lullabies to go to sleep. Also, since we planned to take a vacation, we did not want the babies to become too rigidly attached to a set of conditions that had to be in place before they could fall asleep."*

**Develop a Simple Bedtime Routine to Help Babies Know That It's Sleeptime.**   Even very young babies can "read" signals. If you always turn the lights low, hold babies on your lap in the rocking chair, and sing "Rock-a-bye Baby" or another lullaby at seven-thirty every night, just before putting babies into their cribs, the babies will associate the low lighting, the rocking chair, and the song with bedtime. The ritual helps them wind down and mentally prepare for sleep.

For babies, bedtime routines may be as simple as a bath, a bottle, a song. One family gave their twins bottles in their double stroller *in the house:* "They knew it was mellowing-out time."

***Some Multiples Are "Automatically" in Sync; Others Must Be Helped Along.***   Many identical and some fraternal multiples tend to fall into a coordinated schedule quite naturally. One parent marveled at her identical sons' uncannily similar inner clocks:

> *"They were always on the same schedule. Things happened within a day of one another. If one of them woke up at two A.M., the other woke up at two-ten. They both started sleeping through the night the same week."*

Other multiples' inner clocks seem to have little or no similarity: Jane awakens at 6:00 A.M. and naps from 8:00 to 10:00; John awakens at 7:30 and naps from noon to 2:00 P.M.

> *"I started taking care of my grandbabies when they were six months old, when my daughter returned to work. They did everything at different times: eat, sleep, burp. I thought, Enough of this! I just kept the first one awake until the second one was ready to nap, so I could put them in together. When one baby slept a lot longer than the first, I'd waken the second so he would be ready later to take the next nap."*

***Acknowledge That Children May Have Different Sleep Styles; However This Need Not Preclude Scheduling.***   Sometimes one baby needs more sleep than another. Naturally, the one who needs *less* sleep should not be expected to lie in his crib waiting for his or her twin to awaken. Still, all babies need naps, so put them both in for naps at the same time, even if one sleeps for only an hour and a half and another sleeps for two-and-a-half hours. By assuring the overlap, you get an hour and a half for your own nap or time for yourself.

A mother of twenty-three-month-old boy-girl twins said:

> *"My daughter likes to sleep. She will ask to go to bed. But my son would stay up all the time if we let him. He has lots of energy. He's afraid he'll miss something if he goes to sleep. But we still have him go to sleep at the same time as his sister. We see that he is tired—even if he won't admit it!*
>
> *"And no matter what time we put him to bed, he's up at five-thirty or six A.M. He'll wake up his sister to play. She used to cooperate, but now she wants to sleep longer. He has to learn to play by himself until she wakes up."*

*Shared Bedrooms May Enhance Merged Scheduling.*   Multiples who share a room often babble to one another from their cribs in the morning like neighbors chatting over a backyard fence. They may entertain each other for quite a while, giving you extra time to sleep or shower before going in. Interestingly, one child's nighttime awakening and crying often does not disturb the other(s).

## FEEDING SCHEDULES

Aligning babies' feeding schedules can require some ingenuity (see Chapters 9 and 10 on breastfeeding and bottlefeeding for information on simultaneous feeding). When babies are new you are busy learning how to nurse and/or bottlefeed, and it may be difficult to schedule their feedings for the first weeks or months of life. Dr. Benjamin Spock's classic *Baby and Child Care* (see the Bibliography) provides a detailed guide to infant feeding schedules. Ask your pediatrician to help you assess your and your multiples' needs.

When babies are infants, you may prefer feeding them one at a time, or you might want to feed them together, especially if limited time is a consideration. However, once babies begin solids, such as baby cereal, usually between the ages of four to six months, depending on your pediatrician's advice, feeding them at the same time will move you toward the eventual goal of gathering all of your children together for breakfast, lunch, and dinner.

Evelyn, whose adept scheduling is the envy of all her friends, said:

> *"If one twin is hungry and the other isn't, sometimes I'll try to distract the hungry one so he waits a bit. Or I'll have the nonhungry child eat earlier. To encourage them to wait longer between feedings, I try to get them to eat a little more at each one, without, of course, ever forcing them to do so."*

*Eating at the Same Time Does Not Mean Children Must Eat the Same Amounts or Even Exactly the Same Foods.*   Although most babies share the same menu (breast milk, formula, eventually solids), even identical twin infants may show differences in tastes, appetite, and food sensitivity. When children begin solids, accept that one may eat more than another, either on a given day or routinely, and that's okay (provided, of course, that your pediatrician has ruled out any medical problems or failure to gain weight appropriately).

As children get older, it is increasingly important to teach them to recognize and respect the body's signals of hunger and satiety in order to help them avoid future eating disorders. Encourage children to heed their body signals by following three simple rules: Eat when you are hungry; eat as much as you want; stop when you are full.[5]

*Avoid Allowing Children to Get Overhungry.* Once babies are accustomed to eating solids, you may decide to get them accustomed to three main meals a day. Give them midmorning and midafternoon snacks to tide them over between meals. Some parents like to distinguish snacktime from mealtime for their toddlers by feeding them in different locales. For example, at breakfast, lunch, and dinner, toddlers eat in their high chairs in the dining room; snacktime is in the kitchen, on the porch, or in the stroller during a midafternoon walk.

## SCHEDULES SHOULD NEVER BE "SET IN STONE"

When a schedule stops working, it is often a signal that children are moving into a new phase, such as reducing their number of naps. You have to figure out when to bend. Don't be an army sergeant!

Infants eat more frequently and sleep more than older babies, who tend to eat less often, stay awake longer between naps, eventually reduce the number of naps, sleep longer at night, and have more energy for sustained outings. Notice when children get sleepy and hungry and shape the schedule accordingly.

*"Routine is important, but you also have to be flexible as children move from phase to phase, such as moving from two naps a day to one. When that happened, we started giving the children lunch before nap rather than after. Also, when they were just starting solids, the bottle was a separate event: I would give them their bottles, bathe them, then feed them solids. But when they really became established with eating solids, I gave them the food and bottle together to start getting them used to a three-meal-a-day idea."*

[5]These three rules are adapted from Jane R. Hirschmann and Lela Zaphiropoulos, *Are You Hungry?: A Completely New Approach to Raising Children Free of Food and Weight Problems* (New York: Signet, 1985).

*Recognize That When Children Are Teething or Sick, Schedules Will Change.* With multiples, once one child is sick, another is bound to get sick, too. Illnesses are sometimes traded back and forth for weeks. Try to stick to a schedule as much as you can, and to return to it once illnesses end.

*During Vacations or Day-Long Family Outings, Schedules May Need to Be Temporarily Abandoned.* Do not let this worry you; occasional interruptions of schedules are rarely a lasting problem. Usually babies can readjust to their schedule within a few days. Expecting that there will be a disruption can help you be patient as children get back in the swing of things.

*Involve Your Caregiver in Discussions of Children's Schedules, and Welcome Her Feedback.* Caregivers usually appreciate the guidance a schedule affords. A written schedule gives the caregiver a basic framework for the day and gives children consistency of care. Encourage your caregiver to give you feedback about what is and is not working. She can help you rethink the schedule as children's needs change.

*Adapt Your Scheduling Goals As Necessary.* In addition to synchronizing multiples' eating, sleeping, and play times, a schedule can be planned to meet other goals. For example:

- If you work, you may want your caregiver to give your children a long afternoon nap so they will be awake later in the evening to be with you. (However, if at some point children go to day care, they should probably have an earlier bedtime so they will not be too cranky in the morning.)
- If you are a morning person, you can build the schedule around an early-morning outing.
- If you like to sleep in, plan a later bedtime for the babies.
- If you and your partner want more of the evening to yourselves, you may like the babies to go to sleep early.

Major changes in schedule probably need to be accomplished gradually, over days or weeks. Ask your pediatrician for advice.

***Ask for Help from Other Experienced Parents of Multiples.*** One mother said:

> *"I was so overwhelmed when I brought the twins home from the hospital, I couldn't even figure out when to take a shower. I called a friend with twins, and she became my mentor. She helped me plan my days. She suggested that I make all of the day's bottles the night before, shower when the children go in for their morning nap, and at all other times, nap or rest when they do."*

***Have a Plan in Mind Every Day.*** Although schedules must adapt to children's needs, having a mental framework for the day keeps you focused.

"Otherwise, it's chaos," said one mother of twins. "The children 'know' when I am unsure. They are happier with a routine."

Writing down the day's plan can help keep you (or your caregiver) focused and remind you of errands to run and phone calls to make. Keep several of your written plans to remind you when children are older of how far you've come!

Having a positive attitude toward scheduling will greatly increase your success. If you are ambivalent, your children will sense this; if you are firm and sure, they will be more likely to cooperate. The "discipline is sanity" dad summed up the essence of scheduling: "Everyone gets used to what's supposed to happen." Children adapt and, in fact, usually find routines comforting—so much so that they might be called a kindness. And for parents, schedules and routines can make all the difference between feeling completely overwhelmed—and manageably overwhelmed! As one mother said, "Having the twins on a schedule is heaven. I don't have to feel constantly on duty."

## 🕮 Bedtime Routines for Older Children

Bedtime routines are important throughout childhood. Bedtime is a temporary farewell to parents and to the excitement of living. No wonder children resist it! They forget the cozy pleasures of sleep until they snuggle under the covers. Night after night, they resist and forget, and night after night, parents must help them overcome their resistance and remember how nice bedtime can be.

A bedtime routine not only helps children, it provides a structure on which parents can depend, a step-by-step bridge from daytime commotion to nightly quieting of motion. The earlier parents introduce children to bedtime routines, the happier everyone will be.

Allow half an hour to an hour for bedtime. Rushing is not restful and will only frustrate your attempts to get children to bed. For toddlers and up, bedtime may include toy cleanup, baths and toothbrushing, pajamas, prayers, recaps of the day. Laying out the next day's clothes is a good organizational strategy for expediting the morning routine, and teaches children how to plan ahead. It is also an affirmation that tomorrow is on the other side of bedtime.

Bedtime stories calm children down and promote a love of reading. Although occasionally watching television together can be nice, it generally is not as conducive to parent-child communication and closeness as reading. If there is a show you do not want to miss, consider taping it to watch later.

Margaret Wise Brown's *Good Night, Moon* is the classic bedtime story. A bunny bids good night to a balloon, a picture of three cows jumping over the moon, and other familiar things, as the room gradually darkens with nightfall.

While one bedtime book suffices for babies and young toddlers, older children enjoy being able to choose one book apiece. To eliminate arguing over who gets to sit on your lap, allow Jane to sit on your lap when you are reading her book, while Johnny cuddles next to you, then have them switch places while you read Johnny's book.

### Seal It with a Kiss

The good-night kiss is, for many children, bedtime's essential closure. In *Remembrance of Things Past,* Marcel Proust described the "sense of tranquility" a mother's kiss brought "when she bent her loving face down over my bed [so that] my lips might drink deeply the sense of her real presence, and with it the power to sleep."

Adding to the poignancy of this passage was the belief of the boy's father that good-night kisses were inappropriate for a boy. The belief persists in some families that kisses and embraces are for girls, while hair-tousling and pats on the shoulder are appropriate for boys. Kisses and hugs do not destine a boy for unmanliness. A little boy whose parents have decided he is "too old" for kisses may resent seeing his twin sister suffering no similar deprivation. Both boys and girls need to be cuddled. Many parents notice, in fact, that even when boys and girls reach the age when they gruffly reject public parental displays of affection, they often still welcome hugs and kisses in private.

Yet it is also important to recognize that some children have a low level of tolerance for physical contact—they are simply not the "touchy-feely" type, and their wishes should be respected. Accept that the child who infrequently gives spontaneous physical displays of affection does not necessarily love you any less than her more physically demonstrative twin, who frequently flings his arms around you in spontaneous hugs, sits on your lap, and wouldn't think of going to sleep without a good-night kiss. (Similarly, do not insist that children kiss or hug friends or relatives. The best kisses are freely given.)

### PROMOTE A "NEVER GO TO BED ANGRY" PRACTICE

When one or more of your children has been uncooperative and you are angry, try to effect a reconciliation before they go to sleep, so that the next day can truly get off to a fresh start. Sometimes you may be incapable of finding the right words to bridge the distance. But you can always bestow a good-night kiss and say, "Even though I feel angry, I still love you. We'll talk tomorrow." Children can also learn to say this to one another; it is a way of learning to avoid holding grudges.

## Toilet Training

Many parents worry about how they can toilet train more than one child. One mother was so concerned that she joined a Mothers of Twins Club specifically for information on how other people had toilet trained their multiples. She was pleasantly surprised to find that toilet training was much easier than she had thought, for her two-and-a-half-year-old children helped each other:

> "We had two potties in the bathroom. When one girl went in and sat, the other would follow her and sit down on the other potty. Sometimes they would sit there and chat or read picture books. When either urinated in the potty, we all clapped our hands and cheered."

Oddly, some parents "compete" about whose children are toilet trained first! This is just one example of the emotional baggage attached to what should simply be the learning of an important social skill by children *who are ready*. Establishing healthy bowel habits is so important to children's lifelong physical and emotional health. Never push toilet training or make it into a power struggle. And don't rush to begin early. Ask your pediatrician's advice about when to begin, based on your children's emotional and physical readiness.

The first step is buying potties. If possible, have one for each child. Tell children that when they are ready, they will be able to use the potty just as Mommy and Daddy use the toilet. Praise their efforts to try. Above all, express calm, unpressured confidence that each will learn this skill.

Gradually, as they are ready, introduce each new stage of toilet training. When they seem comfortable with the potty, go shopping with the children and let each choose some "big girl" or "big boy" training pants or underpants. (Few shopping expeditions are more exciting for youngsters!) Experiment with how long children can go without a diaper during the daytime. Instill in them the habit of going to the bathroom before leaving for any outing. Plan bathroom stops when you are out. Sometimes children are reluctant to use strange or smelly public bathrooms. Do not negate their feelings. It is more helpful to agree: "Yes, this bathroom smells yucky, but it's the only one available. I wish it were a nicer bathroom, too." Children may prove to be troupers after all!

If one child toilet trains before the other, do not compare. Never say, "Why can't you go on the potty like your brother did?" Toilet training is a great opportunity to reaffirm children's individuality: "You are learning how your body feels when ready to urinate or have a bowel movement. Isn't it interesting to learn your body's signals? When you are ready, you will use the toilet just fine."[6]

Discuss your toilet-training approach with your nanny, baby-sitter, or day-care provider, if any, to assure consistency. Make sure the caregiver knows not to bribe, threaten, cajole, shame, goad, or otherwise pressure children to "perform." Be clear that you disap-

[6]For more on toilet training, see Chapter 18, "Toilet Training: Helping Children Develop Healthy Bowel Habits," in Sidney E. Wanderman, M.D., with Betty Rothbart, *Hemorrhoids: Warning Signs and Symptoms of Hemorrhoids and Other Bowel Disorders* (Yonkers, New York: Consumer Reports Books, 1991).

prove of fostering competition around toilet training. Commend a child for using a potty, but do not praise so heartily that the other(s) will feel ashamed. Truly, children *will* successfully toilet train when the time is right for them.

## ⌘ Record-Keeping

Many parents of multiples find that creating an informal record-keeping system is key to staying organized and keeping track of each child's essential facts—both short-term (what each child ate today) and long-term (each child's medical history) information. Even parents of one child find such things hard to remember; with multiples, the parental memory is doubly, triply, or quadruply taxed! You may swear you will never forget Susie's chicken pox, Patty's broken wrist, and Herbert's allergic reaction to a new antibiotic. But in the future, when you try to reconstruct your triplets' medical histories, it would not be at all unusual to forget whether Susie or Patty had chicken pox, whether Patty's right or left wrist was broken, and the name of the antibiotic that gave Herbert hives. Of course, your pediatrician keeps such records, but having your own provides important backup, keeps the facts close at hand, and serves as a diary of your children's lives.

There are two types of record-keeping: daily and ongoing.

### DAILY RECORD-KEEPING

*"When [my mother, the anthropologist] Margaret [Mead] planned for my care and feeding, she set out to combine the generosity of most primitive mothers, who nurse their infants when they cry and remain with them constantly, with the resource of civilization, the clock. . . . She would record the hours at which I demanded feeding and then, by analyzing these times, construct a schedule from the order immanent in my own body's rhythms which would make the process predictable enough so she could schedule her classes and meetings and know when she should be home to feed me."*

—*Mary Catherine Bateson,* With a Daughter's Eye
(New York: William Morrow & Co., 1984)

Few parents of multiples can or should even try to match Margaret Mead's scientific approach to childrearing—and one wonders whether her method would have been as successful with multiples instead of one child.

Nevertheless, daily record-keeping does help many parents of multiples through the blur of the first year. While some parents manage daily life quite well without picking up a pencil, others rely on charts to keep track of their multiples' food intake, bowel movements, wet diapers, sleep patterns, medication, and so on. The charts help them keep track of each child and alert them to any significant changes. For example, at the end of the day you may notice that two triplets had plenty of check marks under "wet diaper," but the third child had only one. That may indicate a problem. The chart can be a helpful resource when you call your pediatrician.

Some breastfeeding mothers keep a chart on which they note which breast each child nursed from first at the last feeding. This can be especially helpful when you are alternating breastfeeding with bottlefeeding for triplets or more. A written chart minimizes the chance of mix-ups and helps assure that each child gets his or her turn at the breast.

For working parents, having a nanny, baby-sitter, or day-care center keep a daily record is crucial. The record gives you a window into your children's day. It also fosters the caregiver's awareness of each child's individual needs and patterns.

You can keep the daily record on a legal pad, though a spiral-bound notebook is less likely to get tattered and enables you to keep all the charts together more easily. A chart needs to be nothing more than vertical columns, children's names across the top, with a list of categories down the side. To eliminate the bother of creating a chart every day, some parents draw up a chart, photocopy it, and keep the charts in a looseleaf notebook for a cumulative record.

## ONGOING RECORD-KEEPING

Ongoing record-keeping can range from a brief list of immunizations and childhood illnesses to a detailed chronicle of your children's lives (see page 204). Capturing snippets of daily life makes for nostalgic rereading—not only by yourself, but also, in later years, by your children. Keeping a separate record for each child creates a lasting legacy they will value all their lives. It makes each child feel treasured, independent, and uniquely important. Separate records also reveal that multiples' histories are never identical, even if *they* are.

---

## Ongoing Record-Keeping

Here are some examples of what you might like to record for each child:
- illnesses, medications, immunizations
- first smile
- first time rolling over
- first time sitting up
- first tooth
- first time holding own bottle
- first time drinking from a cup
- when and how child learned to crawl
- first time standing unsupported
- first step
- first words
- first sentence
- first time feeding self
- first haircut (keep a lock of hair for each child)
- first shoes
- first time sleeping through the night
- favorite foods, activities, books, and toys
- cute expressions, anecdotes, new skills
- attachment to a particular toy or blanket
- first day of day care, nursery school, kindergarten
- relationships with family, friends, caregivers, teachers
- childhood pets
- first tooth lost
- anecdotes, typical moments, what makes this child happy, angry, special

---

You may like to use commercial baby books (one per child) for ongoing record-keeping. Some parents like the structure of baby books, most of which have fill-in-the-blank categories. Other parents feel they can never do justice to these "perfect" books and end up leaving them blank (and feeling guilty). Or they want more room to write than most baby books provide or do not like the baby-book categories and prefer to make their own.

For versatility, you can't beat a looseleaf binder. You may want to divide it into sections with index tabs for each child, or keep notes in the column format described above. Don't aim for perfection; although you can use three-hole paper, feel free to punch three holes in the envelope you scribbled notes on at the doctor's office, and put it in the binder as is. You can also use indexed dividers with pockets for such memorabilia as notes from the children's day-care worker. You can also add children's drawings to the divider pocket, but many children are such prolific artists that their artwork will quickly overwhelm your notebook. It may be better to create separate portfolios for each child's paintings and drawings.

Some parents use a computer for family record-keeping. If you regularly use a computer for your work, you can take "record-keeping breaks" and get your children's "files" up on the screen. Some software enables you to use a "word search" feature to locate such events as chicken pox, broken wrists, or problematic antibiotics quickly.

TIPS FOR SUCCESSFUL ONGOING RECORD-KEEPING

*Make Record-Keeping Part of Your Routine.* At the pediatrician's office, go in with written questions and write down the answers, as well as the children's heights and weights, the doctor's assessment of their medical conditions, any shots, diagnoses, or prescriptions. Take notes during parent-teacher or day-care conferences, too.

*Always Write the Full Date* —month, day, *and year* on every note, every document, every photo, and on the back of any of your children's drawings, school papers, and letters that you want to save.

*Consider Keeping a Parenthood Journal.* While ongoing record-keeping is usually viewed as a way of keeping track of children's milestones, you may wish to take it a step further and record your thoughts and feelings about parenthood. Keeping a journal can help you express feelings, vent frustrations, preserve precious memories, and even discover just what is on your mind. Writing can reveal you to yourself. Many writers say, "I never really know what is on my mind until I write it."

The journal need not be elaborate, nor need entries be lengthy. One parent kept her notebook in the kitchen and wrote a few brief lines about the day's activities and her thoughts every evening after loading the dishwasher. Another parent, who worked on her computer daily, typed a journal entry before beginning the day's work.

"What on earth would I write about?" said one mother. "Peanut-butter-and-jelly sandwiches?" A journal is not primarily a "recapitulation" of daily events, but rather a description of your "inner journey." As Ira Progoff wrote in *At a Journal Workshop,* "Even when our lives seem to be uneventful on the outside, the range of content and movement within us is very great. . . . It is truly worth our while to record in our Daily Log without censorship and without judgment."[7]

A journal is especially valuable for parents of multiples, who daily confront the complexities of so many mingled lives.

*Keep Record-Keeping/Journal-Writing Simple and Guilt-Free.* The biggest problem with record-keeping and journals is the stress people often associate with them. Remember, these are not homework assignments but purely voluntary. No one is giving you a grade; there is no one "right" approach. Don't get mired in guilt if you miss a day, a week, even months. Just pick up your pen again when you can.

*If a Journal Is Not Your Style, Consider Alternative Ways to Preserve Memories.*   Around the time of her children's birthdays, one mother wrote each child a letter headed "You at Two" (or Three, Four, etc.). She mentioned notable events and milestones of the last year; most importantly, she described what the child was like right now—not only the laudable things ("You have graduated from double-blade to single-blade ice skates") but other traits as well ("You are still grumpy when you wake up in the morning. We are working on it. At least now you usually cheer up during the ride to school, and you give me a kiss good-bye before running to greet your friends

[7]Ira Progoff, *At a Journal Workshop* (New York: Dialogue House Library 1975).

in the schoolyard."). She saved all of the letters and presented the packet of letters, tied with a ribbon, to each child on his or her twenty-first birthday.

One woman's "journal" consisted of photocopies of her newsy letters to her parents. Another parent did not like to write, but her quick, frequent (and dated) sketches of her kids added up to a picture-journal worth thousands of words.

# Chapter 13

# SELECTING AND VISITING THE PEDIATRICIAN

A pediatrician (or family practitioner) should be your trusted partner in keeping track of each child's growth and development, preventing and treating illnesses, explaining medical issues, evaluating choices, and responding to your questions and concerns.

It is best to select a pediatrician during pregnancy, so the doctor can be part of your children's lives from the very beginning. Ask for recommendations from your obstetrician, friends, and local Mothers of Twins Club or La Leche League members. But do not take recommendations at face value. Ask *why* people like their doctors. A friend may be happy with a pediatrician who "doesn't go into big explanations; we're in and out of there fast." But maybe you *like* detailed explanations and do not mind longer visits.

*"It was important to me to have a doctor who said, 'Come on in, let's check out the problem,' instead of 'Make an appointment.' "*

*"Finding a good pediatrician has been hell. First I went to a big group. I hated it from day one. My kids don't look alike. Crystal has a scar*

*from one side of her body to the other. So it would be easy for the doctor to lift her shirt and say, 'Hi, Crystal.' But the doctors never bothered. They made no effort to tell my girls apart. I finally found a doctor who sees them as more than medical cases."*

Interview one or more doctors before making a decision. Most pediatricians are used to parent interviews. Many do them free of charge, while others charge a fee. To save everyone's time, do some prescreening by phone with the office staff. There is no point making an interview appointment with a doctor who does not take your medical insurance, is inconveniently located, or has no evening or weekend hours to accommodate working parents.

## ⚅ *When Selecting a Pediatrician, Consider:*

- What are the doctor's qualifications? Is he or she board-certified? (If you use a family practitioner instead of a pediatrician, how much of his or her practice is devoted to children?)
- At what hospital(s) does the doctor have admitting privileges?
- Does the doctor have partners? Can your children always see the same pediatrician, or must they rotate? Who covers the practice at night?
- Does the practice accept your medical insurance? How is billing done? Is there any break on fees for multiples?
- Is the office convenient? Check on the availability of parking, proximity to a bus or subway stop, or the round-trip cost of a taxi or car service. Avoid long voyages with sick children.
- Does the office accommodate carriages and strollers? Are there stairs to contend with?
- Is the office clean, inviting, and stocked with appropriate children's books and toys?
- Is the office staff courteous?
- What are the office hours?
- Is the doctor easy to talk with?
- Is the doctor supportive of breastfeeding multiples? Since it is more challenging (but no less rewarding) than breastfeeding single-borns, you will need the pediatrician's encouragement and informed advice. To get a sense of the doctor's commitment to breastfeeding multiples, see whether his or her opinion of

supplementing with formula is akin to your own, how long you can or should expect to breastfeed, how you know whether you have enough milk, and how you can increase your chances of a successful breastfeeding experience.

- How long do patients usually need to wait before seeing the doctor? Entertaining multiples in a waiting room can be trying if waits are long.
- How accessible is the doctor? Is there a "phone-in" hour for questions? Check with other parents about how responsive the doctor is to their concerns, how quickly phone calls are returned, how hard it is to get an appointment, and whether the staff is helpful.
- How big a role do nurse practitioners play in the practice?

## Visiting the Doctor

Take a friend, relative, or baby-sitter with you to assist with the children and transportation. When one mother of triplets must visit the pediatrician alone, she calls from the parking lot and the office staff help her get the children into (and out of) the office. Don't forget toys, books, snacks, and bottles to help the children endure commuting and waiting time.

Make sure the doctor is sensitive to the need to treat multiples as individuals. For example, he or she should use each child's name, rather than saying, "Okay, now let me see the other twin." And ask the doctor to refrain from making comparisons such as, "Why aren't you gaining as much weight as your brother?"

Some parents prefer having their multiples get shots on different days, so they can give more attention to the child who received the shots and may have post-injection fussiness or fever. Of course, additional visits present logistical challenges. Consider whether the benefit outweighs the inconvenience. If you have someone to stay home with the other child(ren), you might like occasionally making doctor visits into special one-on-one time.

The pediatrician should value your feedback and respect your right to question his or her recommendations. In turn, keep your part of the bargain: If the pediatrician ever says, does, or recommends something that bothers you, *say so.* Some parents would rather change doctors than confront the one they have, because they feel intimidated or assume the doctor will not take kindly to their challenge. Give a doctor a chance to respond to your concerns—to straighten out misunderstandings, to minimize unnecessary upheaval for you and your children, and perhaps even to influence the doctor to make changes that will benefit all of his or her patients.

People often assume that a physician's education ends when he or she finishes hospital training. But doctors take continuing education courses to stay current. And they also learn, on the job, through their patients' experiences. Do not hesitate to share literature that relates to your children and their medical conditions.

Many pediatricians will welcome an opportunity to develop a relationship with you and your children, and will greatly appreciate any information on parenting multiples that you can provide. With luck, a little planning, and patience, you will develop a relationship with your pediatrician that you and your children will always treasure.

## ◙ *Chapter 14*

# *I*NSTANT CELEBRITY AND THE (SOMETIMES UN-) KINDNESS OF STRANGERS

◙    All the mall's a stage and all the shoppers gawkers when multiples arrive on the scene. You'd think your triple stroller was a stretch limo packed with rock stars. Of course, as most rock stars could tell you, a crowd's attention is a mixed blessing. Some days you thrive on being the star attraction; other days you would like to shop for socks without an audience.

Whatever your mood, ad libs abound:

"My goodness, are they all yours?"

"You must have your hands full."

"How on earth do you tell them apart?"

"Twins! How adorable."

"How do you cope? I could *never* survive triplets."

Some parents hate the constant interruptions:

*"I was stupefied that people stopped me so often on the street. They saw me as fair game for all their remarks."*

*"I was walking in the mall and this lady shouted, 'Stop that stroller! I want to see those twins!' I felt like saying, 'Who the hell are you?'"*

To discourage comments, some parents devise strategies: Avoid eye contact. Pretend not to hear people talk about or to you.

Yet other parents welcome the attention:

*"I've never minded when strangers come up to talk with me. I'm so cooped up in the house that when we go out, I don't mind talking to anyone."*

One mother notices that her reactions to people's comments are a barometer of how she is feeling that day:

*"People often say, 'I always wanted twins.' On bad days, I say, 'You don't know what you're talking about.' But on good days I feel proud and happy that I do have twins."*

A mother of quadruplets is amused by people's reactions to her brood:

*"People are so confused when they see my kids. They don't know what to call them! They say, 'Oh, you have triplets!' I say, 'Count again!' My kids have been called 'quintriplets,' 'quadtriplets.' You name it, I've heard it."*

The never-ending stream of onlookers' commentary has inspired a cottage industry of "response products" marketed in magazines and catalogs for parents of multiples. Tote bags and T-shirts proclaim, "Yes, they're *Twins!!*" or "Yes, they're *all* Mine!!!" A hat expresses a plaintive appeal: "FATHER OF TWINS . . .which way did they go?"

*"In the supermarket, when people see me with a baby in a Snugli on my chest, they give me a nice smile. Then when my wife comes up and she has a baby in a Snugli, too, everybody says, 'Oh, are those twins?' Obviously they are!"*

When your infant twins are snoozing or your preschool quads are holding hands sweet as a paper-doll chain, complimentary comments are always welcome. But when the twins are yowling, or the paper-doll chain snaps, sending four look-alikes to the far corners of a store, the last thing you need is for someone to mutter, "Better you than me!"

## ▣ Strangers As Angels

*"Once, Abigail toddled out of sight at a flea market. We found her after my husband put Robin up on his shoulders and asked people, 'Have you seen anyone who looks just like this?' "*

—*Letty Cottin Pogrebin, "Twofers," Ms., April 1989*

*"When my twins were little, I could not walk one block without somebody stopping me to look at them. I was like a celebrity. I was so proud of my boys, I loved it when people admired them."*

Strangers are angels when they find your children as captivating as you do. A sincere and well-timed remark about their beauty and cleverness can brighten your day and help you laugh about the chaotic moments of life with multiples. The praise may even feel like a well-deserved reward for all your hard work; some parents dress children alike in order to attract this recognition.

On days when you feel bedraggled, exhausted, or discouraged, the admiration can freshen your recollection of what is so special about your multiples.

*"We were in a pizza place one day with the twins, and they made such a mess. A couple at the next table kept staring at us. Finally, I said, 'We're such a spectacle, aren't we?' They smiled and said, 'Your kids are wonderful. We just found out we are having twins, too!' "*

Yet even compliments wear thin when they are too many and too intrusive. As one mother put it:

*"I began to feel like the constant interruptions deprived me of the right to normal enjoyment of everyday living. I got so tired of people stopping me, I stuck to the side streets when I took the kids out for a walk."*

People are not only fascinated by multiples, they often exhibit a sense of communal pride, even "ownership." They feel emotionally invested in contributing to the well-being of these marvelous children; all well and good, until their investment yields dividends of unwanted advice. A mother who used a plastic rain hood over the stroller felt frustrated by people who shrieked, "Won't those babies suffocate?" The first few times, she patiently pointed out that the hood had ample air vents, that it fit loosely at the bottom, that it came with the stroller, for heaven's sake, and was perfectly safe, was even like a window. . . . After the tenth shriek, however, her patience gave out, and her humor took on a desperate edge. "Suffocate?" she drawled. "Gee, I hope not."

Still, you genuinely appreciate those who are eager to help you. People who hold doors open for the stroller, help your brood board the bus, croon nursery rhymes or mesmerize your children with cat's cradle in the supermarket checkout line, run to give you the pacifiers, bottles, or shoes your children dropped . . . maybe these strangers *are* angels, sent to make your day a little easier.

> *"My husband took our older child and the twins, age five months, to a puppet show in the mall while I went to run an errand. When I went to join them, I saw a woman gently rocking my stroller! I thought, What's going on here! It turns out that while our son watched the puppet show, one twin started to cry, so my husband took him out and fed him. Then the other twin cried, and he tried to rock the stroller with his foot. This woman came up and said, 'I'm a grandmother, here, let me do that for you.'"*

## Devenoming the Sting

> *"It pains me when somebody compliments one of my daughters, who happens to be more conventionally cute, but not the other. Sometimes I wish they were identical."*

People's comments can be a benediction—or a blow. Their thoughtlessness or audacity can leave you speechless, just when you wish you had a retort at the tip of your tongue.

*The Insult of Pity.* Multiples are hard work, but they are a blessing, not a curse. One dad enjoyed wearing a T-shirt whose slogan he could point to when necessary: "Yes, I'm glad they're not yours, too."

A mother of twins has her answer to "better you than me" ready:

*"Some people say, 'Oh, you poor thing. How do you manage twins? I feel sorry for you.'*

*"I tell them, 'I feel sorry for you that you aren't having this experience.' "*

When people say to a mother of quadruplets, "You must have your hands full," she retorts, "Better full than empty."

*The Left-Out Sibling.*   Nothing aches more than having people exclaim over multiples while ignoring their single-born sibling(s). Some parents make a point of saying, "And this is their wonderful big sister. She is a great helper, and a terrific baseball player, too."

*"If They Were My Babies, I Would . . ."*   Unasked-for advice is the bane of every new parent. When you are already chiding yourself for forgetting the children's sweaters, you hardly need the entire world to point out that it is windy and they will surely catch cold.

Yet most people mean well. Many give advice not to make you feel bad, but as a way of striking up a conversation or trying to share their own hard-won wisdom. Although you do not owe people explanations or even a response, you might just say thank you as you hurry by. Murmuring "Hmmm . . ." is quick and lets people know you heard them. The forbiddingly formal "I'll certainly take that idea into consideration" quenches a persistent flow of advice. And when you feel like being gracious: "I appreciate your concern, and we are off to buy new sweaters right now."

*Unkind Comparisons.*   What can possibly be on the minds of people who admire one twin's curly locks, then turn to the other child and say, "Too bad that one got the straight hair"? Counter the tactless remark by saying, "I think both children have beautiful hair." If the person does not get the hint, be more direct: "In our family, we do not compare the children. We feel each is special in her own way."

*"Are They Identical?"*   A fair question. But it is surprising how often people ask this of twins who are obviously boy/girl! The query prompts one woman to answer, "No, he has a penis. She doesn't."

*"Do Twins Run in Your Family?"* One woman's quip: "They do now."

A sibling of twin toddlers answered, "Yes, twins run in our family. They run up and down the stairs and in and out of the house."

*"Are They Pergonal Babies?"* Fertility drugs and *in vitro* fertilization account for some of the increase in multiples today—and for many personal questions. You can respond by tossing the question back: "Why do you ask?" If the asker says, "Just curious," you can smile and respond, "And I'm just private," or "That's privileged information."

Yet some parents do not mind being asked:

*"It's nothing to be ashamed of. They're our babies, even if we needed a little nudge from medical technology to conceive them. And sometimes people who ask are themselves struggling with infertility, or are close with somebody else who is. Their question gives us an opportunity to pass on what we have learned, to help someone else."*

*"I joke about it: 'This is my Clomid son. These are my Pergonal twins.' To me, my kids are miracles."*

Other parents feel strongly about preserving their privacy:

*"How our babies were conceived is no one else's business. I simply say, 'We were just lucky.' We were! We were lucky the drugs worked."*

One questioner would not accept the "just lucky" answer and pressed for details. The exasperated mother of twins found an effective way to have the last word. She smiled and purred, "You really want to know how we conceived? Lots of *great* sex!"

# Chapter 15

# *T*ELLING MULTIPLES APART

*"When they were infants, we colored one girl's toenails pink. It became a joke: 'Where's Pinky?' When we bought them their first pair of shoes, we got one red pair and one blue pair. We did that for years, and teachers appreciated it. But when the girls got older, they did not want to wear red shoes and blue shoes. One girl has a beauty mark on her cheek, but it is small. You have to get close to see it. Very quietly, we tell people to look for it. Just the same, only one of their four grandparents can tell them apart. This hurts the girls' feelings, since their cousins and friends can tell them apart."*

"Which one are you?" It is a question multiples have to get used to. Most learn to respond with patience and good humor and recognize that new acquaintances must learn to tell them apart. But a common follow-up comment can be quite hard to take: "Oh, well, it doesn't matter which twin you are." It matters profoundly. Multiples may not be one-of-a-kind, but they do not like to be seen as merely one-of-a-set. Like everyone else, they need to be recognized as unique individuals and addressed by name.

## ⊠ Active Seeing

*"Nobody sees a flower—really. It is so small, we haven't time, and to see takes time. Like to have a friend takes time."*

—Georgia O'Keeffe

People need to recognize the importance of telling multiples apart—and then learn how to do it. This can be challenging, not only because children are or seem identical, but also because many people do not have highly developed skills of observation. Artists and detectives, for example, are trained to scrutinize faces; they look at the prominence of cheekbones, the shape of eyebrows, the shadings of skin, and the fullness of lips. So an artist or detective may more quickly be able to discern that one twin has a slightly broader forehead, and that the other twin's ears are more delicately formed.

For many people, however, such "active seeing" is a new concept, and they may lack confidence in their ability to master or even attempt it. Parents can help family members, caregivers, teachers, and neighbors by pointing out multiples' distinctive traits. Suggest memory tricks that will help people associate the right name with the right face: "Felicia's face is fuller than Vicky's. Just remember that *fuller* and *Felicia* both begin with the letter *F*."

Older children can take on the task themselves: "I have a scar on my chin from when I fell off a bicycle. Peter does not have a scar." *Peter* and *plain* (unscarred chin) both begin with the letter *P*. A scar, not usually something people point out about themselves, is in this case a handy identifier.

*"It took my husband two months to know who was who. It took me two days. I knew them from the backs of their heads."*

New parents sometimes feel dismayed, even inadequate, when they cannot tell their own infants apart. This is needless guilt. Don't be so hard on yourself, especially when you are coping with a haze of sleeplessness, recuperating from childbirth, and adjusting to life with multiples. Instead of expecting to tell them apart easily, avail yourself of the techniques below for as long as you need them. There is no contest here, no judgment. The better you get to know your babies, the more their unique characteristics will become apparent. Before too long, telling them apart will be effortless.

## ▣ *Techniques for Telling Multiples Apart*

*Hospital Identification Bracelets—At Home.*   Some parents leave on I.D. bracelets for days, even weeks, until they are sure they can tell babies apart.

*Baby's First Pedicure.*   Paint one baby's toenails with nail polish. Fingernail polish, perhaps on only one nail, may also work but is unappealing for thumbsuckers.

*Color Coding.*   Assign each child one color or several colors. Dress Johnny in blue, white, and green; dress Karl in red, yellow, and brown. Or pin ribbons on their clothing.

Interestingly, color coding can stay in children's minds long after parents have discontinued it. One couple dressed their infant daughter, Jade, in green (to match her name) for the first six months. Two years later they were astonished when Jade's twin sister refused to wear a new pair of green overalls. "Those Jade's," she explained.

*Say It with Gold Plate.*   Have one twin wear an ankle bracelet. Or have an I.D. bracelet made for each baby. Add links or different chains as they grow. Ask your children for their ideas, too. One family bought initial pins for their school-age twins.

While you are at it, how about buying I.D. bracelets or initial pins for multiples' siblings, too?

*Trademark Coiffures.*   Allow one twin's hair to grow and keep the other one's short. Of course, this only works if babies have enough hair to grow. Baby girls with scant curls can sport distinctive barrettes.

*Built-In Clues.*   Even identical twins often have subtle distinctions, such as different skin tones or voice qualities. A well-placed birthmark can be an instant deconfuser: "Celia has a small mole on her right cheek; Meg has none."

If both twins have a birthmark, maybe it is not exactly in the same location. Develop a mnemonic device to help yourself and other people: "Both boys have a birthmark near their mouth. But John's is lower, closer to the jaw. Just remember that *jaw* and *John* sound similar."

Write down the "clues" to your multiples' differences, for reference by baby-sitters, teachers, and even yourself.

*Fancy Footwork.*   Color-code babies' booties, toddlers' sneakers, and school-age children's shoes and boots. At a glance, a distracted teacher knows that Henry always wears black sneakers, and Gene always wear white ones. (Of course, the twins can foil this by switching shoes!)

*A Class Act.*   Some people catch on to multiples' uniqueness more quickly than others. One kindergarten teacher, a self-described "slow study," had *all* of her students wear name tags for the first two weeks of school.

A first-grade teacher mixed up twins in her classroom until Max, a particularly observant student, explained why *he* never got confused:

- Tim's voice was higher than Joshua's.
- Tim's skin was a little darker.
- Joshua sat at Table One and Tim at Table Two.

Each morning Max memorized what each twin was wearing so he could tell them apart all day long. The parents' decision to dress the twins differently helped classmates relate to them as individuals.

*Camera-Ready.*   Even parents and children themselves can have a hard time telling multiples apart in photographs. In some group shots, position or pin a name card in front of each child. Or consider always arranging them in the same order:

*"Friends and relatives who see the quads less often can't keep them straight. So [Tammy and Neal Nelson] devised a coding system known as ZACK [or ZACG] order. In pictures, the babies are always positioned left to right in the order of birth, first Zachary, then Aaron, then Christopher and Gene.*

> *"The parents also use color coding to match the boys with such possessions as blankets."*
> —Carol S. Gillespie, *"Four of a Kind,"*
> Pittsburgh Post-Gazette, *May 9, 1993*

Vary your picture-taking. In addition to group photos of the children, take individual pictures of each child and pictures of a sibling with each twin or triplet. And hand the camera to a neighbor once in a while for whole-family pictures that include the ever-present, never-seen family photographer—*you!*

*Film Stars.* When videotaping the children, have them give their names on camera. If they wear different clothing, it will be easier to keep track of who's who throughout the film.

When they are old enough, let them take turns filming, too. Note on the audio the date and who is doing the filming. Let each child give a "show-and-tell tour" of his or her current art projects, collections, schoolwork, wall decorations, etc. Or, with you filming, let each child demonstrate basketball or dance moves or describe what he or she is up to these days.

## You Can't Win Them All

Be aware that no matter what you do, there may be people who cannot or will not make the effort to tell multiples apart. Acquaintances' confusion can be tolerated, but children may feel hurt when family members, neighbors, doctors, or teachers hardly seem to try to tell them apart. Identical teenage girls got so fed up with a teacher who, after knowing them for two years, still asked who was who that they replied, "We aren't telling."

Of course, sometimes multiples must take some responsibility for the confusion. One pair of twin boys confused their grandfather for years with their switch-the-twin tricks. They outgrew their prankishness in their early teens, but it was too late to persuade Grandpa that they no longer played such games. No matter how many times they told him their true names, he refused to believe them!

And then there are people who get so excited about seeing multiples that they lose all sense of logic. Bonnie Eisenberg-Greene, a mother of twins, told the following story in *The Bottom Line,* the newsletter of the Mothers of Multiples of Lower Fairfield County, Connecticut:

> *"[One mother's] boy/girl twins have a four-inch difference in height and an eight-pound difference in weight; her son has dark hair and dark eyes, and her daughter is blond, blue-eyed, and has pierced ears. . . . Yet people are always asking her, 'How do you tell them apart?' "[1]*

[1]Bonnie Eisenberg-Greene, "Are They Identical or Siamese?," *The Bottom Line,* October 1991.

# Chapter 16

# S AME GENES, SAME JEANS? THE PROS AND CONS OF DRESSING MULTIPLES ALIKE

⬛      What should your children wear? For parents of single-borns, this is virtually a nonissue: Children are dressed in easy-care, comfortable clothes that fit. But for parents of multiples, there is another consideration: Should the children be dressed alike?

On both sides of the issue, the arguments are passionate. Those who dress their children alike feel it is one of the "perks" of having multiples. The popular image of multiples—reflected in many children's books, in such films as *The Parent Trap,* and in greeting cards, calendars, and birth announcements geared to multiples—is of dressed-alike children. And when buying baby gifts for multiples, many people automatically choose identical outfits, assuming that they are the "right" gift to give.

Sometimes they are. Many parents take tremendous pleasure in buying or receiving clothing in twos and threes, then watching the double and triple takes of passersby who notice the twins or triplets dressed alike.

Some parents also cite the automatic equality of dressing children alike: No child can claim that another one is wearing something nicer. Yet it can also be inconvenient. If one child stains or tears an outfit, what happens to the other twin's unstained, untorn outfit? Some parents ease up on the matching outfits idea at home, reserving identical clothes for public appearances.

> *"We were dressed alike until we were seven or eight years old. Then I rebelled because my sister was such a slob. She would ruin her clothes, while I was very neat. I wanted my own things."*

Many other parents vociferously object to dressing multiples alike, saying that it diminishes their individuality. They exchange gifts of identical clothing or refrain from dressing the children in those outfits at the same time. One mother was so appalled by identical clothing, she said, "It should be against the law!"

Needless to say, parents who favor dressing alike do not take kindly to such criticism. As one mother said, "Nobody makes a fuss over mother-daughter outfits or team uniforms. So why do they hassle me over my decision to let my twins look like twins?"

The controversy arises from opposite philosophies about raising multiples, and from conflicting perceptions of how dressing alike affects children.


## ▣ *Two Philosophies*

*Dressing children alike* presents them to the world as multiples and emphasizes that they are *different from other children*. "I am a twin," says a look-alike outfit. Such children are more likely to be called "the twins" or "the triplets." Their clothing is a daily reminder of the circumstances of their birth.

*Dressing children differently* makes the statement that these children, though multiples, are *different from one another*. They are presented to the world as being similar to single-born children in their innate individuality. Their dissimilar outfits are intended to discourage people from calling children "the twins," and to encourage people to address them by name.

## ◎ The Effect on Children

*"I dress my girls alike. But one twin is starting to crisscross the Velcro straps on her shoes. I think she is trying to assert her individuality so people can tell her apart from her sister."*

*"Until we were nine or ten years old, our mother dressed us alike. My twin brother was tall and lean, and I was short and chubby. I hated wearing the same clothes, because he always looked better than me!"*

Dressing children alike, by keeping them in a multiples context, urges them to identify with one another. Look-alike clothing, like sound-alike names, announces that twins "go together." It accentuates their bond and downplays their individuality.

Babies and very young children are hardly likely to notice or mind this; they have no other frame of reference. As they get a little older, they may show great surprise to discover that not all children *have* a twin, and that not all twins dress alike. And depending on the children and the receptiveness of their parents, they may press to dress differently. Many parents are surprised by how early children can show clothing preferences:

*"I used to struggle with whether to dress my twin daughters alike. Life is easier now that they are nearly three and pick their own outfits. They rarely choose the same clothes. They have different tastes. Lana loves skirts and tights. Shelley is more easygoing; she likes sweatpants.*

*"But when I'm out with the girls, strangers stop me and scold, 'How could you do that? How could you dress one twin in a beautiful dress and the other in sweatpants?' Why should I have to justify my twins' individual styles to complete strangers?"*

A passerby's judgement of how you should dress your children is best ignored. Yet it is important to remember that all clothing affects how people perceive the wearer. That is why so many colors and styles of clothing exist: to express how individuals see themselves and to influence how they are seen by others. In explaining her decision to dress her twins differently, one mother said, "Interchange-able clothes give people the impression that the *children* are interchangeable." She felt strongly that her twins should be seen—and treated—as distinct individuals.

Dressing alike often has an effect parents do not intend: It makes telling multiples apart much more difficult. This results, so to speak, in multiple frustrations. The children constantly are forced to identify themselves. ("No, *I'm* Henry!") Playmates give up trying to tell who is who and resort to calling them "the twins" and treating them as a unit rather than as individuals. Being called by name is a right that other children take for granted. But it is a right too often denied to multiples whose look-alike clothing confounds people's attempts to differentiate them. Being called "Hey, twin!" or "Let's play, triplet" virtually renders children nameless and makes them feel uncomfortably different.

Teachers and relatives also feel defeated in their attempts to get to know each child when they wear identical clothing. The children's outfits become a burden, an obstacle to normal relationships.

It is revealing that many multiples who were dressed alike as children almost make a campaign of looking different when they get older. While some have fond memories of cute look-alike outfits, others seethe with resentment.

## Seeking the Middle Ground

"Moderation in all things" was Benjamin Franklin's motto, and some parents apply it to the issue of clothing:

> *"Most of the time I dress my boys differently, but I don't make a fetish out of it. For special occasions, sure I dress them alike. Why not?*
>
> *"For example, usually I return most identical outfits that people give us. But when someone sent us embroidered outfits from England, I couldn't return them, and I was glad. Those became their special-occasion outfits."*

Another parent also dresses her twins differently—and also makes exceptions to this rule:

> *"At Halloween, one twin dressed as Peter Pan and the other as his shadow. And for their first-grade play,* The Trial of Alice in Wonderland, *they enjoyed being Tweedledum and Tweedledee.*

*"And when I take the kids on outings to big, crowded places like the amusement park, I dress them alike so I can find them quickly. I don't have to remember what each twin is wearing. Also, I wear bright colors—like a yellow blazer—so they can find me easily, too."*

As with parents who give "equivalent names" to their multiples (see Chapter 8, "Naming Your Babies"), many parents seek out "equivalent clothing." They do not dress children alike, but they choose "separate but equal" clothing, such as similar dresses or sweats in different colors or patterns. If one child demonstrates a preference for a particular color or style, they honor it:

*"One girl loves lace, ribbons, and ruffles, while the other hates all that. To her, the supreme compliment is to say that an outfit is 'plain.' So I take them shopping with me and let them choose their own clothing, as long as it is within my price range and fairly nice looking."*

One mother, wishing to respect her children's disparate tastes, discovered that she had to let go of her own inner pressure to achieve an unnecessary "equality":

*"If I buy a thirty-five-dollar sweater for one of the girls, and it has a certain amount of embroidery on it, then I feel that I shouldn't buy a plainer sweater that costs less for the other one. But she wants the plainer sweater!"*

Another parent realized that she felt more strongly about her twins dressing differently than they did:

*"I never, never dressed them alike. But often, even when they had their own rooms and dressed separately, they'd come downstairs and discover they were wearing similar outfits. They got a kick out of it."*

As children get older, of course, most parents recognize the need to let them decide for themselves what they want to wear, as the growing children discover who they are. The process can be interesting to observe:

*"We always dressed the girls differently. When they became teenagers, they worked even harder to develop their own individual styles. One wore heavy makeup, the other wore no makeup at all.*

*"Since they went to colleges in different cities, they have both re-verted to an all-American classic look, mostly jeans. Now they both look more understated—and more alike than ever before. And they are also more relaxed, more comfortable with each other."*

Ultimately, the children themselves should be allowed to decide how they want to dress. As early as two or three years of age, children often express likes and dislikes about clothing and about dressing alike. Listen to what they say, and try to honor their decisions. You may find that on some days they will want to dress alike and not on other days. Let them decide how they want to appear to the world.

# Chapter 17

# SIBLINGS OF MULTIPLES: ADJUSTING TO HAVING MORE TO LOVE

When twins are born, a single-born sibling often sees the newly multipled family as a Noah's Ark gone awry: "Everyone's two-by-two but me."

And when your child protests, "I want a twin, too!" you cannot do a single thing about it.

> *"My son once said, 'I'm alone. Everyone has company but me. You and Dad share a room. Shannon and Ruthanne share a room. Can't we have another brother?'"*

When you have only one new baby, he or she sleeps much of the time, giving you time for your older children. With twins, triplets, or more, however, you cannot count on synchronized schedules, at least for the first several months. But there are many ways you *can* help your older children adjust to the turmoil and exhilaration of having multiples join the family. The keys to success: Be aware of the siblings' need for inclusion and recognition, and make every effort to prevent the children from feeling displaced in your affections or in the family.

## ◙ Getting a Good Start

*"When our twin girls were born, my four-year-old son ran through the apartment singing, 'I prayed for one, but God gave me two.' He felt like a very special, very proud big brother."*

"These are my new babies!" They may be *your* sons and/or daughters, but to your older children, they are, most importantly, brothers and/or sisters. Amid the anxieties of transition, pride and jubilation also bubble as children respond to the atmosphere of excitement—and seek recognition in *their* new role as the "big brothers" or "big sisters."

Introduce them to "their" new babies as soon as you can. Have them visit you in the hospital, if possible. When they arrive, consider having the babies in the nursery so your older children can have you—and both of your arms—to themselves for this postbirth reunion.

Encourage the children's sense of "ownership" of the new babies: "Here are your new brothers. I bet they want to be just like you when they grow up." Children often enjoy bringing a gift for each baby, such as a drawing or a small stuffed animal. The drawing can be taped onto or near the babies' cribs or isolettes, and the stuffed animals can be perched close by.

Complete this welcoming ritual by presenting your children with gifts "from" the newborns—picture books, drawing pads and markers, or puzzles that you brought to the hospital with you.

## ◙ Who Is Keeping the Children Company?

The importance of having trusted, loved family or friends involved with your children while you are in the hospital and afterward cannot be overemphasized. You and your mate must be with the babies *and* your older children, who may resist the new rationing of time. Having other favorite people around to entertain, distract, and coddle them lessens the pressure on you somewhat and makes this transition an even more special time for the children.

But their companions should not expect children to be unremittingly charming playmates. While some children go along pretty willingly with the program, others resist. Whoever is with them needs to understand that the arrival of multiples is a major, even traumatic, event in their lives, and children may "act out" in response:

> "My parents helped, but they were a little rough on our older child. He was temperamental, and I had to explain to my parents that he had just had twins come into his life! They had to relax with him. I doubly had to care for the twins and protect my older child."

> "My aunt and uncle thought they were doing something terrific when they took our five-year-old daughter to the museum. She acted impossible the whole time. She complained about everything, resisted holding their hands when crossing the street, and threw a tantrum. We had all thought this trip would be a treat for her. Instead, I guess she felt like she was being kicked out of her own home. She wasn't interested in my need to rest. She just wanted to be home."

Grown-ups must not take such behavior personally. Rather, they can try to help the children articulate their feelings and give the children more choice in their activities. If a child doesn't want to go to the zoo, there's nothing wrong with riding bikes on the block or baking cookies at home, as long as you get the break you need in order to tend to the babies and rest.

## ▣ Rituals and Visitors

If you have a ceremony for the babies, such as a bris, baby-naming, or christening, create an honorary role for the older siblings. For example, they can announce the new babies' names, or simply stand with the parents and be introduced to the guests.

One couple created their own baby-naming ceremony for their twin daughters and held it in their backyard. They wrote and photocopied a program for the event, which included poems, announcement of the godparents, and a family tree, with the siblings' roles prominently featured. Their older children were in charge of distributing the programs to guests and gave words of welcome to the new babies during the ceremony; one who was old enough also read a brief passage of text.

Let the older siblings have the fun and honor of unwrapping the babies' gifts while you or another adult make a list of who gave what. (The list facilitates thank-you notes in case cards get separated from gifts.)

When your home is filled with guests, "assign" a relative or friend to look out for the siblings and make sure they do not feel lost in all the hubbub. Alert grandparents, friends, and others that the single-born children's need for attention does not decrease but *increases* with the multiples' birth. Do not let fuss over the babies exclude their siblings.

*"When the twins were first born, we had lots of visitors. It was really important to have other kids visit with whom our older child could play—cousins and friends from nursery school. When all the visitors started fading away, that's when he started to rebel a bit. It helped to ask people to bring gifts for him, not for the twins. I also bought small gifts to reward him for times he was good with the babies. I didn't end up having to use most of them."*

Many guests are sensitive to the needs of older children and bring small gifts for them as well as baby gifts for the new arrivals. However, some people lavish attention on the new twins or triplets and virtually ignore the older children. Tactfully include them by introducing the babies as "Heather and Sammy's little sisters." Let children "over-hear" you praising them to a visitor. By all means, acknowledge what wonderful helpers they are. But avoid referring to them *only* in terms of their relationship to the babies. Report with equal pride that Heather ran very fast in the summer-camp relay race and that Sammy recently learned how to tie his own shoes.

## Expecting Playmates, Getting Reality

Multiples refract the night with their cries, fill the day with their needs. Their older siblings—like their parents—are thrown into up-heaval. Unlike their parents, the siblings did not ask for this.

Furthermore, you may be so overwhelmed caring for the babies that siblings, constantly told, "I'll play with you *later*," can feel like standby passengers bumped from plane to plane—especially if later never comes. And even if later comes, it often has to end too soon:

*"Sometimes I feel bad for my daughter, who is in nursery school. No matter where we are or what we are doing, I have to make sure we are home in time for the babies' two-hour afternoon nap. It rules our lives. But if they don't have their nap, it's hell."*

Your children may feel that they miss you, even though you are right there in the house. Every time they look at you, those babies are there, too! Children may express their feelings in some unexpected ways:

*"When I was nursing the twins at the dinner table, my five-year-old son, referring to my nipples, said, 'I don't like looking at brown at the table. It's very rude!'*

*"I said, 'You have a choice. Either you have me with you while I breastfeed, or you don't have me at all.' He chose to have me stay."*

To complicate matters further, children may have unrealistic expectations of being able to play with the babies:

*"The babies were four pounds, five ounces and five pounds, four ounces. We had built up having twins so much with our son, but the babies were so scrawny, we had to discourage him from touching them."*

These babies are not the full-fledged playmates your children may have envisioned. Instead, you have brought home babies as small as chickens, who don't even smile yet, let alone play ball! Explain that as time goes by, the babies will go through many changes. Ask a librarian to recommend a children's book about how babies grow. Help your children understand that they cannot really compare the babies to themselves:

*"One of the twins is just sitting, but the other is very active, only six months old but already on all fours, trying out rocking motions, taking a few crawling steps. His big brother doesn't understand that his flailing is not intentional and gets angry when the baby tumbles into his way. We have to explain how babies are.*

*"Sometimes he tries to 'parent' the babies the way he sees us do it. He parrots us. 'No, no, no,' he'll say, and gets angry when the babies don't listen."*

Children may also resent the constant noise and even blame the babies for waking them up at night. Again, explain that the babies aren't waking up at night to give anyone a hard time! They awaken because they are tiny and have immature digestive systems and need to eat more often. Assure your children that eventually the babies will sleep through the night. Fervently hope this turns out to be true.

## ⊠ Helpers and Regressors

*"Our seventeen-month-old toddler was fascinated when his twin brother and sister came home from the hospital. He shuttled back and forth between their cribs, unable to decide whom to look at first when they cried. Within a week, however, he had lost interest in them."*

*"At the beginning, our older child wanted to hold the babies and help. He would hold the bottle for two minutes or hold the babies on his lap (with our help). They'd wiggle and waggle. 'Okay, enough,' he'd say. Or we would have to take the babies because he squeezed them too tightly. He loves them—but sometimes he loves them too much. He even tried to butt heads with them!"*

You can use all the help you can get with the babies, but your children may or may not feel like being ready little helpers. While one child may delight in fetching a diaper, helping to burp a baby, or crooning a lullaby, another may wash his hands of the whole affair! Of two sisters, one became a "mini-mommy" to the twins while the other so ignored them that she never uttered their names or looked in their direction. Then there are young men:

*"Our five-year-old entertains the babies. He dances and sings and is a real comedian. He'll sing 'Old MacDonald Had a Farm,' and if one of the babies laughs, he'll sing it ninety times! He's become Chief Entertainer of the Troops!"*

*"Our three-year-old son saw the triplets when they were born. Then he got chicken pox and couldn't visit the NICU, where the babies stayed for three months. When we brought them home, at first he seemed nonchalant. He didn't seem to realize it's unusual to bring home three babies. But then he jumped up and down and said, 'Look at all these babies! We have a really big family!'*

*"He really helped us with the babies. Two of them were on oxygen, and we had to check the oxygen levels in their blood. He knew which buttons to press to turn off the machine when it beeped. He'd also put pacifiers in their mouths when they got fussy."*

Usually, children vacillate, being helpful one minute, dashing away the next. One mother tried to be understanding and not require too much of her older child, until one day when both twins were screaming and she had *had* it:

*"I was feeding one twin and the other twin was screaming, and I needed our son to give him a bottle. He refused. I got angry, put him in time-out, and turned off the TV. I needed him badly, and he didn't come through for me."*

Children may not want to be helpful because they themselves are now so in need of babying. In fact, children often regress when new babies arrive. They wet the bed, have toilet-training accidents, or beg for a bottle after months of being without one. Normally peaceful children may become physically aggressive, hitting and pinching.

*"Our daughter became a pincher, like a crab. She was already four-and-a-half years old. We thought she was old enough not to be jealous. Boy, were we wrong! We couldn't leave her alone in a room with the twins for even a second. The minute we turned our backs, she'd be reaching out to pinch. Yet at other times, she was so sweet!"*

Such regression is understandable. Their world has been turned upside down, their home is now noisy and cluttered with baby things, new babies have moved in and keep everyone up all night, and once-available parental attention is now at a premium. Is it any wonder that children feel like throwing a tantrum, abandoning the potty, or sucking a bottle for comfort?

Parents may find regression exasperating. You have two or three new infants now. You need your older children to be acting their age! It is easy to forget that they probably *are*. When babies are born, their older siblings can suddenly seem like giants. How large they are! How mature, how self-sufficient! This is, of course, an illusion. Yes, two-, three-, four-, and five-year-olds are vastly more competent than infants, but in the grand scheme of things, they are still tiny tots themselves.

## ❧ Do Not Tolerate Physical Aggression

Although physical aggression can be understood, it cannot be tolerated on any level. Firmly explain, "Babies are not for hitting [or pinching]." If the problem is minor, try the time-out strategy, separating the child from the babies for two minutes; use a timer. But if your child does not catch on immediately—and many don't—make sure he or she is never alone or unsupervised with the babies. *Never minimize the very real risk of serious injury.* For example, it is common for toddlers to throw a hard toy into a baby's crib and claim they are sharing, though parents can tell it was an aggressive act. One toss of a hard truck onto a baby's head, or a bassinet knocked over, can cause lasting damage.

Recognizing a child's potential to harm the babies is not a sign of disloyalty or unfair suspicion. You love your older child, and protecting the babies also protects him or her from the traumatic potential of causing injury to a baby. If you see or suspect that your child is being physically aggressive, do not leave the babies alone with your child and immediately consult your pediatrician for help. In some cases, counseling for the child may be necessary. Do not let your sympathy for the child's jealousy interfere with your taking responsibility for all of your children's safety. Do try to help your child express his or her feelings through conversation or dramatic play, and make sure you create time for these to happen.

## ❧ Involving Your Child's School

Notify your child's day-care, nursery-school, or elementary-school teacher of the changes in the family and any regression. This way you can keep track of whether the behavior is continuing in school, and you and the teacher can be mutually supportive in finding ways to help the child adjust.

*"Our five-year-old can chew teachers alive. After the twins were born, he started hitting and throwing temper tantrums. You have to be strict*

*with him. He has overrun quite a few teachers. They stayed in contact with us. When he came home from nursery school, I tried not to focus on the twins. I'd say, 'Why did you have three time-outs in school?' Of course, he'd make up a story about it. But we tried to talk it through."*

Ask the teacher to make the child feel important at school. There may be some fleeting fame among schoolmates now that the child is the older sibling of twins or triplets. But the teacher should assure that the child's main claim to fame is not as a sibling of multiples, but rather for his or her own special qualities and abilities.

Yet also consider whether your child might welcome having the babies be a special "show-and-tell" event:

*"We had sent pictures of the twins for Show and Tell, but our son's big moment was when we took the babies to his nursery-school class. He was on cloud nine, grinning from ear to ear. He was so happy, he kept running around the room."*

## 🔲 Staying Connected

*"I felt so guilty about my older child. How could he sleep at night with all the racket! And I made a mistake with how I arranged child care. The live-in nanny and I took care of the triplets, which left my husband in charge of our son. The effect was to split up the family. It wasn't a conscious decision; it just worked out that way. The nanny was very protective of the babies and kept everyone, especially our son, away from them. If I had it to do over again, I'd hire a night nurse at first, then a regular sitter until they went to school, and not have anyone living in the house.*

*"Our son, who is usually passive and mild, started acting out at school. The situation changed when the nanny decided to leave when the triplets were eighteen months old."*

One mother of a three-year-old and newborn twins took careful note of some rueful advice from her aunt, who also had a set of twins as well as two other children, all close in age: "Be extremely cautious with your oldest child. I lost track of my oldest when I had the twins, and I somehow never did catch up."

The younger mother realized that, indeed, her oldest child had been deposed as "king" since the demanding oligarchy of twins moved in. Because he could pretty much be left to play on his own, she had spent very little time with him. Suddenly, she felt pierced by a sense of loss and distance, and made a concerted effort to spend some one-on-one time with him every day.

> *"I used to read a lot to my son. When the twins were born, I didn't have the time. It was extremely difficult to hold a book when I was breast-feeding! So I switched to storytelling. Sometimes I told fairy tales, but my son liked it best when I made up my own stories—with him as the hero."*

Breastfeeding or bottlefeeding, basic baby care, and bonding keep you connected with your littlest ones. Yet your other children's needs for nurturing, care, and attention are as great, or even greater. Given a choice between using a baby-sitter for a half hour with the babies or a half hour with your older child, remember that the babies won't know or care who is wheeling the stroller, but that your three-year-old will regard a half hour with you as a gift of pure gold.

## Siblings and Multiples Together

### FORMING ALLIANCES

> *"My little boy likes Carolyn better. She is much more easygoing. Daisy, the littler twin, is a fighter. She keeps us all up at night."*

> *"My daughter favors my girl twin, who is very sweet, more than my boy twin, who is a real bruiser."*

Taking sides. Preferring one child over another. Parents strive to do none of these things, but children sometimes can't help it. An older child may gravitate to one twin over another because their personalities mesh better. One twin may take a younger sibling under her wing while the other twin is left out or allies with a different sibling.

> *"One of my twins is much more compassionate and loving toward his younger siblings. I wonder if it's because of the medical difficulties he's*

*had. Maybe taking daily asthma medication has given him a greater sense of vulnerability and helps him relate better to young children."*

Sometimes a twin will feel much closer with a nontwin sibling than with his or her twin. An adult brother of twin sisters still reminisces to his favorite one about the first time he saw her: "I saw you lying there, and I put my hand in yours." Toward this smaller, colicky twin he felt protective and loving; for no particular reason, the other twin more or less annoyed him! Over the years, the bond between the smaller twin and the brother grew, and to this day their relationship is much closer than the twins' own.

*"As a young child, my son thought one twin was gentle and kinder. He'd talk about the 'good doo and the bad doo.' I said, 'Don't you know who's who?' He went into their room, pointed to one twin's bed, and said, 'The good doo sleeps here.'"*

A mother of six children age nine and younger—three older sons, then twin girls, then another girl—says that her children "pair off." The oldest son pairs off with one twin, the youngest son with the other twin, and the middle son with the baby girl ("In his head, she is *his* partner"). This arrangement, neat as a square dance, gives everyone a partner. But in a family of fewer children or an odd number, or where one or more children do not find a sibling to pair off with, an exclusive alliance between twins or between any two siblings can be upsetting. To help counteract this, a parent can try to make opportunities for children to be together separately in different combinations. For example, a parent may schedule two children for a visit to the pediatrician while the other children stay with the spouse or a baby-sitter.

*"My daughter prefers the skinnier, sweeter 'Gerber' baby. Everyone gravitates to that baby. The other twin is big and cranky."*

Siblings' preferences for one twin over another may heighten the twins' own competition and diminish their potential for friendship. The "Gerber baby" does not choose to be more charming; she just is. The cranky baby does not set out to alienate anyone; he would be charming, too, if he could! Avoid labeling twins ("the charming one, the cranky one") and do not allow siblings to label either. Childhood labels are affixed with such a powerful glue, they can stick for a lifetime. "The pretty one, the homely one." "The smart one, the dumb one." Not only do they limit and insult the twins, these labels diminish the ability of everyone in the family to acknowledge the complexity of every individual—including themselves.

## FOSTERING LOVE BETWEEN SIBLINGS AND MULTIPLES

*"My four-year-old sometimes takes on a lookout role. The other day he said, 'Look out, Mommy! The twins are climbing on the kitchen counter!' I scooped them up, and we all trooped off to the living-room couch. My son offered to read to them, even though he doesn't know how to read. It doesn't matter. He turned the pages and described the pictures. The twins looked on contentedly. I leaned back and closed my eyes for a quick one-minute snooze."*

Parents can do much to encourage harmony between multiples and their single-born siblings. Your efforts can build each child's self-esteem and guide all your children toward lifelong friendship.

***Most Important, Give of Yourself.*** Find one-on-one time for your single-borns. Also, actively include them in the multiples' lives. Praise their ability to help, entertain, and demonstrate maturity.

***Do Not Allow Other People's Thoughtlessness to Hurt Your Children.*** Multiples are such magnets for attention that siblings may feel left out in the cold. People who *ooh* and *aah* over multiples probably do not recognize the effect on the siblings they ignore. But you cannot afford to let such rudeness pass unremarked. Let your children know that *you* remember them. Say, "I don't like it when people pay so much attention to the twins and none to you. You are special, too." Even if the stranger is careless with their feelings, *your* sensitivity is all the healing they need.

If you do *not* protest the inequitable attention, the siblings may feel that you think it is okay for people to ignore them; ergo, they may think that you don't really care. And if you become so involved with the multiples that the siblings feel chronically neglected, they may suffer long-lasting damage to their self-esteem. They may blame and take out their rage on the multiples by denigrating, teasing, or belittling them, which in turn can harm the multiples' self-esteem.

***Make Sure the Multiples' Bond Does Not Freeze Out Their Siblings.*** Of course you want your multiples to be close, and their bond is a valuable part of their lives. But encourage a bond with their siblings, too. Occasionally plan outings with one multiple and one sibling.

***Find Ways to Include All of the Children in Activities.*** In one family of twins plus two single-born siblings, all under the age of six, a mother made up a simple game that the children played together and loved. The game seems to symbolize her view of them as unique and competent individuals:

> *"The game used four colors of construction paper, one color for each child. I tore the paper into strips, numbered the strips from one to ten, and hid them around the living room: in between books (with a corner of the paper sticking out), under the sofa cushions, and so on. Each child had to find his or her strips of paper in sequential order. They were very respectful of one another's papers and would never take another child's color. The game taught them to be observant and to cooperate with one another.*
>
> *"When they got older, we did somewhat more complicated things together: treasure hunts, baking bread, making our own jam. All were noncompetitive activities they could all do together."*

***Encourage Togetherness as a Family.*** Reading bedtime stories together (each child choosing a book) is an important family ritual. So is having at least one regular family meal. Around the dinner or breakfast table is where families get up-to-date on one another's activities. That's not to say that dinnertime will be a calm, orderly meeting! When children are spilling milk, playing with their food, and kicking each other under the table, you may wonder sometimes whether they are appreciating your communal effort. But family mealtimes—with the television *off*—reinforce the concept that you are a group of people who belong together. As children get older and schedules more packed, the family meal may become harder to arrange, but it is no less important.

And as a family, play noncompetitive games, build blocks, paint pictures, assemble collages, etc.

*Hold Family Meetings.* Even very young children can learn group problem-solving strategies. Family meetings, where everyone has the right to speak, describe problems, brainstorm solutions, and reach agreements, sensitize children to the feelings of others. They also demonstrate that children have the right to have their own feelings respected.

Some siblings of multiples simmer with resentment even as adults about the attention they felt cheated out of because of the twins or triplets in the family. By being aware of this possibility, you can forestall it and promote a feeling of overall family unity.

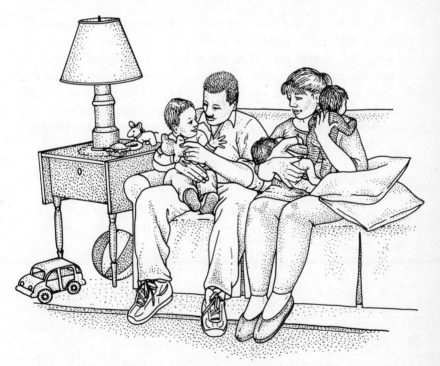

*While Mom breastfeeds one baby and burps another, Dad plays with their older child.*

# 🔹 Chapter 18

# ℒIFE IN AN EXHAUSTED STATE

🔹 Fatigue, U.S.A. Did you ever imagine you could feel this weary? You try to remember what you have read about sleep deprivation. How long does it take for sleeplessness to drive a person insane?

Then again, you are impressed by your own adrenaline supply. Just when you think you can't stay awake another minute, a baby starts crying, and you jump up like a jack-in-a-box, ready to spring back into action. When your children need you, you answer the call.

🔹

*O sleep! O gentle sleep!*
*Nature's soft nurse . . . weigh my eyelids down*
*And steep my senses in forgetfulness. . . .*

—William Shakespeare,
King Henry IV, Part 2

It is wonderful when both of your twins are sleeping, two peas in their respective pods. But when you have triplets, they seem to take turns being "odd man out," a night owl on the prowl for food, while the other two slumber.

🔹

*Weary with toil, I haste me to my bed. . . .*
*But then begins a journey in my head.*

—William Shakespeare, Sonnet XXVII

Your friend Joyce is free this afternoon.

"How can I help you?" she asks.

"Sleep, let me sleep," you beg. You tuck an afghan around your twins in the double carriage and watch Joyce head down the street with them. Free! You are free! You race to your bed, dive under the covers, and wait for sleep. And wait. You can't sleep at all!

You keep thinking of all there is to do.

*"At the end of the first year, a mother of one baby looks like hell. At the end of the first year, the mother and father of twins look like hell."*

No peace negotiator is faced with more delicate questions than: Who gets up when the babies cry at night? Do parents take turns? Do the babies take a bottle or two at night and breastfeed during the day?

*"In the beginning, we alternated babies nightly or by the week: Mom in charge of Annie, Dad in charge of Tina. Now that the kids are two, we alternate nights: One parent sleeps through the night and the other takes care of both children. We also alternate weekend mornings: One of us sleeps late Saturday, the other sleeps late on Sundays."*

Your spouse has the formidable task of keeping up with the babies all day long, so you handle the 2:00 A.M. feeding every night.

You do it with *style.* You set up a chair in the babies' room and a small refrigerator for bottles (theirs) and snacks (yours). You add a TV, with headphones so the noise doesn't disturb anyone. Hey, this isn't so bad. The babies are old enough now to hold their own bottles. You hold one baby in each arm, settle back in the recliner, and channel-surf with the remote until you find a rerun of *Casablanca.*

"Settle back, kids," you murmur. "This is the beginning of a beautiful friendship."

⊠

*Sleep, baby, sleep, thy father guards the sheep.*
*Thy mother shakes the dreamland tree, and from it fall sweet dreams*
*    for thee.*
*Sleep, baby, sleep.*

*Smile, baby, smile, thy mother guards a while.*
*Thy father tends the dreamland tree, and shakes a new sweet dream for*
*    thee.*
*Smile, baby, smile.*

—*Father Gander (a.k.a. Dr. Douglas W. Larche)*[1]

Life is so much more humane when you know you do not have to get up for every feeding. How marvelous when your spouse shares the task, when you set up a schedule in advance.

However: Sometimes sticking to your turn feels impossible. You are so tired, you feel less like a parent than a robot out of kilter. Sometimes you feign sleep, hoping your spouse will take pity on you and cover your shift. Occasionally, the ruse works. Then one night you realize your worn-out spouse is feigning sleep. You take over the shift, hearing a grateful sigh from under the covers when you leave the room.

> *"I usually heard the babies first and brought them in for my wife to nurse. She'd roll from side to side, nursing one, then the other. One night she was so tired, she was almost delirious. One of the babies was crying in the dark, and she had no idea which one it was. She kept saying, 'Who is this child!' I said, 'What's the difference! Get up and feed it!'"*

There are so many variables to consider when figuring out who will take which turns on a given night: work schedules, individual biorhythms, mood, time of the month, how the day has gone. But it is important to decide before you go to sleep, because trying to negotiate in the middle of the night is an invitation to frustration. Last-minute decisions are also often decided by default: Usually, one person gets up more readily. And guess who that is?

Sometimes a stay-home parent feels guilty asking the go-to-work parent to get up at night, since he or she faces a commute and a full

[1] *Father Gander's Nursery Rhymes* (Santa Barbara, CA: Advocacy Press, 1985).

workday the next day. This is a reasonable concern, but these are unusual times, and staying home with the babies is hard work, too. And if the stay-home parent is so exhausted she or he is not functioning well because of exhaustion and the working parent seems to be all business-as-usual, then perhaps the sleep schedule ought to be reevaluated.

❧

Exhaustion plays mind tricks. In the dark of night, you may be seized by fears, doubts, even hallucinations:

*"One night I suddenly woke up in a panic. I thought one of the babies was under the pillow, being suffocated. I threw the pillow on the floor. No one was there! The babies were safe asleep in their cribs."*

*"The combination of postpartum blues and severe sleep deprivation knocked me out. I had lots of help, but it didn't matter. I could not sleep through the night. I can't sit still quietly and let people take over in the kitchen, so you can imagine how I felt about people being with my kids!"*

*"I was so exhausted that we left the babies with my parents and went to a hotel for a night of uninterrupted sleep. All night long, I hallucinated the sounds of my kids crying."*

❧

A mother of twins reminisces about the best advice she ever got from another mother of twins:

*"You know how you're tired, really tired, and you keep thinking to yourself, Soon this will get better? You wait and wait for things to calm down, and they don't.*

*"Well, here's the advice: Stop expecting life to get easier. For at least the twins' first year, get used to living in a blur. Accept it: This is the way life is right now.*

*"When you go with it, when you stop fighting it, that's what makes life easier."*

## Tips for Surviving the Exhausting
## First Months

- *Eat nourishing foods.* Drink plenty of water, plus milk and juice, to keep yourself well hydrated and breast milk flowing. Keep taking prenatal vitamins if your doctor recommends them.
- *Nap* whenever you can; even five minutes.
- *Exercise,* or do simple yoga stretches to reduce stress and restore energy. A ten-minute meditation can also relax and refresh you.
- *Walk!* Walking gets you out—out of the house, out of a feeling of being out of your mind. It can feel therapeutic, even exhilarating, just to be in the fresh air and to get your body moving. For some parents who are caring for babies after years of working outside the home, the leisurely opportunity to notice bushes, trees, and flowers almost feels exotic.

  In their carriage or stroller, your babies are often content or sleeping, so the walk is almost like alone time for you, or time you can talk one-on-one with an older child or a friend.
- *Carve out even five minutes for activities that relax you* and keep you connected with yourself, like playing the piano, reading a page or two of a book, knitting, or keeping a diary.
- *Get help.* (See Chapters 19, 20, and 21.)
- *Do not do today what you can put off until tomorrow.* And don't feel guilty about it!
- *Take pride in your accomplishment:* getting your babies' lives off to a good start.
- *Only set out to do what is really meaningful.* It is probably not meaningful to have a spotless home. It *is* meaningful to cuddle your babies, to coddle yourself, and to make this experience as enjoyable as possible for everyone in the family.
- *Remember: This, too, shall pass.*
- *Look ahead.* When your children are ready, you may want to consider training them to sleep through the night. (See "Scheduling and Routines" in Chapter 12). You may wish to read books on children and sleep.

*Solve Your Child's Sleep Problems,* by Richard Ferber, describes how to help children fall asleep on their own, sleep through the night, cope with night fears, etc. Consult with your pediatrician to assess your children's readiness for the methods Ferber describes and whether they are right for your family. *Nighttime Parenting,* by William Sears, presents another approach, and discusses the merits of a family bed. (See the Bibliography.)

*Part Three*

# HELP AND SUPPORT

# Chapter 19

# GETTING HELP FROM FAMILY AND FRIENDS

*"When my girls were born, my mother-in-law offered to help, even to stay with us for a couple of weeks. But I turned her down. I thought we could handle the twins ourselves, and I wanted to show her that we really didn't need her. That is one decision I have always regretted."*

Caring for multiples can be overwhelming. Even if you are fortunate enough to have a baby nurse when you come home from the hospital, additional assistance is crucial, not only for the weeks following birth, but for the first several years.

Do not be shy about asking for help or too proud to accept it. Perhaps you and your partner *could* do it alone, but why put yourselves to that test? Parents need to protect their health, stamina, and sanity by letting others help them.

## ■ *Grandparents and Other Relatives*

The birth of twins, triplets, or more is a momentous event in a family. Grandparents often regard them with special pride and dearly wish to be involved. Welcome their assistance as much as possible. Parenthood of multiples is not a proving ground for independence.

*"My mother is a notorious night owl. But when she stayed with us after the twins were born, she fell asleep on the sofa at eight o'clock at night. She was more exhausted than I was!"*

*"My parents stayed with us for a month when our first child was born. With the twins, they came for seven weeks, and we pleaded with them to stay longer."*

Some parents or in-laws move in for a week or longer and provide wholehearted help with everything from baby care to making chicken soup with noodles and carrots (just the way you like it).

*"The babies and I lived with my parents for the first three months. I couldn't have made it without them. It's the little things that stick in my mind. My mom ran to the store and bought me two nursing bras, then exchanged them a day later for a larger size. She did piles of laundry and took lots of pictures of the babies. My dad made me a cheese omelette and whole-wheat toast every morning, took the babies out for walks in their double carriage, and fixed the rust spots on my car."*

Granted, not every parent or in-law is easy to get along with. If any help produces more stress than relief, it is not worth accepting. But for the most part, some gentle guidance on your part can remind other family members that you are the parents, you make the decisions, and you set the rules.

Grandparents and other relatives can also help older brothers and sisters adjust to the tumult. Grandma, Grandpa, or Aunt Cindy can take siblings on special outings, make sure they are not overlooked by visitors, and reassure them of their continued and undiminished importance in the family.

## Friends and Neighbors

*"One of my friends came over, put the car seats in her car, and took the babies for a ride so they would fall asleep while she drove around and I could rest."*

Friends are the "second family" we assemble for ourselves. What would you do without your best friend? Your triplets have kept you up for twenty-four hours straight, and you think you will go out of your mind. The moment your friend hears your frazzled voice on the phone, she says, "I'll be right over."

Maybe you are fortunate enough to have a neighbor who means it when he says, "Call any time you need me." He and his teenage son push two carts through the supermarket aisles, one for their family, one for yours.

A parent of a child in your son's first-grade class offers to "drop him off" after school every day, even though your apartment building requires her to make a fifteen-minute detour.

In a Mothers of Twins Club you may find unique support and advice—a group of ready-made friends who really understand what you are going through. Some clubs organize "welcome home" casserole marathons, providing meals for the first month you are home from the hospital.

Call upon your network of family, friends, and neighbors to give you the support you need. If you feel more comfortable helping others than accepting help yourself, now is the time to balance the scales. Letting friends help you strengthens your friendship. One day you will return the favors.

## How Family, Friends, and Neighbors Can Help

All top executives know how to delegate work. Parents of multiples must cultivate that skill, too.

Make a list of the basic kinds of help you need and give a copy to family and friends who ask, "What can I do?" Revise the list as time goes on to cover not only your babies' first few weeks, but their early years, too. And every day, keep a running list of specific errands that must be done. When people offer to help, give them choices: Would you rather run errands? Take the older children out for a walk? Come in and help make dinner? Do an hour's worth of shopping?

Following is a sample "Help Wanted" list to get you started.

## *Help Wanted!*

- Stay overnight or move in for a few weeks to assist with child care, older siblings, and the household.
- Help feed, burp, diaper, and bathe the babies.
- Buy or lend baby equipment, toys, and supplies (see Chapter 11, "Equipment, Clothing, Supplies").
- Throw a baby shower. If possible, request that guests shop for gifts at a store with a "baby gift registry." Or ask them to contribute toward a large gift such as a stroller or a few months of diaper service. In addition to gifts, have people give "coupons" good for an hour or two of help. Or pass around a wall calendar on which they can note days and hours they are available.
- Drive me or my spouse to the hospital to visit our premature or ill babies, or join us there and keep us company.
- Do the family grocery shopping.
- Accompany me or my spouse and the children on walks, outings, doctor visits, and shopping trips.
- Play with siblings.
- Stay with one child while I/we take the other(s) to a medical specialist.
- Baby-sit for an evening, or for just an hour so I/we can get a haircut.
- Spend time with one twin so I/we can have time alone with the other. Then do it again so we can switch.
- Straighten up my house or mop the kitchen floor. Wash the car. Clean out the refrigerator.
- Do errands. Take packages to the post office; pick up dry cleaning.
- Prepare meals—for one night, several, or on an ongoing basis.
- Provide casseroles, spaghetti sauce, or soups for the freezer.
- Wash, cut, and bag fresh vegetables for quick salads or stir-fries.
- Pay for a cleaning service or "lend" us your cleaning person for a day.
- Do laundry.

- Invite one or more children for sleepovers so my spouse and I can spend an evening alone together or take our third grader bowling.
- Visit and play with the babies so I/we can make phone calls, take a nap, or spend time with their older sibling at home.
- Pick up my older children at school or take them to after-school or weekend activities.
- Help write thank-you notes for baby gifts, address envelopes, and mail them.
- Visit neighborhood stores and negotiate discounts on bulk purchases (such as diapers, infant formula, baby food).
- Assist in birthday-party preparation, decorating, activities, and cleaning up.
- Organize other friends to give as little as an hour per week on a regular basis—to help feed the children, prepare dinner, or be welcome company.

# ✦ Chapter 20

# $\mathcal{B}$ABY-SITTERS AND OTHER PARENTS' HELPERS

*"Mrs. Hammond from up the river came down and said she'd take me, seeing I was handy with children, and I went up the river to live with her in a little clearing among the stumps. It was a very lonesome place. I'm sure I could never have lived there if I hadn't had an imagination. Mr. Hammond worked a little saw-mill up there, and Mrs. Hammond had eight children. She had twins three times. I like babies in moderation, but twins three times in succession is too much. I told Mrs. Hammond so firmly, when the last pair came. I used to get so dreadfully tired carrying them about."*
—L. M. Montgomery, Anne of Green Gables

Some couples have live-in help, perhaps even taking out a loan to afford it. Most parents, however, hire regular or occasional baby-sitters to help while one or both parents are home, or to take over while parents work, take one child to a doctor or a music lesson, or have a night out for themselves.

*"My sister-in-law needled me: Get help lined up early. I started making phone calls at the end of my second trimester."*

*"It was hard during the first months just to find time for a shower. It was especially hard because we had no family nearby. For any relief, we had to hire sitters."*

Unless a sitter has multiples of her own or has worked with them before, you and she will be learning together. Here are some ways to assure a smoothly functioning parent–baby-sitter relationship:

*Ask Other Parents for Recommendations.*   But don't just gather names; ask for details of what they like about the sitters they recommend. Are they punctual? Playful? Skillful in getting children to cooperate or take naps?

*Many Mothers of Twins Club Newsletters Have "Baby-sitters Wanted" and "Baby-sitters Available" Sections*   through which you may find an experienced sitter, or even a mother whose own children are grown.

*List Your Hiring Criteria.*   The most important, of course, are a sitter's maturity, responsibility, ability to relate to and care for your children, warmth and kindness, responsiveness to your instructions and authority, and references. A book you may find helpful regarding hiring childcare or household help, costs, training, job descriptions, etc., is *Get Help!: The Complete Guide to Household Help*, by Susan Zolla and Pepper Abrams (see the Bibliography).

Contact the Internal Revenue Service for information on taxes you must pay for your full- or part-time employee(s).

*Safety Is Paramount.*   Do not assume that your baby-sitter knows first-aid or safety rules. Give a quick quiz: What do you do if a baby chokes? What do you do if the baby is on the changing table and you need to get a new box of diaper wipes out of the supply closet? If your sitter does not know the correct answers, ask that she enroll in a baby-sitting and first-aid course through the Red Cross or your local Y or community medical center. Pay for the training yourself, if necessary. Or train her yourself if you are qualified. You may also want her to be trained in infant cardiopulmonary resuscitation (CPR).

The sitter also must be trained or trainable in any special medical equipment, treatments, or administration of medication your children may need.

*Consider Whether You Will Need to Provide Transportation.* It is much more convenient to have a sitter who can walk, drive, or take public transportation to your home, so you do not have to pick her up or take her home. Some parents do pay their sitters' bus or subway fares. In heavy snowfalls or other inclement weather, a sitter within walking distance is more reliable than one who may be delayed or homebound by transit problems. For evening baby-sitting, however, it is a courtesy and an important safety measure to personally escort teenage baby-sitters home.

*Clarify the Scope of Duties.* Are you hiring her only to help with the children, or also to do some cleaning, laundry, cooking, or errands? If so, tell her. Some sitters are willing to do whatever you need them to do. Others exclusively do child care.

Be realistic about how much housework you can expect a sitter to do if she is also responsible for child care. How much can *you* accomplish when with the children? Do they have a regular naptime when you can ask the sitter to do some dishes? Although you have the right to expect the sitter to use the time productively, you don't want her to get so tired that she has less energy to give the children, or so overwhelmed that she skimps on time with them so she can get chores done, or so resentful that she will quit!

*Evaluate Whether to Hire Teenagers.* Of course you want a responsible adult to care for babies and young children. But a responsible teenager can assist you when you are home. Under your supervision, she can hold, rock, diaper, or bottlefeed babies. Or she can fold laundry or clean the kitchen while you breastfeed. She can play with older siblings at home or take them to the park or playground. She can also do errands or shop (from a name-brand-specific list you provide).

Through the Mothers of Twins Club newsletter, you may be able to find a teen sibling of multiples. She may be especially adept at entertaining your rambunctious triplets. You can also ask for recommendations from the guidance counselor at a local high school or from the adult leader of your church, synogogue, or community-center youth group.

*Many Parents Hire Two Teenagers* for both daytime and evening baby-sitting. It costs more, but one teenager may not be able to handle two or more children by herself. Sometimes parents time their departure for post-bedtime hours so children are asleep and the sitters have an easy time. However, if children awaken at night, they can be frightened to discover a strange person there; use this technique only with a sitter your children already know and trust.

*Don't Let Desperation Drive You to Hire Someone Too Young.* If teenagers are difficult to find, some parents feel tempted to hire younger adolescents, even nine- or ten-year-olds. Age is not always an indicator of ability; an exceptionally responsible ten-year-old is preferable to a flaky high school sophomore. But before hiring such young sitters, seriously consider whether they *are* exceptional. Are they truly mature enough and skillful enough to handle the responsibilities and demands of multiples, even if you hire two of them?

On the other hand, it can make a lot of sense to hire a fun-loving ten-year-old to play with your babies and/or other children when you are in the house, close at hand.

*Have Every Prospective Sitter Meet You and Your Children.* Observe the sitter's interaction with your children. Does she seem overwhelmed? Or eager to get to know them? Does she make an effort to tell your twins apart? Do your children seem comfortable with her? Babies cannot tell you what they think, but you can read their nonverbal cues. Always invite older children's comments—and take them seriously. If a child says, "I like Mamie, but she smells," tell Mamie that your children are sensitive to perfume and not to wear it.

*Always Check References Carefully.* Engage people in detailed conversation. Ask them what the sitter's responsibilities were, how long she worked for them, and why she stopped. Ask about her strengths and areas of needed improvement. This is the most important hiring you will ever do, even if you run a Fortune 500 corporation. When in doubt about whether to hire someone, don't.

*If the Sitter Will Need to Drive, Check Her Driver's License.* Find out whether your insurance will cover your sitter, and whether she is comfortable and competent with your car. If she will be using her own car to transport the children, check it out carefully. Emphasize the importance of using car seats and seat belts.

*Heed Your Instincts.*   Both parents need to feel confident and comfortable with the sitter. Even if she interviews well, her references check out, and your children like her, don't hire her if either of you has negative "gut feelings." *You don't have to justify this "illogic" to yourself or anyone else.* A mother's or father's intuition is a valuable decision-making tool.

*Clearly Describe All Work Arrangements:*   hours, days off, wages and tax deductions, whether you will provide meals (a good idea), etc.

*Set Ground Rules.*   While you can do this verbally, writing them down underscores that you are serious about them. For example: No visitors without your permission. Keep the phone free and any personal phone calls brief. No smoking in the house or when out with the children. Never leave a baby alone with a propped bottle or in the bath. No television on school days. Put away toys after playing with them or at the end of the day.

*Review Safety and Childproofing in Detail.*   Tour the house with the sitter. Demonstrate how to open and close gates, cupboard and door latches, etc., then ask her to try. Explain the safety measures you have instituted. Emphasize that safety is always a concern, but especially so with multiples. Together, children can get into more mischief than one alone.

Discuss every safety rule—in front of the children, if possible, so they as well as the sitter know what you expect of them. For example (depending on age): The children must hold the sitter's hand when crossing a street, must put on helmets before riding their bicycles, are not permitted to use the toaster or microwave without the sitter's direct supervision, etc.

*Share Your Philosophy of Child-Raising.*   For example, if you don't like your children referred to as "the twins," say so. Explain their need for individuality.

*Discuss Each Child's Particular Needs.*   Janie likes to hold her toy kangaroo while she drinks her bottle. Rub Kyle's back for a minute when you put him in the crib. Linda loves peanut-butter-and-jelly sandwiches, but leave off the jelly for Sue—and give Melina tuna fish.

*Clarify What the Sitter May Eat.*   You want the sitter to feel at home and relaxed, so be as generous as possible ("Help yourself to anything in the fridge"). Keep fruit and snacks on hand, and perhaps a "snack fund" with which she can occasionally purchase ice cream or other goodies for herself and the children when she takes them out for walks.

*Be Specific About What the Children May and May Not Eat.*   Provide a list of any foods to which children are allergic. Spell out your snack policy. May the children have a midafternoon snack? What should the sitter give them? If children are hungry half an hour before dinner, may she give them a dish of applesauce or some veggies to tide them over?

*Discuss Discipline.*   Do not assume that the sitter shares your aversion to spanking. Some people feel a firm "pat" on the rear end is a reasonable reaction to a child's misbehavior. Spell it out: no spanking. Tell the sitter what she *should* do when children misbehave. For example, she can distract them with a new activity, take them for a walk, separate them, declare a two-minute "time-out" (using a timer is helpful), or turn off the television (if you allow it at all).

*Post Emergency Phone Numbers by Every Phone:*   parents' office numbers, pediatrician, trusted neighbors or relatives, police, fire, and poison information. (See the sample form, page 264.)

*Instruct Your Sitter How to Use the Answering Machine.*
Having it on frees her from having to take messages. However, you need to be able to get through. Show her how to screen calls and pick up the phone when you call. (Also make sure she knows how to use the cordless phone and speaker phone, if you have one.)
When she does answer the phone, insist that she write down all

messages. No busy sitter should try to keep messages in her head! Keep a notebook by the phone. Be specific about what you expect messages to include: e.g., the date and time the person called, the phone number, and the name (ask the sitter to have callers spell their names if they sound at all unclear). If your toddlers tend to walk off with any pencil in sight, tie one to the notebook. (You might need to tie down the notebook, too!)

*Leave a Note by the Phone* before you leave, listing instructions or information. Establish this system from the beginning, so that your sitter gets into the habit of reading it when she arrives. When you are rushing to get out of the house, it can be difficult for both you and her to handle a verbal stream of information. Writing a note helps you think through what the sitter needs to know about that day, such as medicine that must be given, a play date you have arranged, milk that must be bought, or chicken that needs to be defrosted for dinner.

The sitter will find the note reassuring. She will not have to worry about forgetting something important. Always date the note so it does not get mixed up with older ones and remember to close it with a "thank you."

If your sitter's first language is not English, check to see how well she can read it. You may have to keep the note very brief or rely on verbal instructions.

*Suggest Activities.* Some inventive sitters take the initiative in planning activities. Others need more direction. Consider how you want your children to spend their time. Specify whether the sitter should take the children for a daily walk or to the park, weather permitting. A sitter can also escort your toddlers to a weekly neighborhood play group or to story hour at the library. (When the sitter goes out, have her leave a note telling you where they went and what time they left.)

Propose at-home activities, too, such as arts-and-crafts projects, collage-making, water play (such as bathing baby dolls or playing with soapsuds), and simple cooking (such as mashing hard-cooked eggs for egg salad). Be realistic about how much the sitter can handle. Activities should engage children without being overly burdensome for the caregiver. Sitters justifiably may resent activities that require too much effort or cleanup.

## Baby-sitter Information Form

Mother's Name[1] _____

Father's Name _____

Address[2] _____

Phone _____


Mother's Work Address _____

Phone _____ Extension _____

Father's Work Address _____

Phone _____ Extension _____


Child's Name _____ Date of Birth: _____

Allergies, Medications _____

Special Needs _____


Child's Name _____ Date of Birth: _____

Allergies, Medications _____

Special Needs _____


Child's Name _____ Date of Birth: _____

Allergies, Medications _____

Special Needs _____


EMERGENCY NUMBERS

Police _____ Fire _____

Poison Control _____

Pediatrician _____

[1]It is especially important to list both parents' full names if each has a different last name, or if the mother uses her married name at home and her maiden name professionally.
[2]You may want to include cross streets in order to help your baby-sitter give accurate directions to emergency workers, if necessary.

NEIGHBORS OR FAMILY MEMBERS TO CALL IF PARENTS
CANNOT BE REACHED

Name _____

Address _____ Phone _____

Name _____

Address _____ Phone _____

Name _____

Address _____ Phone _____

*Spell Out Your Rules About Television.* If you don't, you may
find your baby-sitter using the TV as a baby-sitter. May children
watch TV at all? If so, which shows or videotapes? By being specific,
you enable your sitter to enforce limits on TV—and head off any
protestations by the children that "Mommy and Daddy always let us
watch that show."

*Share* Twins *Magazine and Other Parenting Periodicals* (see the
Resources section in the Appendix) with your sitter. Point out interesting, amusing, or helpful articles, or those that suggest fun, age-
appropriate arts-and-crafts projects, or other activities.

*Take Good Care of Your Trustworthy, Loving Sitter.* Welcome
her comments and suggestions. Tell her what to do—but also be open
to learning from her. Be forgiving when she makes mistakes, and ask
her forgiveness when you do. Pay her as well as you can. Give her a
raise when possible and a gift and/or cash bonus at Christmas or
Hanukkah and on her birthday.

Encourage the sitter's friendship with your children. Some working parents, even though they depend heavily on their sitter, nevertheless feel pangs of resentment when they notice their children's
closeness to her. Unless you feel that your sitter is trying to usurp
your parental role, openly acknowledge her importance in the children's lives—and in yours. Her relationship with your children may
be an important part of her life, too. Some sitters stay with families
for years and stay in touch for long years after. Children enjoy the
continuity of the relationship. They have another adult with whom
to share childhood memories.

A poignant example of how a baby-sitting arrangement can benefit both family and sitter is that of an American couple whose Chinese nanny, under the Chinese government's one-child-per-family law, was forced to limit her own offspring to one. Caring for the American couple's twins was the answer to her dream: a baby in each arm. Tenderly, she sang them Chinese lullabies.

## Parents' Helpers

Remember that many preteens as well as teenagers look for after-school jobs for only an hour to two hours. Preteens are probably too young to be left alone with young children. But they can help you in other ways. One couple hired a twelve-year-old girl to wash dishes, make salad, and assist with other dinner preparation, and/or walk the dog every day after school from 4:30 to 6:00 P.M.

Another family hired an eighth grader to play with their toddlers for an hour after school so the mother could take a nap. And still another hired an eleven-year-old boy to read stories, draw pictures, and play ball with their kindergartner for an hour every day. Before he left, he packed the child's lunch box for the next day—one less task for the parents to have to think about. The child looked forward to this special hour every day.

## Play Groups

Before nursery school starts, introduce your multiples to other neighborhood children through a play group. It is especially wonderful if your children can become friends with other multiples, perhaps through a play group organized by your Mothers of Twins Club.

At many play groups, parents stay. If you wish to drop your children off (and enjoy a morning or two to yourself), thoroughly evaluate the play-group leader, helpers, program, and facility first.

## Parent Co-ops

Ask your neighbors, friends, and Mothers of Twins Club whether there is a parent cooperative in your neighborhood. By baby-sitting for other members' children, parents "earn" hours of baby-sitting for themselves. There are many advantages: It is free, your baby-sitter is a responsible and experienced parent, and you can make great friends. Of course, when you baby-sit, your spouse has to agree to go it alone at home. A co-op is probably unrealistic when your children are infants and toddlers but may be wonderful when children are at least preschool age.

# Chapter 21

# ℳOTHERS OF TWINS CLUBS AND OTHER RESOURCES

*"I often burst into tears when my husband came home from work. The babies and our older child often were crying, too. It was a madhouse. I found it comforting to join a Mothers of Twins Club and hear other mothers describe the same scene."*

Mothers of Twins Clubs are a mainstay of support in thousands of parents' lives. There are Mothers of Twins Clubs in every state; some large cities have several. The National Organization of Mothers of Twins Club (see the Resources section in the Appendix) provides technical assistance to the clubs, facilitates networking, publishes a newsletter for members, holds an annual convention, refers parents and expectant parents to a club in their area, and helps interested parents establish new clubs.

The national organization does not advocate a single structure, believing that each club must meet the needs of its particular membership. Therefore, the frequency, agendas, "styles," and even names of clubs vary. Most clubs use the "Mothers of Twins Club" name, but some use such names as "Parents of Multiples," "Parents of Twins,

Triplets, and Quads," "Mothers of Multiples." Some clubs have sub-groups, too, such as a "Father's Auxiliary" or play groups for members with specialized needs. Clubs meet in a church, synagogue, library, hospital, or community-center meeting room, a school, or members' homes.

Membership consists mostly of mothers, but some fathers—especially single fathers—do join, and most clubs offer special couples' and family events throughout the year. While acknowledging the importance of fathers' involvement in childrearing, Lois Gallmeyer, executive secretary of the NOMOTC, explained an advantage of a "women-only" club: Many women say of their meetings, "This is the one place I can go and talk about what bothers me. I would not feel comfortable talking about stretch marks or breastfeeding in front of someone else's husband." She also noted that many, perhaps most members would not be able to attend if their husbands did not stay with the children. By enabling their wives to go, they—and the children—also reap the benefits of attendance through the feedback, information, and support she gets.

> "When I speak with the mother of a singleton, I feel overburdened by contrast. But at Mothers of Twins Club meetings, everybody is dealing with at least two children."

While sharing a common mission of offering support and friendship to parents of multiples, clubs differ in several ways. Parents who have access to several usually join the one closest to their home, or may visit them all to determine which club best suits their needs and personal style. For example, some clubs are large, have a set agenda, and frequently have guest speakers. Others are smaller and have more informal rap sessions. One club alternates large meetings, with a planned program and speakers, with smaller, more casual "cope" meetings held in members' homes. Sitting on the floor, eating cheese and crackers and sipping apple cider, women air their problems and trade advice.

> "Through my Mothers of Twins Club I realized that it is very common to feel that you are doing a terrible job with your twins and other children and husband. I didn't feel so alone."

Members frequently offer support beyond the meetings. As Gallmeyer, herself a mother of twins, says, "I have dropped everything,
loaded the kids in the car, and gone to members who called me in
tears. I have sat for hours and hours and hours with an expectant
mom on bed rest at home or in the hospital, helping her relax and
keep her mind occupied." Some clubs set up schedules for bed-rest
visits or for providing nightly hot meals to families in need (sometimes for months).

*"My Mothers of Twins Club provided food for the first six weeks after
I left the hospital. They took turns providing casseroles for dinner. For
some reason, several members were partial to chicken-and-broccoli casseroles, which we quickly tired of. But it was filling, nutritious food that
my husband and I did not have to cook. We were very grateful."*

Gallmeyer gives two examples of the varied types of support
members need. A mother called to ask, "How can I get both babies
and their equipment down to the car [from a walk-up apartment] at
the same time?" Gallmeyer's answer: "You can't!" Together, they discussed options and decided that when the mother was ready to go
out, she would call a trusted neighbor and ask her to help carry the
babies downstairs.

In another instance, someone asked how to respond to a friend
who gave birth to one healthy child and one who died *in utero* as a
result of twin transfusion syndrome. Gently, Gallmeyer explained,
"It is not wrong to send a congratulations card and a sympathy card."
The living twin will be a constant reminder of the other's loss, and
both the joy of the birth and the mourning should be acknowledged.

*"I wish I could have had someone from a Mothers of Twins Club live
with me for the first month to give moral support. I remain grateful for
one club member's answer to my question, 'Why am I crying all the
time?' She said, 'Having twins is very stressful. Don't expect to feel sane
the first year. It's just a blur.'"*

Many clubs offer secondhand maternity and children's clothing
and equipment free, for trade or loan, or for sale at low prices; maintain a reference library; publish a newsletter; hold fund-raising or
social events; and offer bereavement and other crisis support.

# A Visit to a Mothers of Twins Club Meeting

Eighteen women cluster one chilly autumn night in a community center's narrow hallway, waiting for the custodian to unlock their meeting-room door. The member in charge of tonight's refreshments breaks open a package of cookies and rummages in her shopping bag to make sure she brought paper cups for the soda. The club secretary drapes around her neck a sash that features Mothers of Twins Club membership pins. A woman leaning against the wall flips through the pages of a book she is returning to the club's lending library. Somebody admires another member's attractive new purple coat.

"Oh, this isn't new," she says with a laugh. "It's my seventeen-year-old daughter's. She didn't want it anymore, so she handed it down—or rather, up—to me." When this petite mom's five-year-old twin daughters reach their teens, her wardrobe may expand even more.

A gray-haired woman approaches the group.

"You're the Mothers of Twins club, aren't you? I was never really interested before. But now my daughter is carrying twins. Tell me, did your doctors order bed rest for the whole third trimester?"

A chorus of groans answers her. Groans of reminiscence. Groans of resistance. Groans of disagreement with the resisters.

"That's the last good sleep I had!"

"I'm so sick of doctors ordering bed rest as a matter of course. For most women with multiples, there really is no need."

"Tell your daughter it's worth the inconvenience. My triplets were only six weeks early because I stayed in bed."

The custodian finally shows up with the key.

"No, not that room. It's too small," protests the club president. "*This* one, please." A mother of twins develops an authoritative voice as part of her repertoire of coping skills. The custodian complies. The hallway empties, and the meeting soon comes to order.

The president distributes the new membership roster. It includes members' names, addresses, birthdays, and wedding anniversaries, as well as their spouses' and children's names and birthdays. The president also asks members to complete a questionnaire listing their preferences about future meeting speakers, topics, activities, and fund-raising projects.

The newsletter gets passed around, too. In addition to messages from the president and vice president (signed "Twincerely yours"), the treasurer's report, meeting minutes, and family news, it features a list of baby-sitters as well as a section on used items members wish to sell (twin strollers, infant seats, crib bedding, computer desk, a soccer ball, and "like-new" cleats to match). The last page is covered with ads from local businesses, doctors, and dentists who recognize that moms of multiples are plum patrons.

The group votes to broaden the list of circumstances under which the Sunshine Committee sends a card or gift to a member. Someone announces that a beauty salon is looking for identical twins to pose for its "double discount" commercials. The treasurer sells lottery tickets for five dollars each for the state organization's Mothers of Twins Club scholarship fund. The vice president reports that the club will soon finish selecting a freezer it plans to donate to a local hospital for storage of mother's milk.

One mother has invited her pediatrician to be tonight's guest speaker. The doctor, wearing a sharp red suit, perches on the corner of a desk. She fields questions about a broad range of concerns: from ear infections, eating habits, and eczema, to vaccines, vitamins, and the varied sleeping patterns of triplets ("I told one mother of triplets not to even *think* about getting a full night's sleep. Maybe one will sleep through the night. Maybe even two. But three? Never!").

The meeting ends with what many members look forward to most: a chance to socialize over soda and cookies, trading notes about the challenges and pleasures of mothering multiples.

## 🕮 Other Resources

There are many national parent support groups and organizations (see the Resources section in the Appendix). For resources in your community, contact your local Mothers of Twins Club, library, obstetrician, pediatrician, midwife, lactation consultant, community center, mental-health agency, or Yellow Pages telephone directory.

Some parents find that special issues of multiples are not covered or understood as well in general parent support groups. Clearly, groups' helpfulness varies according to their sponsorship, leadership, and members. But whether one has multiples or not, two groups deserve special mention for their attention to parents' special needs:

*La Leche League International, Inc.* "The world's largest resource for breastfeeding and related information" offers advice and encouragement through monthly meetings of more than three thousand local groups throughout the country and by telephone. La Leche League also publishes a journal, *New Beginnings,* and other materials. Many women whose family, friends, or medical practitioners were skeptical of breastfeeding multiples have found that La Leche League meetings and support strengthened their resolve to breastfeed and gave them helpful strategies.

*Parents Anonymous* Provides free self-help support groups for parents who are overwhelmed with the stress of parenthood and seek effective parenting strategies and support. Many groups offer child care or a structured children's program for children of parents attending groups. There are 2,100 groups throughout the United States, serving 15,000 parents and 9,400 children every week.

C/Sec support groups for parents concerned with cesarean delivery are described in Chapter 2, "Pregnancy and Delivery." For parent-care support groups, see Chapter 5, "If Babies Are Premature," and for bereavement support groups, see Chapter 6, "Coping with the Loss of a Child."

Regular support groups can be a consistent and positive presence in one's life. Many parents of multiples also derive much pleasure, support, and affirmation from membership in groups that offer support through newsletters, referrals, phone contact, and/or special events:

*The Triplet Connection*  Sponsors a biannual convention for families of multiples. This "network of caring and sharing for multiple birth families" also publishes a newsletter, has a telephone hot line, and maintains "the largest data bank in the world on multiple pregnancies," for reference by parents, physicians, and researchers. Many parents praise The Triplet Connection's information packet for expectant parents, which provides information on diet, weight gain, prenatal care, and other aspects of pregnancy with multiples.

*M.O.S.T. (Mothers of Supertwins)*  "A support group of families who have or are expecting triplets, quadruplets, or more." MOST provides support by phone during and after pregnancy, provides resources and referrals, publishes a newsletter, and holds an annual family picnic.

*The Twins Foundation*  "An international, nonprofit membership organization established [in 1983] by twins to collect, preserve, and communicate information about twins and twin research." Among its projects are a newsletter and other materials, a voluntary National Twin Registry to facilitate medical and scientific studies, and an Informational Clearing House.

*Twin Services*  Founded "to reduce the high health and psychosocial risks associated with multiple birth" and to enable parents to cope and providers to meet multiples' special needs. Twin Services publishes parent handouts and, for residents of the Bay Area, offers classes, a clothing and equipment exchange, and the Twinline, a "warm line" for advice and support.

*Twins Day Festival*  Takes place annually the first full weekend of August in Twinsburg, Ohio, a town named by identical twin brothers, Aaron and Moses Wilcox, who settled there in 1817. They were also brothers-in-law (since they married sisters) and business partners who died within hours of each other of the same illness.

Twins, triplets, and quadruplets participate in games, a "Double Take" parade, contests, races, entertainment, children's rides, an arts-and-crafts show, seminars, and more. Festival organizers report that about three thousand sets of identical and fraternal twins and other multiples attend each year, for a total number of 85,000 to 100,000 people. Some people go every year, every two or three years, or just once for the experience.

*Part Four*

# PARENTING CHALLENGES AND JOYS

# Chapter 22

# ONE-ON-ONE TIME

In many families, multiples spend virtually all their time together, moving as a group through meals, activities, baths, and bedtime. Through the constant interplay, children develop a uniquely close relationship, and they generally like and need to spend time together. Good thing, too, because logistically, arranging things any other way can be difficult to manage. Parents of multiples constantly wrestle with hectic schedules, never-ending household tasks, and the organizational and emotional challenges of raising two or more. Even so, arranging regular or occasional "one-on-one time" with each child—whether a special excursion to the zoo or a ten-minute walk around the block—can be rewarding for many children and parents.

Many multiples need an opportunity to be seen, and to see themselves, outside the context of their role as twins or triplets. One of the great advantages of being a multiple—you're never alone—can also be its downside. One-on-one time with a parent lets a child bask in your undivided attention, creates shared memories, and opens the world to the child in a new way.

## ▨ Time with Just You

*"I never kept a schedule when my kids were little. In fact, I loved having one sleep and the other one up. I loved that special time. When my daughter awoke in the middle of the night, wide awake and ready to play, I stayed up instead of doing the 'sensible' thing by telling her to return to bed. I was thirsty for time alone with her."*

Parents of multiples want their children to be close, and they want each child to be a strong individual. They simultaneously enhance their children's bond by pointing out their similarities ("You two sure do love strawberries"), and reinforce their individuality by stating that it is fine and normal to have differences, too ("Samantha likes mushrooms in her scrambled eggs, and Arnie likes cheddar cheese. Both ways are good."). These spontaneous opportunities to highlight children's individuality occur throughout the day. One-on-one time builds on such moments.

"Let's take a walk, just you and me" can strengthen your bond with each child. Parents are the most important people in their young children's lives—the stars of the show, the most sought-after companions. One-on-one time lets you lavish the three commodities children most prize and compete for: love, attention, and approval. It also gives both parent and child a chance to explore important questions: Who is this child as an individual? What is his/her relationship with the parent, and with others? How does he/she view the world?

One-on-one time can also create happy shared memories:

*"One of my [six-year-old] sons and I were in the bakery, and the clerk was incredibly cranky. I asked for two cupcakes with chocolate icing. After she put them in the bag, I added, 'Oh, and one with sprinkles.' She rolled her eyes and whined, 'I'm trying to give you what you want.' Her ridiculous reply made my son and me burst out laughing the minute we left the store, and we had a jolly time imitating her all the way home. To this day, we can make each other laugh by whining like her. It's fun having an 'in joke' together."*

## ▣ Blossoming in the Spotlight

Some children, overshadowed by siblings, can flourish during one-on-one time:

*"We had never really thought about having individual time with our triplets; it just worked out that way. Our son Isaac, the smallest, had been so squashed inside the uterus that he was born with a problem with his hip. This first became apparent after he was six months old. When he began to walk at about fourteen months of age, he limped. Not long after his second birthday, he was hospitalized for three weeks of traction, surgery, and twelve weeks in a body cast.*

*"We were with him constantly. My wife took the early-morning-to-midafternoon shift, then I took over until eleven at night. Occasionally, my uncle or our nanny gave us some relief.*

*"Of the three children, Isaac had always smiled the least. He never seemed as happy as his brothers. In part this was due to persistent gastrointestinal difficulties as a baby; in part, it was who he was. But over the weeks in the hospital, he blossomed. It was by far the most time he had spent alone with us, and the attention really turned him around. He showed a new ebullience, real joie de vivre. It created a lasting change in his personality."*

## ▣ The Chatterbox and the Treasure Chest

With another child, too, one-on-one time proved to be a key that unlocked a treasure chest.

Reina, age three-going-on-thirty, was an endearing chatterbox. From first thing in the morning to the last call for "One more good night kiss, *please!*" she burbled with ideas and commentary. She had learned to talk early—and not a moment too soon, for she had a lot to say. If there were such a thing as a three-year-old talk-show host, Reina would be it. Like the comedienne Joan Rivers, her motto would be "Can we talk?" (And talk, and talk, and talk. . . )

Her twin, Cassie, could not have been more different. If Reina was Joan Rivers, Cassie was Marcel Marceau, the French mime: silent. If Reina was a chatterbox, Cassie was a locked-up treasure chest. Her parents were so concerned by her failure to speak that they had her checked for a hearing problem, but she was fine. She just did not want to talk. She pointed to the fruit she wanted, smiled at Big Bird's antics on TV, and stretched her arms soundlessly for one more good-night hug. Although she and Reina were never apart, none of Reina's effusive spirit seemed to rub off.

Finally, it occurred to their parents that perhaps that was the problem: Cassie could not compete with her voluble twin. The parents began splitting the girls up from time to time: Reina and Dad to the supermarket, Cassie and Mom to the Laundromat. Away from Reina, the treasure chest who was Cassie gradually opened, little by little, revealing the thoughts and feelings within. One-on-one time literally gave her a chance to hear herself think—and then to think aloud.

## A New View of the World

To parents, errands often seem banal. To children, a visit to the fruit stand, the post office, and the shoe-repair shop may be intriguing introductions to a complex world. Watch children gawk as the produce clerk balances oranges in perfect pyramids. Kids are fascinated by the Dickensian array of characters lined up to buy stamps, and by the aroma of leather and the humming and thumping of the shoemaker's old machine. No humdrum experiences, these, but rather initiations into the inner workings of the community—especially if you point out and explain the sights. The more their world widens, the more children become open to experiencing new things and meeting new people.

Yet some parents of multiples report a moment of sudden realization that their multiples rarely go anywhere. For walks, yes, and to the park and pediatrician's office, but Main Street may as well be in Sri Lanka for all the kids know. Though their family is bigger, their world is smaller. Suddenly, parents feel that they are cheating their children out of the familiar pleasures that comprise their peers' everyday lives:

> *"About a year ago I realized our triplets were quite shy. The average child accompanies parents to the hardware store, the dry cleaner, the dentist. But it was such a pain to shlep the three that we usually left*

*them at home. They almost had a British aristocratic upbringing, shel-
tered, with lots of time with a nanny.*

*"So we started taking one of the children out to lunch every Sat-
urday, leaving the other two at home with the other parent, rotating it
of course so everybody had a turn."*

There is no doubt that taking multiples along can slow you down,
especially if they are too young to get in and out of the car by themselves or tend to get into mischief. It is one thing to hold a single
child by the hand and dash about from errand to errand and quite
another to shepherd around an entire crew. Allow extra time, and
set out with the goal of enjoyment rather than accomplishment.

## ❧ *Solo Moves*

*"It's a nightmare shopping with my twins. They pull in opposite direc-
tions, get into mischief, or play hide-and-seek. But when I'm out alone
with just one twin, he holds my hand and helps me."*

Strollers for multiples get extra-heavy use. They hold more "strol-
lees" and are used longer. Keeping track of two or more toddlers at
one time can be difficult, so in a mall, or on a crowded street, parents
often keep multiples in the stroller rather than allowing them to run
around. One-on-one time can give your toddler a chance to run and
explore under your undistracted supervision.

## ❧ *For Parents, an Opportunity for a Single Focus*

One October day, while wheeling her twins through the park,
Rachel noticed another mother striding buoyantly through the autumn leaves, smiling at the baby strapped to her chest. Rachel suddenly felt a sharp pang of envy. Although she dearly loved her twins,
sometimes—and she could barely bring herself to admit this—she
felt cheated out of the type of motherhood she had always imagined:
hours of gazing at one small face, the freedom to strap a child onto
her chest and move about the city.

Instead, Rachel sometimes felt like a spectator at a Ping-Pong
match, constantly looking back and forth between her two daughters.

While parents of single-borns casually mentioned trips to the museum, Rachel could barely manage taking both of her children to the neighborhood park. Recently, she had missed an outdoor concert to which many of her friends had taken their children, because she knew her twins would not tolerate staying in their stroller, and she could not face chasing them around.

At first, acknowledging these feelings to herself made Rachel feel guilty and ungrateful. But as she reflected further, she realized that she *could* have what, for her, would be the best of both worlds: the joyful times with her twins and, once in a while, the experience of strapping one twin into a Snugli on her chest and striding out among the leaves.

## One-on-One Time with Siblings

*"The twins had each other, but I didn't have anybody. I wanted a twin, too."*

—adult older sister of twins

An older or younger sibling of multiples may sometimes feel left out, excluded from their special bond. Arranging for the sibling to spend time with just one twin may encourage *them* to build a special bond, too.

## One-on-One Time with Both Parents

Although it may be hard to arrange logistically, consider one-on-one time occasionally with *both* parents. Without the distraction of another sibling present, a child may get a keener sense of how the parents relate to each other and to the child.

## A Matter of Anticipation

If one-on-one time feels like too much of a burden, consider postponing it for a better opportunity. The idea is not to make you feel weighed down; remember that relaxed parents are more likely to have relaxed children. Rather, one-on-one time is something to think about, something to plan for. It is *not* something to feel guilty about not doing more often.

And remember that quality one-on-one time can be brief. Even a five-minute jog to the mailbox and back can be special, if you present it that way. Children savor the anticipation of something nice to look forward to. If you say to one of your children, "Right after dinner, you and I will mail these letters," you have given the child the marvelous message: "I am thinking about *you*." It is labeling an event "special time," letting the child know you want to be with him or her, and following through that make it special, not really the *amount* of time.

## One-on-One Time Is Not for Everyone

Although many parents and children feel strongly that one-on-one time is beneficial, even crucial, some parents strongly disagree:

> *"My kids love to be together, and I think they need to be together. Sure, sometimes they need individual attention, but they should get it within the family setting and not as an artificial setup. When a friend with twins recently asked if I wanted to watch each other's kids sometime so we could both have time alone with one child, I replied that I did not find it necessary, and in fact I think it's a fad. Throughout the day, I find enough opportunities to give individual attention to each child."*

You know better than anyone your children's needs and your own. One-on-one time is not a rigid "should," but rather an option that many parents and children have found valuable.

## Arranging for One-on-One Time

Time is at a premium. Minutes seem to trip over each other, they race by so quickly. It is not uncommon for parents of multiples suddenly to realize that quite a long time has elapsed since they spent time one-on-one with their children.

"Unless I make a concerted effort to have special time with one child at a time," said one mother, "I simply forget to do it."

Consider these ways to make one-on-one time work for your family:

*Assure Children That Each Will Have a Turn and Tell Them When.* ("You and I will go bowling tomorrow." Or "Look, I wrote your name on the calendar for next Saturday morning.") Always follow through on promises; if something comes up (and things often do), reschedule and follow through on *that.*

*One-on-One Time Comes in Many Styles and Sizes.* An entire day or afternoon may be hard to arrange. But how about a one-hour visit to the library? A ten-minute game of checkers? A cuddle-up with a book? Or try just saying, "Let's go out for a breath of fresh air"—no matter what the weather.

*Arrange with Your Spouse for Each of You to Spend Time One-on-One with a Child,* or for one of you to be with one triplet or quad while the others are with your spouse.

*Ask a Family Member or Friend to Stay with Your Other Children* while you are with one, or hire a baby-sitter.

*Let Children Request One-on-One Activities They Would Enjoy.* Make a list, or write suggestions on pieces of paper and let children draw them out of a hat when you present them with the delectable choice of how they want to spend time with you.

*Occasionally, Take Photographs, Use the Video Camera, or Draw Pictures* to commemorate special times together.

*Suggest That Other Family Members Have One-on-One Time* with the children. In one family, the paternal grandmother takes each child out individually to buy a back-to-school outfit, and the maternal grandmother takes each child shopping for a birthday outfit.

*If Time Is Limited, Explore Other Ways to Make Each Child Feel Individually Noticed.* Working parents with limited time can still find ways to relate to children "one on one." Ava L. Siegler, Ph.D., a child psychologist; director of the Institute for Child, Adolescent and

Family Studies in New York; and author of *What Should I Tell the Kids? A Parent's Guide to Real Problems in the Real World*, says:

> *"You can write individual notes to children and put them in their lunch box. You can sing funny little songs on tape and leave them for your kids, so they feel tended to. I think the most important thing that parents need to do is to relate to them as individual people, with their own personalities, their own needs, their own thoughts. Parental interest is a very powerful tool. . . . One of the ways you can help children feel nourished and secure is to let each child know that you keep him or her in mind, even when you're not with that child."*

# Chapter 23

# Overcoming Favoritism

"And Isaac entreated the Lord for his wife, because she was barren: and the Lord was entreated of him, and Rebekah his wife conceived. And the children struggled together within her; and she said, If it be so, why am I thus? And she went to inquire of the Lord. And the Lord said unto her, Two nations are in thy womb, and two manner of people shall be separated from thy bowels, and the one people shall be stronger than the other people; and the elder shall serve the younger.

"And when her days to be delivered were fulfilled, behold, there were twins in her womb. And the first came out red, all over like a hairy garment; and they called his name Esau. And after that came his brother out, and his hand took hold on Esau's heel; and his name was called Jacob. . . .

"And the boys grew: and Esau was a cunning hunter, a man of the field; and Jacob was a plain man, dwelling in tents. And Isaac loved Esau, because he did eat of his venison: but Rebekah loved Jacob."

—Genesis 25:21–28

This passage from the Bible articulates what some parents dare not voice: that sometimes a parent, though loving all of the children, favors one in particular. The common childhood plaint, "You like her more than you like me," a charge roundly denied by parents throughout the world, is in some cases true—and is such a taboo that parents may be unwilling to admit it even to themselves.

Feeling more drawn to one child, more chronically irritable with another, can make a parent feel disloyal and guilty. Parents are supposed to be paragons of impartiality and exemplars of unconditional love. Children are equally yours, equally in need of your love. So why does your affection well up more readily for one child than for another?

A parent who feels a greater affinity with one child may simply be reflecting a truth about human nature: It is natural for different individuals to arouse different responses, even if those individuals are your own children.

Yet natural though such inclinations may be, their unexamined continuation and unbridled expression can damage a family. "Unfavored" children who constantly suffer by comparison with a favored sibling may have lower self-esteem and carry feelings of inadequacy throughout life. They may so resent the favored child as to make it impossible for them to be friends as children or adults.

The child who wears the unwelcome mantle of "the favored one" is also hurt. Being favored is no favor if it is done at the expense of siblings. Set apart by a parent's exclusionary approval, "favorites" may be deprived of their siblings' camaraderie and bruised by their resentment, through no fault of their own. "Favorites" may also feel pressured to live up to a supposed ideal and afraid to make the mistakes that are an inevitable, necessary part of living and learning. And they may get a rude awakening when they discover that the world at large does not automatically favor them.

And finally, favoritism can harm parents' own self-esteem. No one embarks on parenthood wishing to wreak emotional havoc; favoritism often creeps up on a family until it becomes a "given." Yet when parents realize what has happened, they regret having inflicted needless hurt on their children, all of whom they love.

It is crucial that parents who favor a child acknowledge these feelings, not, of course, to children, but to themselves. Denying the feelings denies you the opportunity to work through them constructively. These feelings are not immutable; you *can* overcome favoritism and learn to accept and cherish each child's individual nature.

## ◙ The Seeds of Favoritism

How does it happen that you align with one child over another? Sometimes this can be traced back to the children's births. If multiples were a surprise, you may subconsciously regard one child as the baby you expected and the twin as an "extra."

Was one baby more fragile, perhaps disabled, and in need of extended medical care? Sometimes parents favor this child, who seems to need their greater protection. Or it can work the other way. Perhaps the babies were born prematurely, but one came home first from the hospital. A parent may feel closer with this more robust child, who perhaps cried less, nursed more vigorously, slept through the night first, smiled first. And it sometimes happens that each parent "identifies" more with one child than another. The father who virtually lived with the more fragile child at the hospital while his wife recuperated at home may "look out" for that child, while the mother regards the healthier child as "hers."

Maybe one child looks like or reminds you of yourself or a relative, a similarity that may please or dismay you:

"He looks more like my family, while the other twin looks like my wife's family."

"She's athletic, just like me."

"He's shy and insecure. I was, too, at that age. I worry about him."

"She has her aunt Sophie's stubborn streak."

"He reminds me of my brother. Boy, he made my life miserable. He used to slip ice down my back, pinch me when my parents weren't looking, and yell at me if I even touched his Hardy Boy books."

Even decades after one has become a grown-up, childhood memories can be startlingly fresh. You can still feel the pride of having been a top softball player or spelling-bee champ. You can still feel the sting of having been a socially awkward child who always felt left out. If such memories give you greater empathy, a deeper appreciation of what one of your children may be experiencing, then they are all to the good. But overidentifying with a child may cause difficulties, if you fawn over your Little League star and show disappointment in the "runner-up," or crow over one triplet's report card and scowl over the others'.

If you were a shy child, you might give your own shy boy or girl tips on how to make friends—tips you wish someone had given you. But there can be a fine line between using your past experience to enhance your child's life and trying to revise your past through your child's childhood. Despite all your helpful hints, your quiet child may always prefer to have only one or two close friends and may never metamorphose into a social butterfly. Can you let the butterfly of your imagination go? Can you allow your sociable child to socialize and your introverted child to snuggle with a book, without making either of them feel that they are living out your own fantasies or fears?

## ▣ *Like Oil and Water*

*"I have wonderful twins, but for years I enjoyed being with one more than the other. I felt terrible about it. But one day I realized that I was being too hard on myself. One son is easy and amiable, listens well, and does what I tell him to do. The other is stubborn, argumentative, and high-strung. I love him dearly, but he's tough to be with. So naturally I liked being with the other one more. Naturally! When I realized that there was a genuinely good basis for my feelings, I stopped feeling guilty. I concentrated more on helping the stubborn child become more laid-back—not just for my sake, but for his."*

On any given day, one twin may be more pleasant and the other grumpy, and their moods and your reactions to them can shift accordingly. But sometimes the personalities of a parent and a child seem to clash, an incompatibility that pains them both. Perhaps the best thing that can be said about such a situation is that it is an excellent opportunity for personal growth.

If a child tries your patience, you may question why you are always in such a hurry.

If a child seems clumsy, consider whether you really need to be so particular about how things are done.

If a child's persistent question-asking irritates you, you may learn to appreciate this trait as a sign of a true intellectual. Also be aware that the child's questions may be just a way to engage you; the questions may be a statement: "Be with me."

*Don't negate; negotiate.* Instead of ceaselessly nagging a child who dawdles, awaken her half an hour early on school days. A slowpoke is not a bad person; she is just not a brisk morning person like you and her twin.

Teach a whiner alternative ways of expressing himself. Help him practice asking for what he wants, and praise him when he expresses a need without whining.

Give an active, restless child ample opportunities for physical release of energy.

If you and others in the family are enthusiastic readers but one of your twins would rather sketch fashions or cartoons all day, encourage that child to develop and express his or her own interests.

If you find that you consistently scold one child more, or feel relaxed with one and tense with another and cannot overcome these feelings, consider attending a parenting support group or seeing a counselor. It can be difficult to deal with such issues alone or even with your partner. You may discover that "unfinished business" from your own childhood interferes with your ability to accept all of your children for who they are. Or you may realize that one child "acts out" as a release valve for overall family tensions, or to get your attention. Thousands of parents seek help with the considerable pressures of parenthood; the support and insights you gain may be just what everyone in the family needs.

# Chapter 24

# Your multiples, INDIVIDUALLY AND TOGETHER

Like repeating strands of color woven through a tapestry, these themes weave through the conversations of parents of multiples:

"It's so hard to treat the children equally."

"I know I shouldn't compare them, but. . . "

"Sometimes they compete or fight, sometimes they are best friends."

Such issues seem inescapable—and they should be. For within them lie the keys to how to enhance children's self-esteem, individuality, and relationships with one another.

## The Pressure of Proving Equal Love

*"Children often accuse their parents of being unfair. 'You did this for him, you didn't do it for me'—that number. It got to be a joke.*

> *"Once in a while, I remember, Ed would say 'Larry is your little pet.' I'd agree: 'You're right. Larry is my little pet . . . And you know what? You're my little pet, too.' "*

As surely as your heart beats, it beats for all of your children equally. So sure are you of your equal love that when a child complains, "You love him more than me!" you confidently laugh off this preposterous notion, encircle your child in your arms, and say, "Now, you know better than that."

That's on a good day. At other times, the child's complaint causes the specter of favoritism to rise before you like an accusatory ghost, a mirage of guilt.

To stave off this specter, some parents, virtually from the moment their babies are born, vow to prove their equal love by treating their children with a symmetrically perfect equality. If they achieve this, they think, their children will never be able to accuse them of loving one child more.

Yet perfectly equal treatment is a mirage, an impossible goal. No matter how hard you strive to epitomize equality, to be *beyond reproach,* at some point children *will* reproach you, for that is what children do. They test parents. They prod. They learn to "press your buttons"—especially the button labeled "Accuse Parents of Playing Favorites." But although they may seem to press buttons to provoke you into guilt and giving in, what they really want is to provoke you into reassurance.

This is not to make light of the very real problem of favoritism in a number of families, discussed in Chapter 23, "Overcoming Favoritism." The pressure to prove equal love addressed here is quite a different matter: It refers to parents' feeling that they must continually prove the *absence* of favoritism by allotting their attentions, their time, their kisses, with flawless symmetry.

Where does this pressure come from? Some parents agonize that being a twin, triplet, or quad "cheats" a child of the parents' undivided attention. By treating children "equally," parents seek to even the score and reduce jealousy.

So as early as the first days of infancy, some parents "guard" themselves against showing any favoritism. Some virtually self-monitor how long they hold each baby or how many kisses they give. One mother said, "If I am holding one child, I feel guilty that the other one is in the infant seat on the floor."

YOUR MULTIPLES, INDIVIDUALLY AND TOGETHER

Another said, "I have to divide my time so much, I feel like I'm on a meter, like a taxi."

This feeling—that every gesture, every gift, every sign of affection—must be the same often persists throughout childhood. A father of twins finds himself counting how many houses he walks by with one child on his shoulders before switching children (at which point he will carry the other twin past the same number of houses).

A mother of eight-year-old triplets never compliments one without immediately finding something favorable to say to the other two as well.

A mother of six-year-old boys says, "I feel like I have to give a hundred percent and a hundred percent. When I kiss one, I have to kiss the other. It's gotten so when I yell at one who is misbehaving, he protests when I don't yell at the other twin, too!"

Such vigilance to prove equal treatment can backfire, in several important ways:

**Conspicuous Shows of Equality Do Not Give Children a Realistic Portrait of Life.**   Instead, children get the misleading impression that because they are multiples, their lives will always be the same. One mother said:

> "I struggled so hard to be equal in every way with the twins. Now, I think I was wrong ever to allow them to expect equality. Life isn't like that! You can hope for justice, but it is self-defeating—and unfair to the twins—to hope that each will have equal amounts of luck and fortune."

**By Saying That Everything One Child Gets, the Other(s) Must Get, Too, Parents Actually Foster Competition.**   Children treated with painstaking equality are conditioned to be "on the lookout" for any parental lapse of justice. Thus parents must continually prove that they *are* fair—and condition children to expect the impossible.

> "It is a big mistake to give twins the impression that everything should be equal. I never say, 'You get one cookie, and you get one,' or 'You get a turn, and your turn is next.' If you keep saying things like that, you train them to think that everything one gets, the other must get the same.

*"And I have never held their report cards side by side and asked, 'How come she got this A, and not you?'"*

A mother of identical girls, now grown, had always tried scrupulously to keep her daughters' lives equal. She still remembers how painful it was when, for the first time, the girls' lives diverged:

*"We mothers of twins want good things to happen to our twins at the same time. But when one of my daughters got a special school award and the other didn't, I had to explain, 'Just because you are identical doesn't mean your lives will be identical.'"*

**The Pressure of Proving Equal Love Deprives Both Parents and Children of the Joys of Spontaneity.** Consider the mother who never kisses one twin without feeling compelled to kiss the other. When a child tells a delightful joke, why *can't* a mother feel free to throw her arms around him and plant a kiss on his grinning face? That action treats him like a delightful individual, rather than as a child so yoked to another that the twin must share in that kiss. And the twin who gets the "equality kiss" is really not getting an *equal* kiss! He is getting a "keep things even" kiss.

Similarly, the triplet who has taken the initiative to put away the toys deserves a compliment all her own. She should not have to share her moment of glory with the other two children.

If one child asks for a pretzel, do you automatically give a pretzel to all of them? This gives children the impression that you expect them to move and behave as a group. Instead, ask, "Is anyone else hungry?"

A mother of identical twins said:

*"You can't ever convince children that you are fair when they perceive you aren't fair. So you don't try. You simply say, 'We do our best to be fair, but life isn't fair. You're not the same child as your brother.'*

*"We didn't even call them twins. We called them brothers. When they were three years old and started to walk independently of us on the street sometimes, and people would say, 'Oh, are you two twins?' they would look blank. And we finally realized we had to tell them what twins were before they started to think it was something pathological!*

*"We didn't use the word, and people followed our example. They said, 'Where is your brother?' not 'Where is your twin?'"*

Treating children as individuals is the greatest "evidence" of equal love. You are acknowledging that each child is special, is not a carbon copy of his or her twin, and should not be treated like one.

*"Both children have the annoying habit of eating in the living room and leaving their dirty dishes on the coffee table. The other day I chided my son for leaving his cereal bowl in the living room.*

*"'I do not want you to do this anymore, Joe! We don't want to get ants in the living room.'"*

*"He replied, 'But what about Hannah? She leaves her dishes in the living room.'*

*"I wasn't going to let him off the hook that easily!*

*"'Joe, I am not speaking to Hannah right now. I am speaking to you. I am speaking about your cereal bowl.'*

*"He broke into an abashed smile. I had the feeling that he was relieved that I hadn't fallen into the trap of involving his sister. I think it made him feel more grown-up, more responsible. And I think he liked my keeping the focus on him, just him. It was just him and me talking about that cereal bowl."*

## ⊠ The (Irresistible?) Urge to Compare

*"Everybody who sees the twins compares them, in a way that they would never compare siblings of different ages. And they expect that if one does something, the other one should do it, too. We were adamant about not letting people compare them and not comparing them ourselves.*

*"For example, my father once said when they were about two years old, 'Ed, Larry gave me a kiss. Why don't you give me a kiss?'*

*"I said, 'Don't ever say that to them again. They're different children; they don't behave the same way. You can't expect each child to do what the other one does.'"*

In some ways, to compare is natural. The eye, the ear, the mind all work that way; through observation and comparison we distinguish one person, place, or thing from another. For parents of multiples, it is fascinating to observe how children are similar or different: Joey loves to swim, while Gregory hates to get splashed. Anna has already started to turn over in her crib, while Melanie likes to lie on her back and stare at the colorful animals on the crib mobile.

There is a fine line between *observation* and *comparison*. To say that "Jody hits the ball well" or "Jody is a good softball player" is to acknowledge Jody's athletic ability. This is very different from dubbing Jody "the athlete of the family"—because if Jody is *the* athlete, then that precludes Harry from being an athlete, too. Comparisons are harmful when they essentially rank one child higher; this obscures each child's equal value as an individual. Acknowledge each child's special talents without implicitly or explicitly denigrating the child's sibling(s).

Comparisons can begin during infancy:

*"My twins were born four weeks early. One daughter had problems with her nervous system and thrashed around. It took two people to hold her down. She needed so much attention, I felt I was neglecting the 'good baby.' And then I was horrified that I was thinking of her as the 'good baby.'"*

*"My boy won't go to bed at night. But my girl is 'good' because she will."*

Comparisons can make one child a yardstick for the other's development. Sometimes parents are not even conscious of how they dub one child the "standard" against whom the other(s) must measure up:

*"The girls were slow walkers, didn't walk until fifteen months. One was more energetic when it came to crawling; the other would just sit there and look. I tried to make her crawl so she could keep up with her sister. Then I realized that wasn't a good idea. I had to accept that each twin had her own timetable."*

## CAUTION: THIS LABEL CAN BE HAZARDOUS TO YOUR CHILD'S EMOTIONAL HEALTH

Children are complex beings, yet comparisons can reduce them to labels: "The smart one, the slow one." "The athletic one, the bookworm." In one family, parents persisted in thinking of one twin as "the brighter one" because he had learned to speak earlier than the other. One day a friend pointed out he lacked the other twin's ability to count backward! Both twins were bright, notwithstanding the fact that one spoke sooner.

Labels are for multiples as typecasting is for actors: "occupational hazards" that limit people's ability to see their full scope of possibilities. Typecasting actors and actresses confines them to certain types of roles (a tough criminal type . . . a warm, parental type . . . a sex object). Some performers become so locked into their "type" that they are locked out of roles that could show the versatility of which they may be capable. Labeling a child can have the same effect. A child who is always called "the athletic one" or "the bookworm" may feel bound to live up—or down—to the label.

The actress Patty Duke has played a diverse range of roles during her career, but she got a taste of the limits of typecasting when she played the dual roles of (biologically impossible!) "identical cousins" on *The Patty Duke Show*, a situation comedy. "Patty" was the bubbly, outgoing cousin. "Cathy" was the demure, conservative one:

"I separated the characters by examining my own mannerisms and then figuring out which ones I would be able to give up in order to animate the other character. One takes longer strides and when she sits down, she doesn't necessarily cross her legs. The other wouldn't dream of sitting down without crossing her legs at the ankles. One has very erect posture, the other slumps. One is very vivacious, the other looks more cerebral. One is going to talk louder and be left-handed, the other the reverse.

"It was an interesting acting exercise in some respects, but it was also . . . annoying not to be able to perform either character fully because of the restraint of keeping them separate, having to eliminate certain things I might have done for one character because it belonged to the other one. No human being is either that perky or not perky. Although Sidney Sheldon had developed the roles as a device to use all parts of me, I felt as if I didn't get to use any. It was like asking a ballet dancer to dance only from the waist down."[1]

Typecasting children not only defines them in terms of how they compare with one another; the practice also obscures the fact that childhood is a time of so many changes. A shy four-year-old may evolve into a self-assured teen. A "slow child" may simply be in a "preaccomplishing" stage. History is full of stories of eminent people who as children were delayed in learning to speak, had poor grades,

[1]Patty Duke and Kenneth Turan, *Call Me Anna: The Autobiography of Patty Duke* (New York: Bantam Books, 1987).

or seemed unremarkable or even odd. For example, in *Microbe Hunters*, a collection of biographical tales of great scientists, Paul De Kruif wrote that Louis Pasteur was "only a plodding, careful boy whom nobody noticed particularly." Lazzaro Spallanzini "was a strange boy who lisped verses while he fashioned mudpies." Instead of studying, he "sneaked away and skipped flat stones over the surface of the water, and wondered why the stones skipped and didn't sink." (Years later, before beginning his research on microbes, he wrote a scientific treatise on "the mechanics of skipping stones"!)[2]

Of course, not all "slow" children achieve professional prominence. Yet *all* children have wonderful qualities of their own that should not be eclipsed by a label. When parents help their multiples recognize that each is special in his or her own way, they both increase their children's self-esteem and provide an affirming way to look at other people as well.

Furthermore, it is very common for multiples to "flip-flop," switching characteristics that once seemed to typify them. For example, when Nancy and Emily, identical twins, were young, Nancy was always seen as the "dominant" twin and Emily as the "follower." When Emily was eight, she complained, "Nancy gets everything her way. She always goes first."

Emily's mother countered, "But, Emily, you were born first."

"That's not true! You're just saying that to make me feel better!"

Around fourth grade, Nancy and Emily traded traits! Emily became downright bossy (and continues to be so to this day), while Nancy mellowed. So dramatic was the change that until their mother realized what was happening, she began to mix them up for the first time.

Another problem of labeling is that it disregards the fact that children may simply have dissimilar learning styles and pace. For example, let's say that twins, Nora and Fred, take violin lessons. Nora catches on more quickly, while Fred seems slower, laborious. They overhear their parents calling Nora "the talented one."

Yet the world has many violins and many violinists. Some musicians show aptitude from the beginning and stick with it. Yet others, to use the analogy of "The Tortoise and the Hare," are like tortoises who get a slow start but through discipline and hard work improve

[2]Paul De Kruif, *Microbe Hunters* (New York: Pocket Books, 1926).

steadily. A great beginner may prove to be a "rabbit" who is initially capable but doesn't stay in for the long haul.

Thus, calling Nora "the talented one" has several pitfalls. Nora may feel pressured to live up to the label, thereby perhaps losing some of the pleasure of playing. Or she may feel obliged to stick with the violin even though a year later she would much prefer taking up pottery. Fred, who really enjoyed the violin, may feel he should give it up because Nora has been dubbed "the talented one." As one twin in a similar situation said, "Violin is 'taken.'" Yet nobody owns an art. Why label anybody?

On the other hand, if a child finds a special niche, it may be that much more delicious if it *just so happens* that the other children in the family have no particular interest in it. No competitive tension exists. While absorbed in making music or running track or sculpting, the child enjoys a sphere all his or her own, an opportunity, as Virginia Woolf wrote in *A Room of One's Own,* to "escape a little from the common sitting-room and see human beings not always in their relation to each other."

## A Devastating Silence

An adult twin said that the "unspoken competition between multiples can be life-shattering, especially if one twin is smarter or more athletic than the other *and nobody talks about it.*"

In their desire to protect their children's feelings, parents sometimes avoid speaking about conflicts that are quite obvious. They may simply not know how to talk about such issues or may feel that silence is a delicate solution.

Silence, like pictures, often speaks louder than a thousand words. The problem is, it speaks within children's imaginations, where it may paint horrific (and unwarranted) visions of parental disapproval or disgust.

It can be hard to figure out what to say, but it might help to realize that listening to your child is equally important. Seek or create opportunities to bring such issues into the open.

For example, let's say your son Frank is the Little League team's Babe Ruth, but his twin, Anthony, is an unremarkable player. If you are silent about the situation, Anthony may erroneously assume that you disdain him in comparison with Frank.

Talk with Anthony about his own game: "You had a good throw to first base in the fourth inning," or "I noticed that you really tried hard today to support the rest of the team." Anthony will appreciate your interest—and may articulate what's on his mind: "Frank's a much better player than I am." This gives you the opportunity to honestly say that you are proud of Frank, and also proud of Anthony. Do not deny Frank's abilities—they are there for the world to see, and it would be unfair to Frank and patronizing to Anthony to pretend otherwise. But do make sure Anthony understands that you value each child as special.

Ava L. Siegler, Ph.D., a child psychologist, says:

*"You want to find a child's strengths and build on them, and recognize the child's vulnerabilities and help the child address them. What parents often do is to obliterate, or deny, a difference ('Oh, he's not so good at climbing, you can climb too'), instead of addressing it with the child ('Yes, Jonathan does climb much more easily. Now, that means that you are going to have to work a little bit harder to climb fast, and I can help you do that. Or, if you don't feel like climbing, maybe we should go into the swimming pool and learn how to swim.'). Give children an option— either to compete, or to step out of that particular race and put themselves in another place. . . .*

*"Certain parents are very good at creating an atmosphere in which one can be oneself and competition is not the name of the game: 'You compete with yourself, we love you both, we accept you both, you're not in a race with each other.'*

*"The degree of loving feelings that kids have for each other again has to do with the atmosphere that parents create—because all siblings have rivalry; twins are just going to have it in a more heightened way. . . . What mitigates against rivalry, against aggression, is love. If you love somebody, you're happy for their successes. . . .*

*"There are some families where they create a sense that there's only one pie, and if one child gets more of that pie, the other gets less. It's the pie theory of life. In other families, the parents are able to convey to children that family life is not like a pie; there's enough love for everybody, and everyone can have their piece. If one person has a very big piece, it doesn't mean that somebody else is going to have less."*

## THE FLIP SIDE OF COMPARISON

Some parents are frustrated when comparisons reveal a *lack* of contrasts. One mother said:

> *"People advised us to look for interests where our twin daughters diverged and encourage them. It was frustrating when they didn't manifest different interests or aptitudes. I felt pressured to emphasize their individuality, and a way to do it didn't present itself."*

Another parent, too, reported the uncanny, even disconcerting, similarities of her twin daughters' favorite activities: Scrabble, reading, gymnastics, and guitar.

Some multiples, especially those who are identical, share the way they look, the things they like to do, and their areas of talent. This similarity does not mean that they are not true individuals; they are individuals who are highly similar. This is by no means a "wrong" way to be a twin; like other children, they should be allowed to be who they are.

> *"Both of my daughters studied piano. When it was time to choose an instrument for the school band, they both chose clarinet. The teacher protested to me, and I suggested to the girls that one choose the flute or the French horn. But they both really wanted clarinet. Finally, I thought, what am I hassling them for? To make the teacher happy? To please the world? I told the girls that if they both want to play the clarinet, fine. The school requires them to stay with an instrument for a year. After that, if either or both change their minds, that's fine, too."*

## ▦ Typecasting by Gender

> Jack be nimble, Jack be quick,
> Jack jump over the candlestick!
> Jill be nimble, jump it too,
> If Jack can do it, so can you!
>
> —Father Gander (a.k.a. Dr. Douglas W. Larche)[3]

[3] *Father Gander's Nursery Rhymes* (Santa Barbara, CA: Advocacy Press, 1985).

With boy/girl multiples, typecasting sometimes is based on gender. Is Angie a "tomboy," but is Gordon just a "boy"? Maybe they are both simply active children! Yet researchers have shown that many parents treat male and female children differently even as infants, in ways that may limit children's abilities along gender lines. One summary of such research includes such examples as:

"Girls are cuddled significantly more."

"Mothers imitate the vocalizations of girl infants more frequently."

"Parents encourage competence in boys, but foster interpersonal expressive skills in girls."

"Parents are more likely to interrupt a girl than a boy."[4]

Fortunately, today more people are aware that a girl playing with a truck is no less a girl; she is a person who enjoys making that truck move. A boy playing with a doll is no less a boy; perhaps he is emulating his loving father.

In *Growing Up Free*, a book about nonsexist childrearing by Letty Cottin Pogrebin (see the Bibliography), she described a moment that illuminated her own inadvertent "gender typecasting" of her twin daughters and their younger brother:

*"One day, I brought home a miniature basketball hoop with a light, spongy ball. As I affixed the hoop to the closet door in my son's room, my husband stopped me.*

*" 'Why in the world are you putting that up in David's room?' Bert asked. 'He's three years old and barely three feet tall. Besides, the girls are much better athletes.'*

*"We moved the basketball set to Robin and Abigail's room while I bemoaned all the sex-role-connected decisions—such as basketball-equals-boys—that I must have been making since our children's births. That week alone, I remembered giving comb-and-mirror sets as Halloween party favors to girls, and matchbox cars to the boy guests. . . .*

*"Bert reported his sins: One day in the car with all three children, he'd found himself exclaiming, 'Hey, David, look at that big crane!'—even though Robin and Abigail were also in the backseat gawking at the impressive machine."*

[4]*Beginning Equal: A Manual About Nonsexist Childrearing for Infants and Toddlers*, (New York: Beginning Equal: The Project on Nonsexist Childrearing for Infants and Toddlers, a joint project of the Women's Action Alliance, Inc., and the Pre-School Association, Inc., 1983).

Just as being a twin or triplet or quad should not limit a child, neither should being a girl or a boy. Make available a wide range of toys and experiences to your male and female children, and let them gravitate to those they like best.

## Multiples' Unique Bonds

*"My triplets change in formation, like an amoeba. Sometimes all three are together, or just the two girls, or one boy and a girl, then all three again."*

*"I was intimidated for many years about talking with my twins about their relationship, even about asking whether one twin was angry with the other. I felt it was taboo to invade a relationship so private and special and significant. Being twins is the closest human relationship I can imagine. In a way, their relationship was unknowable. But I also felt that even though it was incredibly intense and good, it was also fragile."*

To some degree, virtually all twins, triplets, or more have between them a delicate and necessary tension: a tension of cooperation and differentiation, of a need to be together and a need to be separate.

Dr. Jane Greer, a psychotherapist who has worked with many multiples and their families, says that this process is the way multiples determine the degree to which they want to emphasize their *individuality* versus their *"twindividuality,"* or unity. Every set of multiples, says Dr. Greer, has its own unique ratio of individuality to twindividuality. Some want to be close and spend great amounts of time doing the same things. Others wish to move in separate directions. For many, the patterns change depending on the multiples' age, interests, degree of similarity and difference, goals, and circumstances.

Dr. Greer identifies four types of twin bonds (which also applies to higher multiples as well). She identifies these bonds as:

- *the bond of equality*—twins try to keep things the same between them
- *the bond of complementarity*—twins divide areas of experience

in ways that can complement each other ("You do the cooking, I'll do the cleaning.")

- *the bond of being indifferent*—twins who push to be different from one another by negating completely, minimizing, or making very light of the fact that they are twins. In order to pursue individuality, they feel they must free themselves of the twin relationship by denying that it is an important aspect of their life.
- *the bond of competition*—twins have all-out rivalry, trying to outdo, overpower, one-up, and compete with one another

Identical multiples are more likely to have similar temperaments and patterns of development, and to demonstrate bonds of equality or complementarity. They may tend more to filter out sources of conflict. Yet they also need to learn that it is okay *not* to be the same in all things:

*"One of my twins tends to copy the other, even in what he has for breakfast. I try to explain, 'If you have milk and your brother has juice, you're still brothers.'"*

Fraternal multiples are as alike or as unalike as any brothers and sisters, and theoretically equally likely to demonstrate any of the four types of bonds.

Dr. Greer ascribes the differences between identicals' and fraternals' bonds in part to the way they are seen and treated by the world at large:

*"Identicals tend to be compared in terms of similarities: 'You look just like your brother, and do many of the same things.' So identicals feel a constant pushing toward similarity. This can increase their closeness and lead to their working out a certain complementarity and balance, keeping the rivalry in check.*

*"With fraternal multiples, on the other hand, people compare in terms of differences: 'Gee, you don't look anything like your brother.' This constant comparison can fuel competition and result in more rivalry and friction."*

Dr. Greer points out that not only do many identical and fraternal multiples have different experiences; some fraternal twins have even had the disconcerting experience of being told by identical twins that fraternals are not "really" twins. Some identical twins feel they have more of a connection and that their twinship is more "authentic" than that of fraternal twins!

Both identical and fraternal multiples must cope with being treated by others as "different," in some ways, from single-born children. Many multiples resent this:

> "My girls didn't like being twins. They felt that people did not look at their faces, did not see them as people, did not call them by name but called out 'Hey, twin!' The girls were so frustrated, one of them once said that at birth, one twin should always be given away!"

Such feelings underscore the importance of treating multiples as individuals (never called "the twins," for instance). If the world at large cannot be counted on to be sensitive to multiples' feelings, at least the family can.

> "Having twins is wonderful and extraordinary. But I think twinship is more a hardship than a blessing. It is hard to have another person of the same age, the same gender, the same parents, in the same family at the same time. Twins always have to share their life experience. It's never just their own. But it is also true that their interplay can produce greater festivity within the family."

## MULTIPLES AS MUTUAL COMFORTS

Because multiples have each other, they bond differently with parents than do single-born children who, by definition, have a more single-minded focus on parents. Of course, multiples still profoundly need their parents! Yet, as Dr. Greer says:

> "Twins can be more self-sustaining and self-contained because of their twin partner. Single-borns might start crying after half an hour of being left alone. But twins can self-soothe one another. They can suck each other's toes, pat each other's heads, snuggle, and derive a certain sense of warmth and security, so that the twin becomes almost a sort of transitional object, the extension of soothing that is associated with mother's soothing qualities. The twin can really serve that soothing capacity."

Multiples' bond may intensify, even be an effective "survival mechanism," at times of crisis, when they turn to each other for comfort. Dr. Greer studied twins who were placed in foster care at about age two following their parents' divorce, and stayed until a parent reclaimed them and regained custody when the twins were about six. She found that "having each other as self-soothing transitional objects inhibited what otherwise could have been much more developmental arrest and impairment."

Parents are often surprised to discover that multiples can serve as such comforts and resources for one another:

> *"We had the babies share a crib for the first two months. They are cosmically aware of each other. Now one will try to catch the other's eye, but the other will be off in a cloud.*
>
> *"Now [six-month-old] Johnny is so active, Amber less so. Amber is is his favorite toy. He grabs her, sucks on her. But she doesn't cry. She doesn't seem to mind."*

> *"My twins shared a crib for the first four months. One day I walked in to see one twin sucking on the other one's toe. They often reached out and touched each other, sometimes sucking on each other's arms. When they got older, they called each other 'Dee Dee,' as if one name sufficed for both. 'Come on, Dee Dee,' one twin would say to the other, pulling her over to play."*

> *"When my six-year-old twins go somewhere for the first time, such as when we decided to join a new church, they hold hands. I love it that they always have each other for support—but I don't want them always to depend on each other."*

Just the same, multiples are far from a self-contained unit; proximity to and approval from parents is still paramount:

> *"The girls have a big room full of toys, but they don't want to be in it unless I'm there. They want to be near me. They like to do what I do. So when I'm in the kitchen, I give them wooden spoons and pots or a toy kitchen set."*

While most parents are grateful that their multiples have "built-in playmates," some feel excluded by their children's close bond:

*"I felt very shut out by my twins. They were loving until first grade or so. Then they weren't allowed to talk in school and had so much to discuss with each other when they got home that they would disappear into their room. I felt so left out. I didn't feel that I could discuss this with singleton moms. They wouldn't understand."*

But many parents are moved and intrigued by their multiples' interplay:

*"Both [five-year-old] boys have cerebral palsy. Jimmy has walked since he was three and is fully ambulatory. Carl recently completed surgery, got full braces, and is just starting to walk, too. Jimmy is protective of Carl, but they fight like normal siblings as long as they are on the floor.*

*"Carl is the main instigator. He can't do as much as Jimmy, but he can—and does—tell Jimmy to do something that gets them into mischief, like trying to turn on the car keys. Carl also tells Jimmy to fetch him things if Carl doesn't feel like getting them himself.*

*"Every day, Carl needs to have stretching exercises, which are painful. Jimmy says, 'Don't stretch Carl, it hurts him.' Then Jimmy volunteers to be stretched, too."*

## LANGUAGE

*"One of my twins spoke more clearly than the other, but he understood his twin's language better than I did and would translate for me. When the other twin said, 'Etta bood,' his brother explained, 'He's saying it is a bird, Mommy.'"*

*"The twins make up their own words, like* bowie *for* pacifier.*"*

*"Especially between ages two and a half to three, the twins spoke their own language. I didn't understand what they were saying, but they did. I didn't feel left out, though. I liked the closeness between them."*

*"I had heard twins sometimes have delayed language development. Not to worry. My girls talk all day while they follow me around."*

Multiples often develop language "shortcuts"—words, expressions, or sounds whose meaning only they understand (until parents catch on). Toddler twin girls, for instance, made distinctive two-syllable squeaking sounds, which baffled their parents. Finally, their mother realized what they were "talking" about. They were imitating the back-and-forth squeak of the playground swing. The sound was a request to go to the park!

Some parents are concerned that their multiples' language development will be slowed by their unique communication with one another and by their lessened need to be understood by their parents, since they are already understood by one another. And some parents are alarmed at exotic tales of *idioglossia*, a condition in which twins or other multiples develop a language of their own; in extreme cases this language is so exclusive and impenetrable by others that the children are effectively in a closed world of their own. Such instances are rare.

While multiples may indeed have somewhat slower language development than single-borns, most do catch up by the early grades and show no long-term problems.

To encourage multiples' language development:

- *regularly spend one-on-one time with each child.* This is especially important if one child is verbally dominant.
- *talk to children often, from early infancy.* Murmur endearments, name things, describe what is going on, tell stories, recite nursery rhymes. Read to them often.
- *use each child's name frequently.* This acknowledges their individuality and also reminds you to address separate remarks to each, from time to time, instead of primarily speaking to them as a group.

## MULTIPLES' DEVELOPMENTAL STYLES

*"One of the most enjoyable things about being a mother of twins is watching them both grow up at the same time. Also, one of the most important things to remember is that you cannot expect them to be the same person on the inside. Twins differ from the outside to the inside no matter who they are or who you want them to be."*

Some multiples seem to have an almost rhythmic give-and-take. One woman compared her identical twin daughters' development to a game of leapfrog:

*"In their progress and learning, first one would learn a skill, then the other, then one twin would jump ahead and the other would follow. They alternated, building on acquired knowledge. Neither was always a leader or a follower."*

The mother of identical twin boys still marvels that:

*"They sometimes learned motor skills within minutes of each other. Larry did most of the motor skills first, and Ed just watched him and copied him, which I thought was rather clever, because he didn't have to go through all the practicing. It was so dramatic with the crawling. Larry practiced crawling, rocking back and forth. Ed just sat there and watched! Larry figured out how to crawl, and Ed just got up and did the same thing!"*

When multiples develop in markedly dissimilar ways, parents sometimes feel split. They do not want to "favor" the quicker child or the slower one; they try to find ways to hold on to their vision of each child as an individual.

## TRIPTYCH

When a mother of four-year-old triplets discusses her children, her words are the equivalent of a triptych, a three-panel painting in which each panel is different yet complements the others. She is intrigued to see her sons' separate lives unfolding simultaneously, different from yet somehow complementing the others:

*"Sean is outgoing and somewhat blithe. He likes to take social and physical risks. On the beach, he thinks nothing of flirting with ten-year-old girls. He is eager to learn about the world. He even taught himself to read, announcing one day that a hubcap said Toyota! He spelled out the word Dad in blocks long before the other two were ready. I was an early reader, too. For Sean and me, learning to read was a way of solving the mystery of older people. Sean is unbelievably brave. He once pulled out his own stitches, from a cut in his lip. But if his brother is wearing his shirt, Sean will cry for half an hour.*

*"Isaac is extremely curious. When I cook, he likes to help and wants to taste every ingredient, sample every dish. He has a very sophisticated palate. Like the wise child in the Passover seder, Isaac asks questions*

*about everything. He is very interested in life and death. He asks, 'Was the food we eat ever alive?' Once he insisted that a chicken on a deli rotisserie was waving at him. He asks, 'Were puppets ever alive? What about statues?' About skeletons of animals in the museum, he quietly said, 'They were once alive, but they are not alive now.' He is a poet. In our family, when the kids bump themselves, I let them suck a piece of ice. One day Isaac was upset and said, 'Ouch! I hurt my feelings. I need a piece of ice.'*

*"Obviously, Will is the same age, and about the same height and weight as his brothers, but he seems younger, more babylike. He is happy sifting sand through his hands or watching Sesame Street. He is very affectionate, cuddly, and charming, very easy to parent. I worry most about him, try to give him more attention. He just can't do all the same things as his brothers.*

*"Sometimes I feel that Will focuses most on his mom and dad, Isaac focuses on his brothers, and Sean's eyes are on the outside world."*

### THE FLIP-FLOP PHENOMENON

It is common, but often baffling, for multiples to "flip-flop," i.e., reverse patterns or assume behaviors that *had* seemed to belong to one another. For example, if one second grade twin "always" is better at math and the other loves reading, they might "flip-flop" in fourth grade, with the reader scoring higher on math tests and the mathematician triumphing on reading tests.

An elementary school team's soccer coach was confounded by the flip-flopping of twin players, both of whom appeared to be equally good athletes during tryouts. Yet it frequently seemed that the girls alternated having "off" and "on" days. The bemused coach said, "Just when I think I know which girl is the better player, they surprise me and it's the other way around."

## When Children Fight

*"Though utterly unlike in character, the twins got on remarkably well together, and seldom quarreled more than thrice a day."*

—Louisa May Alcott, Little Women

*"When I choose toys for my twins, I ask myself, 'Will they kill each other with this?' During a fight, a toy hammer, a baseball bat, a xylophone stick can be dangerous weapons."*

Conflict between siblings is normal, expected—and often frustrating. When children fight, parents sometimes feel like failures. You try and try to get them to understand the principles, the worthiness, of peaceful interaction—and then they're at it again!

*"One day, I heard myself shrieking, 'Peace, peace!' I felt so hopeless, so pathetic. I felt I was fighting a losing battle against their fighting."*

It can be dizzying, even disorienting, to witness how children can be best friends one minute, fierce enemies the next, and then back again to being pals. It's like watching the weather switch from lightning storms to placid sunshine to wild tornadoes in the space of an hour. Sometimes you may even feel a bit foolish for taking a quarrel so seriously, when the children forget about it so soon. And sometimes you may feel that you can never bask in peaceful moments too confidently, for another squall may happen any minute.

*"We never relaxed when the twins were little. There was so much potential for hurt or trouble."*

*"My triplets have random bursts of aggression when they fight over toys. Sometimes one demonstrates a sudden desire to clank the others over the head. But they are also affectionate, like puppies. They maul and hug and kiss and roll around on the floor."*

Parents of multiples are often surprised and distressed to discover how early fighting begins, how vicious it can be, and how difficult it can be to stop:

*"From the time the twins started to crawl until they were about four years old, they showed fierce anger when they competed for toys. It was a primitive rage, horrifying and amazing. Sometimes they hit or pulled hair.*

*"The worst was when they started to bite each other. The doctor said it was totally unacceptable and to stop it. But we asked how? We tried everything but biting them back. We tried ignoring, spanking, separating, talking, holding up the bitten arm and saying to the biter, 'This hurts!' Nothing did any good—until one night, when they were about four years old.*

*"We were in a phase of trying to ignore them whenever they fought. We had invited people for dinner, and the girls were upstairs. Suddenly,*

*we heard a hideous, bloodcurdling shriek. We declined to go upstairs. Our guests, who had no children themselves, were skeptical, but we explained our tactic of denying attention when the girls fought. Then we heard another scream. This time we ran upstairs. Blood was flowing down one girl's face from a bite in her forehead. It didn't need stitches or leave a scar, it was just very bloody. I don't even remember which one was the biter. But both were terrified by the experience, and they never bit each other again."*

Keeping a vigilant eye on children can be exhausting, and often parents jump in just in the nick of time:

*"There was a little fenced-in area we called 'the corral.' The twins played in there. But I had to keep an eye on them all the time. Once, one put the handle of a pail around the other one's neck! Another day, they managed to open the gate. One ran one way, one the other. They tried to outdo each other."*

Children's fighting can make parents question their own fundamental competence (not to mention their sanity)—especially if they have had unrealistic expectations that they would be such good parents that *their* children would not fight!

In *Between Generations: The Stages of Parenthood*, Ellen Galinsky describes how some television sitcoms can perpetuate such unrealistic views of family life:

*"When one child in a family says to another, 'I hate you so much,' or when they all turn into a writhing, squealing mass of pounding feet and arms and shrill voices—it's hard for parents not to feel, 'I must have done something wrong' or 'It's my fault.' But if they have separated their own identities from those of their children, and they see family life as having ups and downs, they tend to overcome their initial discomfort more quickly than if they see family life as television sit-coms picture it—parents always home in the magazine-fresh living room reading the paper, in the spotless kitchen stirring one pot which miraculously turns into a full-course dinner, with endless time and patience to listen to their children's minor scrapes and hassles (which happen conveniently one at a time) and judiciously resolve these problems (in a half an hour's time)."*[5]

[5]Ellen Galinsky, *Between Generations: The Stages of Parenthood*, New York: Random House, 1981.

When children's fights persist, you may feel that "nothing is getting through," or that they are destined to be lifelong warriors. Yet if you consistently emphasize (and model) resolving conflicts through talking, listening, and loving, children will, over time, learn to shun bloodshed, cultivate a sense of humor about molehill-size issues, and arrive at fair and creative solutions.

Some ways you can help children achieve this goal:

*Model Effective Ways to Handle Anger and Frustration.* Check out your own behavior. Do you yell at other drivers on the road—or do you point out to children how you avoid reckless drivers or wait patiently at a Stop sign until the driver in front makes the turn? Do you loudly scold a child who spills juice—or do you try not to make a big deal out of it and just hand the child a sponge to wipe it up? Try to make the atmosphere of your home peaceful.

If you were hit or yelled at as a child, or if your parents did not stop siblings from hurting, even terrorizing, one another, you may find yourself passing these "traditions" on. Or you may fear repeating your parents' ways, but do not know what to substitute. Try taking a parenting course in conflict resolution. Or read *Siblings Without Rivalry* and *How to Talk So Kids Will Listen & Listen So Kids Will Talk*, by Adele Faber and Elaine Mazlish, to learn constructive techniques for handling conflict. *He Hit Me First: When Brothers and Sisters Fight*, by Louise Bates Ames with Carol Chase Haber and the Gesell Institute of Human Development, is also a good source of strategies for coping with children's fighting, rivalries, tattling, bossiness, and so on. (See the Bibliography.)

*Show Children What a Good Relationship Looks Like.* If you and your spouse argue frequently, perhaps children are imitating your example or expressing their dismay at your behavior by fighting with one another. Sometimes children unconsciously act out to distract parents from their own conflicts, or even to unite them. Counseling can help you and your spouse find more effective ways of addressing your differences and coping as a team with children's squabbles.

*Listen to What Children Are Fighting About and Address Recurring Problems.* If children are constantly at war over space, perhaps you can rearrange their room, put up room dividers or assign personal shelves and drawers, or give them separate rooms. If children fight over TV, require them to work out an agreement about which show(s) they will watch before allowing the TV to be turned on. Turn the TV off if fighting resumes.

*Use Nonphysical, Noninsulting Ways to Discipline Children.* For example, have misbehaving children sit in a chair in "time-out." This can and should be brief—only a minute or two for little children, five minutes for children in early elementary school, somewhat longer for older children. Use a kitchen timer to let children know when time-out is over.

Be careful not to insult your children. Hurtful words can damage children's self-esteem. Instead of negatively labeling a child ("You hit your sister? You are a bully! You never learn!"), convey your objection to a behavior in kind, but firm language ("We do not hit each other; use words to tell your sister how you feel.")

*Consistently Separate Children Who Are Physically Fighting.* Many multiples feel excruciatingly unhappy when separated from one another. Children will learn quickly that hitting and punching are unacceptable.

*Set Standards of Behavior.* Some examples: No hitting or other physical attacks. No one may be excluded from play. No put-downs or name-calling. Use courtesy words like "please," "thank you," "you're welcome," "excuse me." Avoid rude phrases like "shut up" and "none of your business." If children use such language because they have heard it in a friend's home, acknowledge that other families may speak and behave differently, but that your children must abide by the standards that you, as their parents, set.

*"Catch" Children Behaving Well.* Let your children know how excited you are by their skill in deciding who would turn the jump rope first. Commend their cooperation in stretching sheets and blankets over chairs in the living room to create a fabulous tent.

Articulate how special their relationship is: "You two are so lucky to have each other," and "Look how fast you finished the dishes; isn't it great to be triplets? You three really worked out a good system for working together."

Remark on how ingenious the children were to pool their allowances so they could buy a toy they could play with together.

Let children know you notice and appreciate their attempts at improvement: "Cara, I noticed that you made a fist but stopped yourself from hitting Julie. You were angry, but you used words instead of hitting!"

***Make Sure Each Child Feels Protected in Your Home.*** Staying out of children's fights and letting them work things out on their own is sometimes effective, especially if children are staging battles just to attract your attention. But a nonintervention policy can be disastrous if a child does not have the strength or ability to stand up for him/herself. One researcher wrote:

> *"The position of nonintervention assumes that siblings are physically, psychologically, and mentally equal, that each can cause the other equal pain, and that if left to settle their own differences they will discover through trial and error that fighting is not the best way to solve problems. It must be recognized that these assumptions are unrealistic. Identical twins constitute the only sibling dyad having any likelihood of physical equality; mental and psychological superiority and inferiority will exist in any sibling relationship. To refuse to intervene is to assure one child tyranny over another, particularly if differences between them are great."[6]*

***Help Prevent "Restlessness" Fights by Making Sure Children Get Enough Exercise.*** Children need physical outlets for their energy. Sometimes the best remedy for fighting is not scolding or separation or time-out, but biking, basketball, jogging, or just walking around the block. Tell kids that you will take them to the park for relay races, and watch quarreling cease, as if shut off by a switch, as children rush to find their sneakers and jackets.

Of course, a relay race is hardly the solution to a fight over baseball cards at bedtime. But do reflect on whether your children get enough exercise in general. Do they have a decent gym program in school? (Unfortunately, due to budget cuts and overcrowding, some schools have cut back on their gym programs.) How much do your children actually move during the course of the day? How much do they sit? Children who take a school bus, who have little opportunity to move about in school, and who automatically turn on the TV when

[6]J. C. Bennett, "Nonintervention into Siblings' Fighting as a Catalyst for Learned Helplessness," *Psychological Reports* 66 (1990), 139–45.

they come home may have few outlets for their energy other than picking fights with their brothers and sisters.

As with adults, exercise promotes self-esteem, relaxation, health, and a happier disposition. If you think your children could benefit from more exercise, consider having them walk to and from school instead of taking the bus, take after-school swimming or dance classes at the local Y, make regular treks to a playground with you or a baby-sitter, or participate in family dance or workout sessions at home (perhaps with an exercise video geared to children).

*Limit or Eliminate TV.*   What role does TV have in your children's lives? Many parents have found that limiting or eliminating TV helps to promote exercise and sports, reading, creative play, and family communication.

Also, evaluate the shows your children do watch. Are children mimicking the rough talk, belligerence, insolence, or violence of the characters? Discuss the situations and characters with your children. Exercise your parental prerogative of determining which shows are worthy of your children's valuable time—and which shows deserve to be turned off.

*Have Family Meetings.*   These can be convened on an as-needed basis or as a regular Sunday night event. Use meetings to settle arguments (like who is responsible for feeding or walking the dog) *and* to discuss enjoyable topics (like planning a menu for the weekend camping trip). Family meetings help teach children such skills as brainstorming and decision-making and promote family togetherness.

*Seek Family Counseling if Your Consistent Efforts to Stop the Children's Fighting Are Ineffective.*   Family counseling can help all of you learn to function better as a family. In some instances, you may wish to have one or more children evaluated to see if behavior problems have a physical basis (such as allergies) or require psychological intervention.

## The Value of Fighting

How can something that gives you such a headache be *valuable*? Yet children who are learning to "fight well" are honing constructive skills and forming positive attitudes that will help them all their lives long—in the workplace, in the community, in love and family life. Twins who come up with the solution of dividing a cupcake in half instead of fighting over it are forging crucial skills in compromise. From cupcake battles to disputes over nations' territories is not as far a leap as it seems!

Every fight is really an opportunity for you to help children learn:

- *to express their views.* Learning to articulate "I want" is one of the most important lessons in life. It strengthens children's sense of self and enables them to clarify short-term and long-term goals.
- *to listen to others.* Active listening teaches one about the world and about each individual's perspective of the world. It is one of the most important and valued, yet neglected, life skills.
- *to explore ways to achieve agreement.* Practice at problem-solving promotes competence, self-esteem, trust, and creativity.
- *to honor the right of others to have their own opinions and to be treated with respect.* Children are egocentric by nature; learning to respect others helps them develop compassion and require respect in return.
- *to value others' individuality and to insist on their valuing yours.* Especially for multiples, this is key to reducing competition and enhancing cooperation.
- *to achieve these goals without inflicting or having inflicted upon them intentional bodily or emotional harm.* Home and family must be a safe haven. Perhaps children who learn and benefit from the skills of peacemaking will grow up to make the world at large a more peaceful place.

### ❧ *Happy Birthday to One and All*

For twins or triplets or quads, every birthday is both a commemoration of their debut into this world and a reminder that their debuts were shared.

In some families, multiples' "births-day" is celebrated with a single cake and a single rendition of "Happy Birthday." Other families feel it important to emphasize that this occasion is actually a collection of simultaneous individual celebrations. They may have separate cakes or cupcakes and candles. Some parents have each child decorate part of a single homemade birthday cake in his or her own way. "Happy Birthday" may be sung to each multiple in turn.

As multiples get older, they are sure to have their own ideas about how they want to celebrate. They may want a shared birthday party or separate ones, on the same or different days, with similar or quite different guest lists. How multiples want to celebrate their birthdays is very indicative of where they are—this year—in their process of bonding with or individuating from one another. It is usually a good idea to allow multiples to have a strong say in birthday planning. At the same time, remind children of the limits of the family budget. Separate celebrations need not be costly to be fun. Nor should parents feel that they must overextend their finances to accommodate their children's wishes.

Allowing multiples their separate celebrations affirms their diversity: One child wants to go bowling; the other wants to play miniature golf. Everyone can have a good time, and the children are spared having to agree on a single birthday activity (although there is also something to be said for the cooperative process that such joint decision-making requires).

In some families, however, "diversity" is not so benign. For example, one teenager, when angry with her twin, shut her out of her separate birthday party, forcing her to stay upstairs in her room alone while the party guests (who included some friends of hers) carried on downstairs. Years later, that memory still stings. Sibling love cannot be dictated, but one child causing deliberate pain to another should not be tolerated as a form of individual expression. Such incidents may cause lasting rifts if they are not worked through.

If multiples choose this occasion to create strife instead of celebration, they may be revealing a need for help in learning to live comfortably with the fact that they are multiples. Try to help them express their underlying feelings. If necessary, consider family counseling.

### GIFT GUIDANCE

When multiples request identical gifts, it reflects their similar interests. But when multiples are *automatically* given identical gifts, it often reflects the gift-giver's *assumption* that the children are the same, or an attempt to eliminate jealousy and competition.

People who do not know children well can hardly be resented for trying to minimize gift-related conflict. But one hopes that closer friends and relatives will tailor gifts to each child's interests and tastes. To help people buy individually desired gifts, some parents have children "register" at a toy store that has a gift registry. (One mother, who had never heard of a gift registry for children, was so shocked when another mother asked, "Where are the kids registered?" that she thought the woman had confused them for a pair of newlyweds!)

Even less welcome than identical gifts is the "shared gift." A mother of preschool-age twins complained:

*"It makes me furious when people give my children a single teddy bear to 'share.' Neither girl can call the teddy bear her own, or give it a name, or sleep with it every night. And it's an imposition on me: by giving a shared gift, people set up a situation where children are almost bound to argue over a toy instead of enjoy it—and I have to do the peacemaking!"*

A father of twins is also indignant:

*"Nobody would give half a gift to a single-born child for his birthday. So why do they feel it's okay to give twins only one gift? Isn't it kind of like saying that two twins equal one person? People don't have to spend a lot to give each twin his own present."*

Young children enjoy opening gifts as much as they enjoy the gifts themselves. They often value separate small items, like a book or puzzle or stuffed animal, more than a single shared gift, even something large like a riding toy. An exception might be the gift of a shared experience, like tickets to a circus or a trip to an amusement park.

Similarly, when multiples attend other children's birthday parties, each child will probably enjoy making a separate birthday card and taking a separate present so each can participate in the ritual of handing a gift to the birthday child. To reduce the financial strain of giving separate bithday gifts, some resourceful parents stock up on reduced-price board games, toys, stuffed animals, books, and children's clothing at special sales or discount stores. One mother keeps several bags of such gifts in the rear of her closet; another hides them in the attic. Shopping "in bulk" saves not only money, but time.

## ▧ Puberty

Body changes during puberty provide an opportunity for support—or yet another arena of competition. One eleven-year-old girl said she was especially glad to be in a separate fifth-grade class from her fraternal-twin sister. Her classmates avidly compared one another's physical development and traded rumors on which girls in the class had already gotten their menstrual period. Because one twin was markedly more physically developed than the other, it was a relief for both not to be side by side so much in public view. Identical twin girls are far more likely to begin their menstrual periods at around the same time, although this is by no means guaranteed.

Opposite-sex twins may face similar issues, especially since girls tend to mature earlier. Boy-girl twins who were once roughly the same height may suddenly find the girl substantially taller and more filled out. When the boy's growth spurt kicks in, of course, he may equal or excel his sister's height.

As puberty progresses, some boy-girl twins take solace in having someone of the opposite sex with whom to compare notes. In *Sex and the American Teenager*, a sixteen-year-old girl describes the feelings she and her twin brother share:

*"Every day, just about, something new seems to be happening to this body of mine, and I get scared sometimes. I'll wake up in the middle of*

*the night and I can't go back to sleep, and I toss and I turn and I can't*
*stop my mind; it's racing fast. . . . I worry [that my face] will break*
*out . . . but so far it hasn't, and I think of my sizes, and I can't get it out*
*of my head—the chest size and the stomach size and what I'll be wearing*
*and whether I'll be able to fit into this kind of dress or the latest swim-*
*suit. . . . My brother isn't doing too good, either! He's got acne, and he*
*can't shave without hurting himself . . . because of those pimples. . . .*
*He's a nut about taking showers. Two a day! He's always using deo-*
*dorant. He's got all that hair under his arms. So do I! We will have our*
*'buddy talks,' and a lot of the time we just ask, 'When will it end—so*
*we can just have a body that looks the same, from one week to the*
*other?' We're in this together, my brother and me, and my friends."*[7]

## Twins in a Family of Twins

If there are other multiples in your family, be aware that they may
serve as "role models" for your own.

Carla, a mother of twins, was also the daughter of an identical
twin, an experience that strongly affected how she raised her own
twin daughters. While she dearly loved her mother and aunt, she had
grown up hearing each say a frightening thing: "I couldn't live without my sister. If God were really good to us, He would kill us in a
car crash so one would not have to survive the other."

When Carla had twins, she was determined to encourage them
to express their individuality. She placed them in separate classes in
school. She allowed them to dress differently. She spent one-on-one
time with each child.

And while she reveled in her mother's and aunt's loving devotion
to her daughters, she worried that her daughters would get the impression that their grandmother and great-aunt's way of being twins
was the way twins are supposed to be: so extremely close that they
could not imagine life without one another. She realized that discussing this concern openly with her daughters was important. She
wanted to make sure they knew that she did not expect or want them
to take the same position.

[7]Robert Coles and Geoffrey Stokes, *Sex and the American Teenager* (New York: Harper & Row,
1985).

## ⊠ Multiples' "Potential"

Multiples: close, resisting closeness, too close. This is the ongoing dance of birth-partners, as they try to figure out how close or how separate they want to be. The story of Tina, age sixteen, reveals the "dance" of one set of identical twins:

> "I feel sad when I see twins who aren't close. Being a twin is like having a gift. Twins who are rivals aren't using their twinship to its full potential.
>
> "When my sister learns a lesson, she passes it on, and I do the same. So we aren't the average sixteen-year-olds, because we have learned 'double' the life lessons. Only twins who appreciate their relationship get the benefit of this earlier maturity and understanding.
>
> "I also feel that being twins helps us adjust in different situations, like our parents' divorce. Both of our parents were devoted. I guess Dad was more lenient, spoiled us more. He always said kids should be the most important things in parents' lives. Mom taught us a lot about how to behave, how to appreciate things, how to become independent. But wherever we are, when we're with each other, we're at home.
>
> "In our rock band, I play drums, Marian plays bass. The rhythm section has to be tight. Being twins helps that tight connection. It helps when we play basketball. You have to know where the other players are on the court. We can feel each other's presence on the court. It helps us to make good passes!
>
> "One night we were visiting relatives and shared a bed. I dreamed we were floating around the house. We looked back at our bed and saw ourselves sleeping there. When I woke up, Marian said she had the same dream. Another time, we both dreamed that we were being chased by a big bear.
>
> "We are quite different. I'm more cautious, she's more reckless. We have many of the same friends. But it doesn't work to be friends with anyone who doesn't like my sister and tries to be friends with me.
>
> "Until one or two years ago, I felt I knew my sister better than I knew myself. I spent time analyzing her. One night I dreamed that I had my sister's face. Now, I spend more time analyzing myself, figuring out who I am. I started keeping a diary. I realized that when I am in a situation and my sister is not there, like if she's absent from school, I feel lost. We are stronger when we are together.

*"Recently, we were separated for the first time. My sister went away for the weekend to visit friends. I was invited, too, but I didn't feel like going. Suddenly, in the middle of the weekend, I felt so lonely, like an emotional breakdown. It hit me: I can't see my sister."*

## LINKING, SEPARATING, REUNITING, REPEATING

Your set of multiples is unique, and so is each child within that set special in his or her own way. Allowing children the freedom to explore how they want to express their individuality as well as their bond is a challenge unique to parents of multiples.

It can be hard to know when to intercede and give guidance, and when to step back—just as it is hard for the children to decide when to pull together and when to pull apart. Together, as a family, you explore this never-ending, always changing dance.

🖾 *Chapter 25*

# SCHOOL DAYS, SCHOOL DECISIONS

🖾   Together or apart? Many parents, teachers, and principals assume that twins, triplets, and other multiples are always better off in separate classrooms: They will be known more as individuals than as multiples, avoid competition and comparison with one another, and have a chance to develop their own academic and social skills outside of the context of being a multiple. Some schools translate this assumption into policy: Multiples are never put in the same class.

Separate classes *are* beneficial for many multiples. Yet the decision should not be based on assumptions and one-size-fits-all policies, but on the individual children's needs. Some multiples do better together. They gain comfort and strength from each other's presence and, in the early grades or even through elementary school, would find separation traumatic.

Keeping such children together doesn't mean they will never thrive on their own. Rather, there are many ways to encourage individuality. Although some multiples do beautifully in separate classrooms from the start, some need separation to be a more gradual process. Others are able to develop satisfying social relationships and achieve academic success while remaining in the same classroom. As the children grow and change, the school decision may need to change, too. A choice that was right in day care, preschool, or kindergarten may no longer fit in fourth grade or seventh.

Consider the following factors in deciding what is best for your children and your family. Explain your preference to the school principal. If the school has an "always separate twins" or "always keep twins together" policy, you may be able to have it waived for your children. Even better, you may encourage the school to adopt a policy of making decisions about multiples on a case-by-case basis, in consultation with parents, and with regular assessments to determine the continuing validity of the decision.

## ⬛ How Do the Children Handle Separation from Home and Parents?

*"One day, one of my boys got sick in kindergarten. When I went to pick him up, the other one was crying, 'Take me home, too!' So I did."*

Children are often excited about starting school, but also tearful and anxious about separating from their parents. Most schools recognize that this separation is a major event in young children's lives and structure the beginning of school as a series of small steps. For example, they may have children stay for only an hour on the first day, two hours on the second day, and so on, until they have built up to a full session by the end of the first week.

What schools may not acknowledge as frequently is that for multiples beginning school, separate classrooms puts them through two separations: from their parents and from one another. They are, in effect, facing "twin separations." They may be better able to understand and accept separation from parents; after all, parents are too old to be in their class and too big to fit in those tiny seats! But they may have a hard time understanding why they need to be split up. The separation may feel to them like insult added to injury—a wrenching apart that devalues their bond and deprives them of a means of support.

Some parents, therefore, even if they think they will prefer separate classrooms down the line, choose to keep their multiples together during day care, preschool, and/or kindergarten and the early elementary-school grades. One mother said that being together gave her twin daughters a comforting home base within the classroom:

> *"The girls look out for each other. One recently started to cry because she had painted at the easel, but her sister didn't have a chance."*

Children may differ in their feelings about separation. One four-year-old girl acclimated to nursery school quickly and appeared unconcerned or unaware of whether her twin brother was happy. When their mother dropped them off, the little girl gaily danced into the classroom—while her brother cried, clinging to their mother and begging her to stay.

If children want to be together and you want them separate or the school requires it, consider working out a compromise. For example, if their classes go to the cafeteria at the same time, can they be allowed to sit at the same table and eat lunch together? Can they play together at recess? Can they ride the same bus home? Can they be partners when their classes combine for field trips? Can they visit one another's classroom on occasion? If one child falls and gets hurt, will the school allow the twin to leave class and comfort her?

If you want the children separated, one option to consider when children are just beginning school is registering them for different half-day programs. One couple, for example, after researching nursery schools, decided that one school was vastly superior to the others. The problem was that it could not offer the children separate full-day classes, yet the parents felt strongly that the children should not be together. Their solution was to choose the half-day option, sending one child to the morning session and the other to the afternoon session. An advantage was that the mother got to spend one-on-one time with each child.

Another mother also chose different half-day kindergarten classes for her twin daughters and called it "the best thing I ever did." She said:

> *"I never had one-on-one time with the girls before. And I knew that once they entered first grade, I would not have this chance again. I started to see their little personalities develop. One of my girls was so feisty and verbal. The other was more quiet. She loved peering at ants and other bugs and saying, 'Look at this insect, Mommy.'"*

The different half-day solution is not an option for working parents who need a full-day program. It also may not suit many at-home parents who feel the need for a break from the children and time for themselves. Separate round-trip commutes may also prove impractical unless children travel on a school bus with convenient stops, or drop-offs and pickups are coordinated with other parents or caregivers.

### ⊠ Do Your Multiples Want to Be Together? Would They Be Upset If They Were Apart?

*"There was never any jealousy between us. If we fought, it was only about little things, like whether the radio was on my side of the bedside table or hers. We were always very close, and also each of us was different. Our mother recognized this. She never said, 'You have to be your own person.' We each did what we wanted—and often it ended up being the same thing the other one was doing!"*

*"I remember in second grade the teacher put my [identical] twin brother and me in separate spelling groups. He was in the group with the smartest kids, and I was in the next best. I felt that she had made a mistake; I should be in the excellent group, too. When the teacher gave words to his group to spell, I silently mouthed the answers. She noticed me doing this, laughed, and let me switch into his group."*

Are your children relatively cooperative with one another, or often at each other's throats? Does one dominate, or are they pretty much equal in terms of who takes the lead? How they relate at home or in nursery school can help guide your decision about whether to keep them together in elementary school.

Some multiples are usually in sync, flowing cooperatively through their days with a minimum of fighting. In some cases, the multiples' ability to harmonize with one another actually makes them more appealing playmates for other children. One such set of six-year-old identical twins was kept together in school because they were so much happier that way. They easily made friends with other children, who were drawn to their peaceful, sunny natures.

Another set of identical twins the same age was equally close, but they communicated only with each other. Separate classrooms were not possible in their small school, and the twins may have found separation too upsetting anyway. Their teacher called the parents. She suggested that they invite other children over to play so that the girls, who were quite shy, could get to know their classmates one-on-one, not in a group. This helped the twins feel more comfortable with the other children and provided a gentle way to open up, but not disengage, their attachment.

Some twins are so attached that separation even within the same classroom can be devastating. Dr. Jane Greer, a psychotherapist who has worked with many multiples, recalls such a situation with twin boys who had always sat together in school because seating was by alphabetical order. One day in fifth grade, however, the teacher decided to change the seating plan. She had one boy sit in the front row and one in the back. A couple of months later, the boy in the back row acted so remote that his mother called Dr. Greer in a panic: "He's staring out the window, he's not concentrating, he's not working, they want to have him tested by a psychologist."

When Dr. Greer asked if there had been any recent changes at home or in school, the mother said, "Well, the teacher moved them." Dr. Greer recommended that the mother tell the teacher to move them back together for the time being and let her know how the child was doing. The boy became reinvolved in the class.

Dr. Greer noted that when multiples have a very difficult time separating from each other, the parents and school must negotiate their separation in a way that is "much more measured and much more supported, perhaps with a counselor, perhaps with a parent at home, before it's suddenly thrust upon them. If the twins are struggling around separation to the point where it interferes with the ability of either one's ability to function, to do the work at hand, then they're going to need support to work through the attachment."

She notes that an excessively intense attachment could come about for a variety of reasons, such as if the family moves, there is a change in family composition, parents are having marital difficulties, or a grandparent becomes ill. A therapist might work with the parents, the entire family, or the multiples, depending on the circumstances. Dr. Greer recommends choosing a therapist who has worked with multiples before and is familiar with the issues they often face.

"Many therapists are unfortunately uninformed when it comes to twins," she said. "They will push separation in instances when it really can be detrimental."

## ▧ Are Multiples Better Off Apart?

Some multiples' disparate temperaments and styles place one or both at a disadvantage. If one twin is dominant, a separate classroom may give the other twin some breathing room:

*"When our twins were three, we asked the nursery school to put them in separate groups, because the boy tried to rule the girl. During Show and Tell, for example, he wouldn't let her talk. When she got up to talk to the class, he interrupted and told them what she had brought before she had a chance."*

Similarly, if one child has an easier time making friends, the other may perpetually feel that he or she suffers in comparison:

*"We requested separate classes for the girls. Different schools would have been even better. Their social evolution became tagged to each other's. The less outgoing one hitches a ride on her sister's friendships. This puts stress on the friendship and on the girls' own relationship."*

Yet there is by no means a rule that if multiples are quite different they are better off in separate classrooms. They may be able to coexist quite happily, each carving out his or her own niche. Or, one child may be dominant but not in a way that injures another; their feelings of contentment at being together may override the benefits of separation:

*"Our triplets' distinct identities really come out in nursery school. Sean, who is very outgoing, plays a lot with the other kids—and thinks he is older than his brothers! Isaac, who is devoted to his brothers, parallel-plays in Sean's vicinity. And Will, who is loving and babylike, follows Isaac.*

*"Will is so shy, he rarely even goes near the teacher, preferring to stay with Isaac. But Sean adores her and likes to sit on her lap every day. One day Isaac was out at his physical-therapy appointment, and for the first time Will sat on the teacher's lap—just so he could be near Sean."*

## 🪆 *Do Children Have Different Abilities?*

*"My triplets were in different nursery school and kindergarten classes. But when they were in first grade, we moved to another city when I got a one-year fellowship. There, the three were put in the same class. One girl is not as strong academically, and for the first time in her life she was compared with the other two children. She came home crying, 'I didn't realize I was stupid!' When the year was up, all three returned to separate classes at our regular neighborhood school. She started bubbling again and regained her confidence."*

If a school genuinely encourages *all* children to work at their own pace, plans individual courses of study for each child, and evaluates children not on the basis of comparison with their classmates but on the basis of each child's individual progress, then having differing abilities may not pose a problem. But if, for example, one twin consistently does better than the other, *both* children may suffer. The self-esteem and confidence of the child with lower grades may be damaged. The child with higher grades may feel guilty or remorseful about the pain his or her success causes the twin, and may even hold back in class in an effort to "equalize things." Or, since children are sometimes insensitive to others' feelings, the higher-achieving child—and classmates—may tease the less academically adept twin.

The teacher's skill in such a situation can make all the difference. Ideally, teachers guide students to understand that *everyone* has both strengths and areas of needed improvement. But some teachers do not emphasize this, or are unable to make this point convincingly or frequently enough, or are so pressured to produce high reading and math scores that they themselves become impatient with slower students.

Children may experience separate classes as a relief from the physical and academic comparison to which multiples are so often subjected:

*"My twin brother and I were always in the same grade school and junior high school classes. We would help each other out. But he didn't do as well. Now he is in a different school. People do not mix us up. The*

tension is off. *Now I feel that he has his own life, I have mine. You can't always be so attached."*

## How Difficult Is It to Tell Children Apart, and How Likely Is It That They Will Be Compared?

*"The girls' teacher couldn't tell them apart, which I found very upsetting. I let each girl pick out a pin to wear every day. One got a star pin, the other chose a dog."*

Identical multiples or fraternal multiples who look very much alike may find being in the same class very frustrating if teachers and class-mates cannot tell them apart. As one boy said:

*"A teacher we've had for two years in a row still doesn't know who we are. He doesn't take the time to tell us apart. He only knows us by where we sit."*

In school, where children should be finding new ways of com-municating and expressing themselves, being seen as "one of the twins" instead of as individuals can make them feel cheated of the individual recognition they deserve. One little girl said to her mother, "I don't want to be a twin anymore, because people mix us up."

Multiples may also face unrelenting comparison, even by teachers who intellectually know better:

*"The girls' teacher tries to treat them as individuals. At parent-teacher conferences, after we talk about Tina, she'll say, 'Now I want to speak with Sally's mother.' But then she still compares them! She'll say things like, 'During class discussion, Sally answers more questions than Tina.' And I must admit, I feel mixed about pointing this out. I want to know about both kids, but I am interested in how they compare."*

One mother of twins tried to turn the comparison to her chil-dren's advantage. When she found out that the girl was better at math and the boy better at spelling, she encouraged them to help each other.

Yet for other parents, hearing the teacher compare their sons' "good" and "bad" behavior was the deciding factor in putting them in separate classes. At home and at school, their son James was the easier, "angelic" child, while Eli was rebellious. (Their downstairs tenant once said, "Gee, I always hear you screaming, 'Eli! Eli!' ") The parents hoped that separating the twins in school would relieve James of the pressure to always need to be "good" and would relieve Eli of the pressure of being compared to James.

Asking your children whether they want to be in separate classes may reveal whether they have feelings about potential comparison. When twins who had always been in separate classes had the opportunity to be in the same fifth-grade class, their mother asked them what they wanted to do. Her daughter Mandy answered, "I wouldn't like to be in the same class. I would be afraid that the teacher would compare us and see that Meryl is smarter."

Her mother replied, "I do not agree with you that your sister is smarter, but I do agree that some teachers do compare." She honored Mandy's desire to continue being in separate classes.

### ▣ Can the School Accommodate Your Wishes While Still Meeting Each Child's Educational and Social Needs?

The notion of separate classes may seem less attractive if those classes are separate—but not equal. One mother described this situation:

> "I really wanted my twins in different classes, so that each had a chance to develop his identity. But in my school district, there were only two schools with programs for gifted students, and each school had only one gifted class per grade level. It seemed ridiculous to send them to two different schools, and I did not want to exclude either boy from the program. So they are in the same class—and it has worked out fine.
>
> "In kindergarten, however, one of the twins was upset when the teacher decided they should sit at separate tables. I made a joke out of it by changing around everybody's seat at the dinner table. I got him used to the idea that he could be in the same class as his brother without having to be at the same table. I reassured him, 'You're still twins, even if you are not next to each other.' "

For another set of twins, parents had to decide how to deal with the fact that they were no "even match." One child learned more quickly and read earlier and more avidly, while his sister seemed to progress more slowly. Their parents were sensitive to the possibility that seeing her brother in the more able "Bluejays" reading group could make their daughter feel inadequate in comparison. The principal gave them the option of transferring their daughter to a slower-paced class, and at first this seemed the ideal solution.

But the more the parents thought about it, the more uneasy they felt. In their school district, as in many others, once children are "tracked," i.e., placed into "slower" or "brighter" classes, they tend to stay in those classes for their entire school career. Tracking, in fact, is one of the most controversial issues in education today. Proponents of tracking argue that bright children should not be slowed down and that slower children should not have to struggle to keep up. Opponents of tracking assert that mixing children of different abilities within the same classroom gives a richer learning experience to all of them. They also point out that traditionally, slower classes have fewer "enrichment" options and special activities than brighter classes do.

This girl's parents decided to keep her in the same class as her brother. They shared their concerns about comparisons with the teacher and asked her to find ways to acknowledge their daughter's talents as well. If she couldn't be a "Bluejay," she *could* be applauded for her dexterity at dodgeball and her tender attentiveness to the class hamster. The parents' and teacher's concerted efforts to avoid comparisons enabled both children to thrive in the class.

This decision may not suit all families, or even be available. For example, when children are of widely disparate abilities, the school may require them to be in different classes—and it may be appropriate for them to do so. Some schools for gifted students not only state that admissions are based on each individual child's test scores and other admission criteria; they specifically stipulate that no exceptions will be made for twins or other multiples!

A mother of fourth graders, looking back on her daughters' schooling thus far, said, "If I knew then what I know now, I would have put them in separate schools." Their school had only two classes per grade, plus a policy of always separating twins. One daughter, Deena, was placed in a challenging class, while the other twin, Eve, ended up, by default, in the "quieter," less demanding class. The girls' scores on standardized tests were pretty much even (although they did "flip-flop" sometimes, alternating higher and lower scores). Yet Deena was the more focused student—quite possibly as a result of her participation in the more challenging class.

Even when opportunities arose for Eve to join Deena's class for special programs, such as an advanced reading group made up of selected children from both classes, their mother felt that the school made decisions based on the girls' "twinness" rather than their individuality. There was palpable reluctance to having the girls together and "hypersensitivity" to their interaction. The first week of the joint reading group, the teacher called the mother and said, "I notice that when Deena gives good answers, Eve looks at her own paper."

The mother said, "Well, isn't that natural? Don't all students check their own answers against those of their classmates?" The teacher backed down, acknowledging that the mother had a point! Yet the mother feels that the school's overvigilant attention to presumed "twin issues" has ultimately done her daughter Eve a disservice. She says:

> "You always want the best for your children—and I feel that Eve was shortchanged. Two separate schools would be hard in terms of transportation and so on. But at least I would know that each girl was being treated as an individual, not as a twin. I discussed the separate schools idea with the principal recently. He said he had never suggested it because 'most moms would not be willing to do the driving.'
>
> "I believe that separate schools are a good idea for twins if a school has only two classes per grade. There's no 'choice' then."

In a different twist on the issue of choosing the best school, when identical boy twins entered junior high school, their parents discovered that the school had some rough students, and a number of the parents' friends were pulling their children out of the school and registering them for private school. Yet when these parents offered this choice to their sons, the boys turned it down: "What are we going to learn about real life in a private school?" they asked. The boys were in separate classes, yet being in the same school enabled them to give one another support and company so that together, they successfully developed the coping skills and the ability to relate to people of many different backgrounds that they felt they needed in junior high school and throughout their lives.

## Which School Choice Is Convenient for You?

*"Having twins streamlines my life. There's only one stage to go through at a time. The children have the same activities and a built-in playmate; I don't need multiple car pools or different day-care plans."*

As much as you want to do what is best for your children, do not neglect taking your own needs into account. If the only way you can place your children in separate and equally good classes is by putting them in different schools, is it worth the inconvenience? Can you handle transporting children to and from different schools? Attending separate PTA meetings? Building two (or more) different support networks with other parents? Juggling parent-teacher conferences on Open School Night? If children attend private schools, will you end up paying significantly more than if the children attended one school, which may offer a discount for multiples? Will schools' separate fund-raising overburden you?

## School As a Social Learning Experience

School serves a twofold purpose: academic and social learning. School is your children's "social laboratory," where they learn about friendships and relationships with others. Some multiples, especially those who get along quite well together, attract other children's friendships. Perhaps this is testimony to the fact that these multiples have had to develop good "sharing skills" and be sensitive to another child's needs as well as their own. One father was startled to hear from another parent that his twins were such popular class "leaders" that some classmates asked their parents to buy clothing similar to that favored by the twins.

One fairly common dilemma is when a quieter twin is outdazzled by his or her more outgoing, friendly twin. It is essential to help the quieter child identify children with whom it will be possible to build satisfying friendships. Above all, avoid comparing multiples. One woman, who was always the "socially awkward twin," feels that her self-esteem was permanently damaged by her mother's consistent—

and constantly verbalized—delight in her bubbly twin sister's monumental social success.

Especially when multiples are in separate classes, they may develop some separate friendships. A classic example of a "parental turning point" is when only one twin is invited to a schoolmate's birthday party. Both the uninvited twin and the parents feel the sting of rejection. One mother said she felt "insulted" and would not let the invited twin attend.

Yet most often such an invitation is *not* a rejection of the other twin, but rather a normal event in an ordinary friendship. Children invite their friends to their parties—not their friends' brothers and sisters. If they are not friends with the other twin, then an invitation to that twin would be an artificial gesture of obligation, not a gesture of friendship. If multiples are truly to be treated as individuals, they must be allowed to develop separate friendships and those friendships should be honored and allowed to take their normal course.

*"In third grade, Daphne was invited to a birthday party, and her sister Laura wasn't. It was the first time this ever happened. The mother had called me in advance to ask if it was okay, and I said yes. At first Laura was hurt not to be invited, since Sheila—the 'birthday girl'—knew her, too. But she also knew that Sheila was really Daphne's friend, not hers. I let Laura invite a friend over to play while Daphne attended the party."*

## College Choices

Throughout the years, decisions about staying together or moving apart should be made on their individual needs, not on the basis of any arbitrary rule. This is true even—and especially—when multiples are ready for college. Dr. Greer says:

*"What I encounter a lot with parents, particularly when it's time for twins to go off to college, is that some parents feel that they need to push their kids to go off to separate schools. I say you can't make an arbitrary determination that they should go their separate ways. You really need to factor in certain elements: Have they been separated before? How is each doing in school? Do they want to be apart? How far are they planning to go away from home?*

*"The fact is that going off to school is a very big adjustment for anybody. And if that's suddenly going to be the first time that twins are*

*separated, it can be really damaging, in the sense that one or both of them may not be able to cope with the enormity of the separation from family, from twin, and the pressures of adjusting to college. So there have been twins who married prematurely, who had emotional struggles, who dropped out of school because of the pressures, who needed to return to a safer home base. Now I'm not saying that that's the rule of thumb, but I am saying that there tends to be the notion that twins should be separated. Sometimes they need to be, but sometimes they don't."*

One pair of twin girls had always prided themselves on their strong individual identities, and assumed they would go to separate colleges. They did not even apply to any of the same ones. Yet when the time came to separate, they—and their parents—were surprised by how excruciating the experience was. Their mother said, "The girls had no clue to how bonded, how attached, they were."

They had shared a room, a home, and their lives for over seventeen years; now, as one girl put it, "I felt like part of me was being ripped away. I had never experienced pain like that in my life."

Yet they proceeded with their plans to attend colleges in different states (and ran up astronomical phone bills!). Ultimately, one transferred for her last two years to her sister's school. She said she had decided it was a better school—and claimed that it was simply a nice "coincidence" that her twin sister was there.

## Memories in the Making

*"There were four sets of twins in my kindergarten. One day the local newspaper sent a photographer. We all got dressed alike that day. It was kind of fun."*

*"My [identical] twin brother and I never switched classes. We didn't think it was an amusing idea at all. We wanted to maintain our own identities."*

Childhood memories generally center on family and school. Whether your children are in separate classes or together, many of their schoolday memories are likely to include their status as multiples. One school principal, in fact, says that one reason he entered the field of education was to right the wrongs he had experienced as a student, when teachers did not bother to tell him and his twin brother apart. A high school student bitterly remembers how being a twin blinded other people to who he was as an individual:

> "You struggle your whole life for independence, sometimes you hate the person you resemble most. People are always trying to group you: 'Oh, there are the twins.' But at least we didn't look much alike. Some other twins in my school were identical. They got so sick of people pointing and talking that one twin routinely walked five feet in front of the other to avoid the attention."

For one fifty-eight-year-old identical twin, who is also the grandmother of identical twins, schoolday memories of bygone days mix with present-day memories-in-the-making:

> "In kindergarten they tried to separate my sister and me. It was terrible. We cried and carried on until they gave in and put us together. She sat on one side of the classroom, and I sat on the other.
> "We switched classes a lot in high school. I was good in history, and my sister was good in English. So I took history tests for both of us, and she took the English. It was great—we only had to study for one test! We never got caught.
> "My daughter, who has twin girls, age ten, recently said, 'Twins don't do that kind of thing anymore, Mom.' But then her daughters begged her to let them switch classes on April Fool's Day! She permitted it, on the condition that the switch was a one-time thing. The girls wore the same clothes to school that day. All of their classmates knew the girls so well, they knew who was who. But it took their teachers a little while to catch on! The other children were delighted. They thought the switch was the most fun and exciting thing that had happened all year, and many went home and told their parents about it that night. My granddaughters are carrying on a family tradition!
> "Recently, my sister and I took the same college adult-education course. I took the Monday class; she took the Wednesday class. We got the same answers wrong on our tests!"

## ▧ The School Path

Whether your multiples share classes or not, school will present many challenges not only for them, but for you as their parent. A

341

SCHOOL DAYS, SCHOOL DECISIONS

school's lack of familiarity with "multiples' issues" may require you to become the school's "teacher." If your children are being compared, by teachers or even by you yourself, you must find ways to eliminate or minimize comparisons and keep awareness focused on each child's individual qualities, triumphs, and needs.

For your multiples, learning to navigate school successfully, supporting one another while recognizing one another's individual paths, prepares them for navigating adult life as well.

# Chapter 26

# HANDLING STRESS

It is no betrayal of your love for your children to acknowledge that raising them is hard work. From multiple night feedings to multiplied diapers to just having more kids to keep track of, the demands on your mind, body, and heart are nonstop. It's a struggle to feel caught up and in control; to get sufficient rest may seem an impossible dream.

Unrealistic expectations of how life "should" be can contribute to stress. Many parents have vivid mental pictures of how parenthood is *supposed* to be: parents who are always patient with babies and gracious with each other, babies whose cries quickly cease when you pick them up, a household that practically runs itself. Abandon hope of ever attaining this. Real life is too interesting to be so perfect.

And be careful, or you might exacerbate stress by falling into the disquieting exercise of comparing your situation with that of parents of single-borns. You may find it a bit exasperating that your neighbor's one-and-only is the first to toilet train, to speak in complete sentences, and to see the Cézanne exhibit at the museum. Meanwhile, you struggle to keep your kids from using potties as goldfish bowls.

You urge them to say "apple juice" instead of "ju." And the thought of transporting triplets to the museum is so overwhelming that you haul out the basket of broken crayons and attempt art appreciation at home.

"If I had one kid," said a mother of triplets, "I bet I could raise it with my eyes closed and my hands tied behind my back!"

At the playground, a mother of twin toddlers enviously notices the relaxed way that parents of single-borns stand around talking. She says, "I can't afford to take my eyes off the girls for a second. If I talk with a friend or look for a shovel in the sandbox, the girls disappear! I look back and forth so constantly, I feel like I'm doing eye exercises!"

You try not to compare your twins or triplets with one another; why subject *yourself* to comparisons with other parents? That includes other parents of multiples. You can always find someone better organized than you. More resourceful, unruffled, moneyed. Learn from others, let them inspire you, but avoid debilitating comparisons. If you are doing the best you can, in all likelihood, your children are thriving.

## The World's Most Difficult Question

The myth of the "ideal" parent casts a heavy shadow; it hovers like an oversized genie ballooning over a golden flask, a phantasmic embodiment of parental wishes. Every parent has his or her own notion of what the ideal parent is; whatever it is, it isn't really human. If the ideal parent is unfailingly calm and kind, then you do not measure up if you occasionally yell at the kids to hurry up already, the bus is here. If the ideal parent spends endless hours baking and drawing and reading to children, then as a working parent you cannot possibly come close with your bags of store-bought cookies, hasty glances at children's artwork, and pleas to *please* choose a shorter bedtime story tonight.

Many parents are so knotted with guilt, so aware of their imperfections, that they have a hard time acknowledging what they do well. They feel lucky to have their children, yet should also remember that their children are lucky to have them as parents, too.

Occasionally, it's a good idea to force yourself to confront the World's Most Difficult Question, a stop-you-in-your-tracks query that makes most parents gasp, stammer, and draw a blank:

*"What are you most proud of about how you parent your children?"*

It's a tough question, all right—not because you haven't done many things well, but because you may focus too often on what you haven't done "well enough." You could probably rattle off a long list of your parental/household/spousal deficiencies. But can you meet the challenge of listing your successes? If necessary, ask for help from your spouse, your best friend, even your children, if they are old enough (and in a good mood).

## 🕮 *Time Off*

*"I put myself second, third, and finally eighteenth. I don't mean to be a martyred mom, but with twenty-six-month-old twins, life is hard. I feel like I have given up my life. My self-esteem is shot. I feel so isolated."*

When children misbehave, putting them in "time-out" is an effective mode of discipline. It separates them from the other children and gives them some quiet time to calm down.

Parents need "time *off*"—a chance to separate from children and restore equilibrium. When the stress gets to you, when you find yourself needing to put your children into "time-out" a few too many times, it's your turn for time off.

Yet many parents of multiples, absorbed in parenting, working, managing, put their own needs last:

*"The first year, I went out less than five times! I felt guilty taking a break or leaving the house. I thought, 'They have to share me as it is.' Now I know I could have left. I didn't realize they got comfort from each other."*

Children are more adaptable and flexible than we often give them credit for. Not only can they adjust to having parents go out; they learn valuable life lessons from the experience:

• When parents go out, they always come back.
• Taking breaks is reasonable and necessary.
• Making time for oneself is important.
• And so is making time for friends.

- People who are responsible for others also have a responsibility to take care of themselves.

Time off for parents is not selfish; it is natural and reasonable. You hope that when your children are parents, they will take time off, too.

*"Sometimes the only way I get out is by splitting up my kids. I'll drop one off with my mother and one off with a friend. It's complicated to split them up. I have to deal with all the logistics. It's time-consuming to shlep them all over the place and juggle things. But it's necessary for my mental health."*

If you cannot allow yourself a break just for the pleasure of it, then do it for the kids. Give them the pleasure of seeing a smiling, emotionally renewed parent bounding through the door after a gym workout, a heart-to-heart talk with a friend—or an overnight date with your spouse at a local motel. Replenish your energy so you can have more to give.

*"My one big outing is a manicure every two weeks. My nails are the last vestige of the woman I once was. I feel like I'm barely holding it together, but when I see someone I know, I want them to say, 'You look wonderful!' I don't want to look as haggard as I feel.*

*"When I was driving to my manicure appointment the other day, some guy whistled and said, 'Hey, Mama.' I burst out laughing. Little did he know just how much of a 'mama' I am!"*

## ✿ Stressed-Out and Had It!

If parenthood feels like an unrelenting pressure, you may need more than the occasional "time off" to help you cope. If you feel depressed or overwhelmed, tend to yell a lot, have the urge to hit your children, or actually do give physical vent to your frustrations, a support group of other parents can be immeasurably valuable in giving you effective means of handling the stress of parenthood (see Chapter 21, "Mothers of Twins Clubs and Other Resources"). If problems persist, consider seeing a mental health counselor for help and support.

It can cheer you up just to hear that other parents are facing the same kinds of things you are.

Margaret Thatcher, former prime minister of Great Britain and a mother of twins, once described the stress of parenthood:

*"I worried all the time. Of course, ninety percent of the time you worry about things that don't happen, but still you worry."*[1]

A mother of quadruplets who are almost four years old says:

*"There are times when I just have to walk into the other room and catch my breath. I'll remind myself: God doesn't give people more than they can handle. Then I'll look up and say, 'Are you sure I can handle this?' That puts a smile on my face, and somehow the kids eventually do calm down."*

One group of mothers of multiples discussed what they do when they "bottom out" from the stress:

"I eat."

"I tune them out by walking out of the room."

"We made the basement into the indoor equivalent of the back-yard—indestructible! When I've had it with our [eight-year-old] kids, I send them downstairs to play by themselves."

"I take the kids outside. If I'm in the house too long, I go crazy. Once when the kids were sick, I didn't step out of the house for five days. It actually gave me the shakes to be cooped up like that."

"I fill the tub and give the kids a bath—even if it's the middle of the afternoon. The bath often calms them down. What do they call that—hydrotherapy? I sit on the bathroom rug so I can keep an eye on them. While they're busy with the bath toys, I tune them out and flip through a fashion magazine or a catalog."

"I call my sister. Even a two-minute conversation with her cheers me up."

"I see my therapist."

"I ask a neighbor to come over so I can go out jogging."

"I reach out to others, especially friends from the Mothers of Twins Club."

"I put on the kids' favorite video. It's twenty minutes of peace."

[1]Chris Ogden, *Maggie: An Intimate Portrait of Margaret Thatcher* (New York: Simon & Schuster, 1990).

"I tell my husband I need a break and walk out. When the kids were infants, he'd plead, 'Don't leave me alone with them!' "

"I hire a sitter or drop the kids off with my parents. Even one hour of food shopping without the kids is great."

"I'm usually okay if I take a shower every morning before I get the kids."

"When I'm feeling down, I shower *and* blow-dry my hair."

"I cry. Sometimes the kids cry, too. My husband will walk in and see us all crying."

"I keep thinking, this is temporary. In a few more years, they'll be in school, and I'll have my life back."

---

### *Looking Ahead to Looking Back*

A mother of twins said, "People say childhood goes so fast. But when you're living it, it doesn't feel fast at all!" Yet gradually and inexorably, these years will melt away into memories.

Remembering that the stressful times of parenthood will pass can help give a sense of perspective, as shown by the following excerpts from a speech by Fabia Mahoney, a mother of triplets (two girls and a boy) and an older son, to the Montgomery County (Maryland) Parents of Multiples Club:

---

*"I have come a long way since the time I sat crying on the sonogram table at Georgetown University Hospital and they sent in two doctors to comfort me and offer congratulations, to now, when I'm looking at the prospect of four teenagers in a few years. Believe it or not, the house seems empty when even one of them is away.*

*"The day after that fateful sonogram, I was on the phone to the twins club, whose help was the key to our recovery and the source of all comfort. Being a former newspaper reporter, I immediately went to work, setting up interviews with families with triplets and one with quads.*

*"When I was very obviously pregnant, a young bank teller gushed, 'Is this your first?'*

*" 'No,' I said, 'it is my second through fourth.' A shocked pause, and I could see her lips moving, as though she were counting. Finally, she asked, 'Twins?' My impression is that people cannot count to three.*

*"Even people who know me well still ask, 'How are your twins*

*doing?' As if the magic boundary between twins, with which they are somewhat familiar, and higher multiples, is somehow too much to fathom.*

*"But as I read the Triplet Connection newsletter—with its news of triplets, quads, quints, and even a set of sextuplets—I feel very ordinary indeed. . . .*

*"I was lucky enough to have a vaginal delivery. They were a good size when they were born—all over four pounds—but still had problems that kept them in intensive care for a few days before they were sent to the intermediate nursery. They couldn't suck, so they were fed by tube, wired from head to toe and tucked into little incubators resembling toaster ovens.*

*"After they got home, my husband and I and our nanny organized ourselves into hospital-like shifts that covered the twenty-four hours, so the house was lit up and buzzing day and night. The situation was complicated because the babies came home on apnea monitors that were so sensitive that they went off day and night, even when there was nothing wrong. . . .*

*"My theory about fraternal triplets is that, in some ways, they are easier than twins. Because there are more of them, they aren't so tightly knit that you are excluded—mine never developed a twin language, for example. They are close, but on the other hand, more dispersed because there are literally more people to relate to. And the three of them keep busy from morning till night.*

*"I've had a hard time disassociating myself from 'group mentality.' I still yell, 'Hey, guys,' when I mean the three of them and I have caught myself yelling, 'Hey, guys' while trying to attract the attention of just one of them, to my embarrassment. Then there are times I've been laughed at because I mixed the girls up or groped through all four children's names before I found the right one.*

*"As the triplets grow older and don't necessarily dress alike, have the same friends, or do the same activities, I have had a hard time letting go of thinking of them as a Group of Three—of the time long ago when I dressed them alike and burst with pride every time someone noticed. I had to bite my tongue this year when Brenna refused to buy the same cute bathing suit as her sister. Yet many times the girls purposely dress alike, down to the socks, and announce that they're 'twins.'*

*"My best advice for managing multiples, especially if you work, is to plan a menu for the week, keep a running shopping list, cook the*

*meals the night before, plan vacations months in advance, and use lots of bleach!"*[2]

## ▣ *A Solacing Connection*

In the midst of the tumult of raising multiples, parents often find themselves asking out loud, "Is it this hard for everybody? Do other people's children drive them this crazy? Am I an incompetent parent—or is this really as tough as it seems?"

Next time you feel this way, instead of addressing the air, pick up the phone and call another parent of multiples. You are not alone. And, with your call, that parent is not alone, either.

[2]Reprinted by permission.

# Chapter 27

# Your multiples as
# Lifelong friends

In the darkness of the womb, before multiples ever see one another, before consciousness—perhaps that is when their bond begins to form. Some multiples fantasize that they communicated telepathically before they were born, sharing ancient, timeless dreams. . . .

Others imagine that, even as fetuses, they jostled for position. Maybe there was a race to see who would be born first! Was their first fight *in utero*?

"To this day," says one woman, "my sister still blames me that she was born with a scratch on her nose."

Then babies born together become babies raised together. Suckling at the breast, their bodies touch; drinking from bottles, their eyes meet. They smell and taste the same mother, nuzzle into the same father's soft beard. They hear the same household sounds: the mysterious churning of the dishwasher, the tweets of the pet canary, their sister's giggle as she makes faces at them.

Older still, they splash together in the bath, toss oatmeal from their high chairs—and are plopped back into the tub again. On a

green woven rug they tumble over, under, and around each other like puppies or kittens.

Every day, every night, through every stage of childhood, they witness one another growing up, until at last they pass through adolescence and become adults. And then . . . what?

Many multiples are lifelong friends, cherishing their unique intimacy.

But some are estranged, embittered. Their childhood resentments have built up like layer after layer of toxic sludge, and they cannot let go. They miss out on the unique kind of intimate friendship that only multiples can have. As one identical twin said, "How can anyone *not* be friends with his or her twin?"


## A Rare Opportunity

Being a multiple is an opportunity to be lifelong friends with a person or people who have known you and been known by you since (even before) birth, through countless shared experiences. Some multiples' disparate interests and personalities may preclude them from having as intimate a relationship as others may enjoy. Yet at minimum, all should be able to enjoy a peaceful, nonacrimonious, supportive relationship.

Their friendship may be one of their most valued relationships:

*"My twin gives me the only uncritical love I've ever had in my whole life."*

*"My sister and I are each other's bottom line. She is more likely to talk with me about her problems than with her husband."*

*"My twin and I speak on the phone two or three times a day. When I was pregnant, she went in for a pregnancy test!"*

One man takes such pleasure in being an identical triplet, he bubbles over with a vaudevillian glee:

*"When Dad discovered he was the father of triplets, he said, 'Boy oh boy oh boy!'*

*"Of course, I know how it happened. Dad worked in government. He had to do everything in triplicate!"*

Yet even when multiples are grown, and are friends, the issues that they faced as children are still with them:

*"I guess I have the need to prove myself competitively. I always tried to climb a tree higher, jump farther, risk more than my sister—and we are both risk takers. My vacations tend to be outdoor, physical, competitive trips: hiking, mountain climbing.*

*"I always did slightly better in school than my sister, which gave me conflicting feelings. I wanted to do better than her, and I also didn't want to. I think our competition in grade school and high school is why I work freelance today. I am not in direct competition with anyone, as I would be if I worked in a competitive, hierarchical organization. I can be on my own, only competing with myself, not with anyone else.*

*"The worst day of my life was when my sister got married. I was inconsolable for quite a while. For a time, I hated her husband. Eventually, he and I got close, but sometimes I felt that he confused us and transferred his feelings of his closeness with my sister to me. Nothing ever happened between us, of course, but there were overtones of being*

*a 'substitute wife.' I never talked about it with him or my sister, but I think he realized it around the same time I did, and we drew more apart.*

*"The impulse to be close with my sister is enormous, but the impulse to survive as an individual is also enormous. It's all about intimacy versus separation."*

Competition. Comparison. Togetherness. Individuality. These issues resonate not only during childhood, but throughout multiples' lives. How they are addressed when children are young will affect not only their relationship with one another, but also their future relationships with spouses, children, friends, and coworkers.

So, as a parent, when you refrain from comparing your multiples, you are helping each child nurture a strong sense of self that will fortify him or her throughout life.

When you accept each child as an individual, you help free all of them from the need to compete with one another. During adulthood, perhaps they will also feel less pressure to compete with others.

## ❀ *Setting Your Sights on the Future*

A man who had always feared heights became a father of identical twin boys who loved nothing more than climbing tall trees and scaling high fences. Up to the top of a chain-link fence these toddlers would climb, and once on the top, they liked to hold on with one hand and wave proudly to him. It took all his self-control to keep from shouting, "Get down! Get down!" Yet he was determined not to saddle his sons' futures with a fear that had hampered him all his life.

Symbolically, he did not want to be a dad who said, "Don't aim high."

In many ways, parents guide their children to aim high—to aim, for example, for academic, artistic, or athletic achievement. At least equally as important is achievement of a healthy family closeness—the ability to nurture enduring and supportive relationships with parents, with siblings. Multiples, especially, have the potential for an incomparably rewarding lifelong friendship. Lay the groundwork by teaching them the skills of communication and conflict resolution. Show them how you can celebrate each child's successes without comparing them to anyone else's. Insist that they respect one another's right to safety from physical or emotional attack. Caution them about the danger of holding a grudge.

As children, multiples were always there for each other to play with. As adults, they can *still* be there for one another—friends who can offer love, support, and understanding for years to come, blessings in one another's lives.

# Appendices:

## Glossary
## RESOURCES
## BIBLIOGRAPHY
## BOOKS FOR CHILDREN ABOUT TWINS AND TRIPLETS

# $\mathcal{G}$LOSSARY

*alpha-fetoprotein (AFP):*  protein normally synthesized by a fetus's liver, yolk sac, and gastrointestinal tract. Abnormal AFP levels may indicate fetal neural-tube defects, such as spina bifida and anencephaly.

*alpha-fetoprotein test:*  prenatal test of a woman's blood or amniotic fluid to detect fetal brain and spinal-cord abnormalities

*amniocentesis:*  removal of a portion of amniotic fluid, either to test for chromosomal abnormalities that could indicate Down syndrome or other disorders, or to relieve polyhydramnios

*amnion:*  membrane continuous with and covering fetal side of placenta. The amnion becomes the outermost layer of the developing fetus's skin.

*amniotic fluid:*  liquid that surrounds the fetus throughout pregnancy

*amniotic sac:*  thin-walled bag that contains the fetus and amniotic fluid throughout pregnancy

*anemia:*  condition in which blood plasma increases faster than the number of red blood cells

*binovular:*  of or pertaining to twins from two fertilized ova; also called dizygotic or fraternal twins

*breech:*  condition in which the fetus, instead of presenting headfirst at the time of childbirth, is turned so its leg(s) and buttocks face the cervix

*cesarean section:* surgical method of childbirth in which a woman's abdomen and uterus are incised and the baby is delivered transabdominally

*chorion:* membrane enclosing the fetus

*chorionic-villi biopsy:* prenatal test for chromosomal abnormalities

*chromosomes:* threadlike structures in the nucleus of a cell that transmit genetic information

*Clomid:* trademark for a nonsteroidal fertility drug

*conjoined twins:* identical twins whose bodies are connected; also called Siamese twins

*dizygotic:* of or pertaining to twins from two fertilized ova; also called binovular or fraternal twins

*Down syndrome:* congenital condition caused by a chromosomal abnormality; characterized by varying degrees of mental retardation and multiple defects

*ectopic pregnancy:* dangerous condition in which a fertilized egg begins to mature in the Fallopian tube instead of the uterus

*epidural:* anesthetic injected in a space at the base of the spinal cord

*episiotomy:* linear incision from the vagina toward (but not into) the anus, made by the practitioner at the time of delivery

*fallopian tube:* one of a pair of ducts opening at one end into the uterus and at the other end into the peritoneal cavity over the ovary. Each tube serves as a passage through which eggs are carried to the uterus and through which spermatozoa move out toward the ovary.

*forceps:* large, gently curving tongs that the practitioner may use to help move the baby through the birth canal

*fraternal twins:* twins resulting from two eggs being fertilized during the same sexual intercourse, or during separate sexual intercourses during the same menstrual cycle; also called dizygotic or binovular twins

*gestational age:* age of a fetus or newborn usually expressed in weeks dating from the first day of the mother's last menstrual period

*hernia:* defect in the muscle wall that allows an organ to slip out of place

*identical twins:* twins formed when a single fertilized egg divides in half; also called uniovular or monozygotic

*intrauterine growth retardation:* impeded or delayed fetal development and maturation due to genetic factors, maternal disease, or fetal malnutrition caused by placental insufficiency

*in vitro fertilization:* laboratory insemination of eggs; the fertilized eggs are then implanted in the uterus

*low birth weight:* weight of babies less than five pounds, eight ounces at birth

*neonatal intensive-care unit (NICU):* hospital unit containing special equipment for the management and care of premature and seriously ill newborns

*oxytocin:*   hormone prescribed to stimulate contractions in order to induce or augment labor, and to contract the uterus to control postpartum bleeding. Pitocin is a trademarked name for oxytocin.

*Pergonal:*   trademark for a drug used to treat anovulation and infertility

*perineum:*   area between the vagina and anus

*placenta:*   vascular organ through which woman and fetus(es) communicate. The fetus receives oxygen, nutrients, and antibodies to infection and excretes carbon dioxide and waste products.

*polyhydramnios:*   abnormal condition of pregnancy characterized by excess of amniotic fluid

*preeclampsia:*   abnormal condition of pregnancy characterized by the onset of acute hypertension after the twenty-fourth week of gestation

*pregnancy reduction:*   selective abortion of one or more healthy or impaired fetuses while allowing other(s) to survive

*prematurity:*   birth prior to the thirty-seventh week of pregnancy

*respiratory-distress syndrome (often called hyaline-membrane disease):*   acute lung disorder of the newborn. The condition occurs most often in premature babies and in babies of diabetics.

*Siamese twins:*   see **conjoined twins**

*singleton:*   child born from a nonmultiple pregnancy; also called a single-born child

*sonogram:*   see **ultrasonography**

*spina bifida:*   congenital neural-tube defect in which part of one or more vertebrae does not develop completely, leaving a part of the spinal cord exposed.

*superfecundation:*   fertilization of two or more ova released during one menstrual cycle by spermatozoa from the same or different males during separate acts of sexual intercourse

*superfetation:*   fertilization of a second ovum after the onset of pregnancy, resulting in the presence of two fetuses of different degrees of maturity developing within the uterus simultaneously; also called superimpregnation

*supertwins:*   triplets or higher multiples

*toxemia:*   hypertensive disorder of pregnancy including presence of bacterial toxins in the bloodstream; also called preeclampsia

*transverse lie:*   condition in which the fetus lies horizontally across the uterus. If the fetus does not turn, safe vaginal delivery is impossible, and a cesarean section must be performed.

*Turner's syndrome:*   genetically determined condition that is associated with the presence of one X chromosome and no Y chromosome and that is characterized by an outwardly feminine body with incomplete and infertile gonads

*twin transfusion syndrome:* unequal nourishment of identical twins who share the same placenta

*ultrasonography:* prenatal test performed to explore reasons for vaginal bleeding, pelvic pain, and frequent miscarriage; confirms gestational age and ectopic pregnancy and determines the position of the fetuses

*vacuum extraction:* process in which a cap applied during childbirth to the baby's head creates a vacuum, which helps the baby slide out through the birth canal

*vanishing twin syndrome:* unexplained loss of one embryo during the first trimester despite the survival of other(s)

*VBAC:* vaginal birth after cesarean

*version:* manual repositioning of the fetus by the practitioner in order to facilitate vaginal birth

*zygote:* fertilized egg

# $\mathcal{R}$ESOURCES

## ⬛ *Periodicals*

*American Baby,* 475 Park Avenue South, New York, NY 10016
*Baby Talk,* (distributed free through retail stores), 636 Avenue of the
   Americas, New York, NY 10011
*Child Magazine,* 110 Fifth Avenue, New York, NY 10011
*Double Talk,* P.O. Box 412, Amelia, OH 45102
*Family Fun,* P.O. Box 929, Northampton, MA 01060
*Parenting,* 501 Second Street, San Francisco, CA 94017
*Parents,* 685 Third Avenue, New York, NY 10017
*Triplet Connection,* P.O. Box 997, Stockton, CA 95209
*Twins Magazine,* P.O. Box 12045, Overland Park, KS 66212
*Working Mother,* 230 Park Avenue, New York NY 10169

## ⬛ *Organizations*

*American Academy of Pediatrics,* Publications Department, P.O. Box 927,
   Elk Grove Village, IL 60009-0927; phone 1-800-433-9016

*Center for Loss in Multiple Birth, Inc. (CLIMB),*  c/o Jean Kollantai, P.O. Box 1064, Palmer, AK 99645; phone 907-746-6123

*Center for the Study of Multiple Birth,*  Suite 464, 333 East Superior Street, Chicago, IL 60611; phone 312-266-9093

*Cesarean/Support Education and Concern (C/Sec),*  22 Forest Road, Framingham, MA 01701; phone 508-877-8266

*Compassionate Friends,*  P.O. Box 3696, Oak Brook, IL 60522-3696; phone 708-990-0010

*Family Resource Coalition,*  230 North Michigan Avenue, Chicago, IL 60601; phone 312-341-0900

*International Society for Twin Studies,*  c/o Adam P. Matheny, Jr., Ph.D., The Louisville Twin Study, Child Development Unit, Department of Pediatrics, University of Louisville, Louisville, KY 40292; phone 502-852-5134

*International Twins Association,*  c/o Lynn Long, 6898 Channel Road, Minneapolis, MN 55432; phone 612-571-3022

*La Leche League International, Inc.,*  P.O. Box 1209, Franklin Park, IL 60131-8209; phone 1-800-LA LECHE

*Learning Disabilities Association of America,*  4156 Library Road, Pittsburgh, PA 15234; phone 412-341-1515

*Mothers of Supertwins (MOST),*  P.O. Box 951, Brentwood, NY 11717-0627; phone 516-434-MOST

*NAPSAC (International Association of Parents and Professionals for Safe Alternatives in Childbirth),*  Route 1, P.O. Box 646, Marble Hill, MO 63764; phone 314-238-2010

*National Organization of Mothers of Twins Clubs, Inc.,*  P.O. Box 23188, Albuquerque, NM 87192-1188; phone 505-275-0955

*Parent Care, Inc.,*  9041 Colgate Street, Indianapolis, IN 46268-1210; phone 317-872-9913

*Parents Anonymous,*  520 South Lafayette Park Place, Suite 316, Los Angeles, CA 90057; phone 1-800-421-0353

*Parents of Multiple Births Association (of Canada) (POMBA),*  4981 Highway #7 East, Unit 12A, Suite 161, Markham, Ontario, Canada L3R 1N1; phone 905-513-7506

*Triplet Connection,*  P.O. Box 997, Stockton, CA 95209; phone 209-474-3073 or 0885

*Twinless Twins Support Group,*  c/o Raymond W. Brandt, 11220 St. Joe Road, Fort Wayne, IN 46835; phone 219-627-5414

*Twins Day Festival,*  Twins Day Festival Committee, P.O. Box 29, Twinsburg, OH 44087; phone 216-425-3652

*Twin Services,*  P.O. Box 10066, Berkeley, CA 94709; phone 510-524-0863

**Twins Foundation,**   P.O. Box 9487, Providence, RI 02940-9487; phone 401-274-TWIN
**U.S. Consumer Product Safety Commission,**   Washington, D.C. 20207

## ▣ Mail-Order Buying for Parents of Multiples

Here are some mail-order sources you may like. Most offer free catalogs upon request.

### ITEMS FOR PREMATURELY BORN BABIES

| | |
|---|---|
| La Petite Baby | 404-475-3247 (call collect) |
| Preemie Store | 1-800-O-SO-TINY |
| Preemie Wear | 1-800-992-TINY |
| Commonwealth Premature Pampers | 1-800-543-4932 (in Ohio 1-800-582-2623) |

### ITEMS FOR PARENTING MULTIPLES

| | |
|---|---|
| A Baby Carriage | 1-800-228-TWIN |
| Four Dee Products (Nurse-Mate pillow for breastfeeding) | 1-800-526-2594 |
| La Leche League | 708-451-1891 |
| McGills | 402-592-0000 |
| Mainly Multiples | 1-800-388-TWIN |
| Twincerely Yours | 904-394-5493 |
| Twozies Plus | 1-800-52-TWINS |

### CLOTHING AND CLOTH DIAPERS

| | |
|---|---|
| After the Stork | 1-800-333-KIDS |
| Biobottoms | 1-800-766-1254 |
| Hanna Andersson | 1-800-222-0544 |
| Seventh Generation | 1-800-456-1197 |

## SAFETY AND HOME PRODUCTS

| | |
|---|---|
| One Step Ahead | 1-800-274-8440 |
| Perfectly Safe | 1-800-837-KIDS |
| The Right Start | 1-800-LITTLE 1 |

## BOOKS

| | |
|---|---|
| Bank Street Bookstore | 1-800-724-1486 |
| | (in New York State |
| | 1-800-439-1486) |
| Chinaberry | 1-800-776-2242 |

## TOYS

| | |
|---|---|
| Animal Town | 1-800-445-8642 |
| Child Craft | 1-800-631-5657 |
| Play Fair Toys | 1-800-824-7255 |

# $\mathcal{B}$IBLIOGRAPHY

## ❧ *Twins, Triplets, Quadruplets, and More*

Ainslie, Ricardo C. *The Psychology of Twinship*. Lincoln: University of Nebraska Press, 1985.

Alexander, Terry Pink. *Make Room for Twins*. New York: Bantam Books, 1987.

Bryan, Elizabeth M. *Twins, Triplets and More*. New York: St. Martin's Press, 1992.

Cassill, Kay. *Twins: Nature's Amazing Mystery*. New York: Atheneum, 1984.

Friedrich, Elizabeth, and Cherry Rowland. *The Parent's Guide to Raising Twins*. New York: St. Martin's Press, 1984.

Gromada, Karen Kerkhoff, and Mary C. Hurlburt. *Keys to Parenting Twins*. Hauppauge, New York: Barron's Educational Series, 1992.

Noble, Elizabeth. *Having Twins* 2nd ed. rev. Boston: Houghton Mifflin, 1991.

Theroux, Rosemary T., and Josephine F. Tingley. *The Care of Twin Children: A Common-sense Guide for Parents* 2nd ed. rev. Chicago: The Center for Study of Multiple Gestation, 1984.

## ▣ *Pregnancy*

Caplan, Ronald M., with Betty Rothbart. *Your Pregnancy: Reassuring Answers to the Questions of Mothers-to-Be*. New York: William Morrow and Company, 1992.

Eisenberg, Arlene, et al. *What to Eat When You're Expecting*. New York: Workman, 1986.

Friedman, Rochelle, and Bonnie Gradstein. *Surviving Pregnancy Loss*. Boston: Little Brown and Company, 1982.

Rothman, Barbara Katz. *The Tentative Pregnancy: Prenatal Diagnosis and the Future of Motherhood*. New York: Viking, 1986.

## ▣ *Premature Birth*

Harrison, Helen. *The Premature Baby Book: A Parent's Guide to Coping and Caring in the First Years*. New York: St. Martin's Press, 1983.

Henig, Robin Marantz, and Anne B. Fletcher. *Your Premature Baby*. New York: Rawson Associates, 1983.

Homan, William P. with Betty Rothbart. *The Hernia Book*. New York: Consumer Reports Books, 1993.

Manginello, Frank P., and Theresa F. DiGeronimo. *Your Premature Baby*. New York: John Wiley, 1991.

Sammons, William A. H., and Jennifer M. Lewis. *Premature Babies: A Different Beginning*. St. Louis: C. V. Mosby, 1985.

## ▣ *Breastfeeding*

Eiger, Marvin S., and Sally W. Olds. *The Complete Book of Breastfeeding*. New York: Bantam Books, 1987.

Gromada, Karen. *Mothering Multiples: Breastfeeding and Caring for Twins*. Franklin Park, IL: La Leche League, 1985.

Keith, Donald M., Sheryl McInnes, and Louis G. Keith, eds. *Breastfeeding Twins, Triplets, and Quadruplets*. Chicago: Center for Study of Multiple Birth, 1982.

Pryor, Karen. *Nursing Your Baby*. New York: Pocket Books, 1991.

## ⑧ *Parenting*

Ames, Louise Bates, with Carol Chase Haber and the Gesell Institute of Human Development. *He Hit Me First: When Brothers and Sisters Fight.* New York: Warner Books, 1982.

Faber, Adele, and Elaine Mazlish. *How to Talk So Kids Will Listen & Listen So Kids Will Talk.* New York: Avon Press, 1982.

———. *Siblings Without Rivalry.* New York: W. W. Norton, 1987.

Ferber, Richard, M.D. *Solve Your Child's Sleep Problems.* New York: Simon & Schuster, 1985.

Greer, Jane. *Adult Sibling Rivalry.* New York: Crown, 1992.

LeShan, Eda. *When Your Child Drives You Crazy.* New York: St. Martin's Press, 1985.

Pogrebin, Letty Cottin. *Growing Up Free.* New York: McGraw-Hill, 1980.

Sears, William. *Nighttime Parenting.* New York: New American Library/Dutton, 1987.

Siegler, Ava L. *What Should I Tell the Kids? A Parent's Guide to Real Problems in the Real World.* New York: Dutton, 1993.

Spock, Benjamin, and Michael B. Rothenberg. *Dr. Spock's Baby and Child Care* 6th ed. rev. New York: Pocket Books, 1992.

Stoppard, Miriam. *The First Weeks of Life.* New York: Ballantine Books, 1989.

Wanderman, Sidney E., with Betty Rothbart. *Hemorrhoids: Warning Signs and Symptoms of Hemorrhoids and Other Bowel Disorders.* Yonkers, NY: Consumer Reports Books, 1991. See Chapter 18, "Toilet Training: Helping Children Develop Healthy Bowel Habits."

Zolla, Susan, and Pepper Abrams. *Get Help!: The Complete Guide to Household Help.* New York: Crown Publishers, 1983.

# $\mathcal{B}$OOKS FOR CHILDREN ABOUT TWINS AND TRIPLETS

One of the greatest gifts parents can impart to children is a love of reading. Your multiples will be especially interested in books about twins and triplets—and in discussing them with you.

## ❧ Nonfiction

Ingram, Jay. *Twins*. New York: Simon & Schuster, 1988. Examines the subject of human and animal twins; scientific studies of twins; unusual stories of twins.

Rosenberg, Maxine B. *Being a Twin, Having a Twin*. New York: Lothrop, Lee & Shepard, 1985. Describes the experiences of several different sets of twins, both identical and fraternal.

Williams, Gurney. *Twins*. New York: Franklin Watts, 1979. Describes the occurrence of identical and fraternal twins and the growth and development of people who are twins.

## ❧ *Fiction*

### PICTURE BOOKS

Abolafia, Yossi. *My Three Uncles*. New York: Greenwillow, 1985. A young girl learns how to tell her uncles, who are identical triplets, apart.

Carey, Valerie. *Harriet and William and the Terrible Creature*. New York: E. P. Dutton, 1985. Adventurous Harriet and her twin, William, who likes to stay at home, fly in a spaceship to a distant planet.

Cleary, Beverly. *The Growing-Up Feet*. New York: Morrow Junior Books, 1987. Twins' feet haven't "grown up" enough for new shoes so they get bright red boots instead. (Also by Beverly Cleary: *Janet's Thingamajigs*. New York: Morrow Junior Books, 1987. *The Real Hole*. New York: Morrow Junior Books, 1987. *Two Dog Biscuits*. New York: Morrow Junior Books, 1986.)

Lindman, Maj. *Flicka, Ricka, Dicka, and the New Dotted Dresses*. Chicago: Albert Whitman, 1939. Triplets' new clothes do not prevent them from doing a kind deed. (Also by Maj Lindman: *Snipp, Snapp, Snurr and the Magic Horse*. Chicago: Albert Whitman, 1933.)

Mitchell, Adrian. *Our Mammoth*. San Diego: Harcourt Brace Jovanovich, 1987. Twins discover a mammoth frozen inside an iceberg at the beach and take it home for a pet. (Also by Adrian Mitchell: *Our Mammoth Goes to School*. San Diego: Harcourt Brace Jovanovich, 1988.)

Pirani, Felix. *Triplets*. New York: Viking, 1991. Triplets who look so much alike that no one but their parents can tell them apart decide to fool people, but their dentist can still tell them apart.

Seuling, Barbara. *The Triplets*. Boston: Houghton Mifflin, 1980. Triplets go into seclusion when their parents, teachers, and friends keep confusing one with another.

Smith, Wendy. *Twice Nice*. Minneapolis: Carolrhoda Books, 1989. Though content to be an only mouse, Theolonius learns to love his new twin sisters.

### STEP-UP BOOKS (BEGINNING CHAPTER BOOKS)

Adler, David A. *The Fourth Floor Twins and the Disappearing Parrot Trick*. Fourth Floor Twins Series. New York: Viking Kestrel, 1986. Two sets of twins launch a wild chase when the "disappearing parrot" in their school talent-show magic act really does disappear. (Also by David A. Adler: *The Fourth Floor Twins and the Skyscraper Parade*. New York: Viking Kestrel, 1987.)

Bach, Alice. *Millicent the Magnificent*. New York: Harper & Row, 1978. The adventures of bear twins with a circus bear. (Also by Alice Bach: *The Most Delicious Camping Trip*. New York: Harper & Row, 1978.)

Flournoy, Valerie. *The Twins Strike Back*. New York: Dial Press, 1980. Tired of being teased about being twins, Ivy and May decide to take action on their eighth birthday.

Hoban, Lillian. *The Case of the Two Masked Robbers*. New York: Harper & Row, 1986. Raccoon twins track down the robbers who stole Mrs. Turtle's eggs.

Hutchins, Patricia. *Which Witch Is Which*. New York: Greenwillow, 1989. Although Ella and Emily look alike, their choices of food, games, and colors at a birthday party help the reader tell them apart.

Ross, Pat. *M and M and the Bad News Babies*. New York: Pantheon Books, 1983. Mandy and Mimi discover a way to make the unruly twins for whom they baby-sit into perfect angels.


## SPANISH AND ENGLISH STEP-UP BOOKS

Garcia, Maria. *The Adventures of Connie and Diego*. San Francisco: Children's Book Press, 1987. Tired of being laughed at because they are different, a pair of multicolored twins run away to ask the animals where they belong.

McKissack, Pat. *¿Quien Es Quien?* and *Who Is Who?* Rookie Reader—two editions, one in Spanish, one in English. Chicago: Children's Press, 1983. Even though Bobby and Jimmy are twins, they often like different things. Includes word list.


## INTERMEDIATE LEVEL

Cleary, Beverly. *Mitch and Amy*. New York: Morrow Junior Books, 1967. Adventures of nine-year-old twins equally matched in abilities but very different in personalities.

Cooney, Caroline. *The Paper Caper*. New York: Coward, McCann & Geoghegan, 1981. Twins visit their aunt and uncle and become involved in discovering the thief of a stolen computer program.

Follett, Ken. *The Power Twins*. New York: Morrow Junior Books, 1990. Twins are taken by their uncle, who turns out to be an alien, to the capital of the Galactic Empire.

Hope, Laura Lee. *Bobbsey Twins' Wonderful Winter Secret*. Bobbsey Twins Series. New York: Grosset & Dunlap, 1962. Classic tale of the adventures of twin detectives.

Markham, Marion. *The Halloween Candy Mystery*. Dixon Twin Series. Boston: Houghton Mifflin, 1982. Twins use their powers of deduction and scientific expertise to catch a burglar on Halloween night. (Also by Marion Markham: *The Thanksgiving Day Parade Mystery*. Boston: Houghton Mifflin, 1986.)

Singer, Marilyn. *The Case of the Cackling Car*. New York: Harper & Row, 1985. Detective twins interrupt their Texas vacation to search for a missing girl. (Also by Marilyn Singer: *The Case of the Fixed Election*. New York: Harper & Row, 1989. *The Hoax on You*. New York: Harper & Row, 1989.)

## AGES 11–14

Aaron, Chester. *Out of Sight, Out of Mind*. New York: Lippincott, 1985. Teenage twins are pursued by the Russians, who want to use their ESP powers.

Cohen, Barbara. *The Long Way Home*. New York: Lothrop, Lee & Shepard, 1990. Sally's relationship with an elderly bus driver who recites Shakespeare's stories helps her cope with the problems of her mother's cancer and being separated from her twin sister at summer camp.

DuJardin, Rosamond. *Double Date*. New York: J. B. Lippincott, 1952. Teenage twins discover that being twins is more fun when neither is a carbon copy.

Hall, Lynn. *Murder at the Spaniel Show*. New York: Scribner, 1988. The adventures of sixteen-year-old twins at a dog-breeding show.

Hamilton, Virginia. *Justice and Her Brothers*. New York: Greenwillow, 1978. An eleven-year-old and her older twin brothers struggle to understand their supersensory powers.

L'Engle, Madeleine. *Many Waters*. New York: Farrar, Straus & Giroux, 1986. Fifteen-year-old twins are accidentally sent back to a strange biblical time period.

McGraw, Eloise. *The Trouble with Jacob*. New York: M. K. Elderberry, 1988. Twelve-year-old twins' adventures in western Oregon.

Mulford, Philippa. *The World Is My Eggshell*. New York: Delacorte Press, 1986. Sixteen-year-old twins learn to adapt to change and to form individual identities.

Paterson, Katherine. *Jacob Have I Loved*. New York: Crowell, 1980. Feeling deprived all her life of school, friends, mother, and even her name by her twin sister, Louise finally begins to fight back.

Pevsner, stella. *Sister of the Quints*. New York: Clarion Books, 1987. Thirteen-year-old Natalie's life undergoes chaotic changes when her stepmother has quintuplets.

Rabe, Berniece. *The Orphans*. New York: E. P. Dutton, 1978. An orphaned twin brother and sister living in rural Missouri during the Depression finally find a permanent home.

Sachs, Marilyn. *Thirteen Going On Seven*. New York: E. P. Dutton, 1993.

Adjustments of radically different twins, one who seems to excel at everything and another who struggles with a learning disability.

Scoppettone, Sandra. *Playing Murder: A Novel*. New York: Harper & Row, 1985. Seventeen-year-old Anna and her twin brother realize that their circle of friends may conceal a real murderer.

Sleator, William. *Singularity*. New York: E. P. Dutton, 1985. Sixteen-year-old twins stumble across a gateway to another universe, where a distortion in time causes a dramatic change in their competitive relationship.

Williams, Kate. *Who's Who*. Sweet Valley High Series, Francine Pascal, creator. New York: Bantam Skylark, 1990. One of a series of books in which identical twins' adventures prove that they are carbon copies only on the outside.

# ℐNDEX

hospitals and hospitalization, 8
arranging transportation to, 72–73
Level III, 39, 82–83
NICUs in, see neonatal intensive-care
units
nurseries of, 89–90
packing for stays at, 73
and planning for babies' birth, 39–40,
72–73
premies and, 82–83
selection of, 39–40
siblings' visits to, 77–78, 231
hyaline membrane disease (HMD), 96–
97
hypertensive disorders of pregnancy, 55
hypothermia, 97

idioglossia, 310
individuality, 305–310, 325
birthdays and, 320
equality and, 297, 305–306
language development and, 309–310
and multiples as lifelong friends, 353
school and, 336, 340
and types of twin bonds, 305–306
infant formulas, 144–146, 152
infant seats, 168, 181, 182
infant swings, 168–169
infections, susceptibility to, 97–98
inguinal (groin) hernias, 100
intercoms, 169
intrauterine growth retardation (IUGR), 56,
95
intraventricular hemorrhages (IVHs), 92,
99–100
in vitro fertilization, 7, 28, 217

jaundice, 97, 121

labor, 26, 39, 62–67
bed rest and, 49–51, 53
everyone in family affected by, 75
and finding out early about pregnancies,
24–25
HUAMs and, 47–48
premature, 7, 57, 82
lactation consultants, 123–126, 130, 142
La Leche League, Inc., 40, 71, 124–125,
131–132, 136–137, 140, 143, 160,
208, 274
language development, 309–310, 343
lap one, seat one position, 151
laundry, logistics for, 183–185
left side, lying on the, 45, 62
limousine strollers, 170–171
low-birth-weight babies, 57, 64
bed rest and, 50, 52

categorization of, 95–96
survival of, 81

Madsen, Midge Thurin, 104–105
Mahoney, Fabia, 347–349
maternity clothes, 42–43, 62
Mead, Margaret, 202–203
mealtime, logistics of, 182–183
miscarriages, 26, 55
bereavement services for, 104
and confirming multiple pregnancies, 31–
32
pregnancy complications and, 59
and telling siblings about pregnancies,
76
Mohrbacher, Nancy, 131–132, 136n
Mothers of Multiples, 223
Mothers of Supertwins (M.O.S.T.), 275
Mothers of Twins Clubs, 51, 54, 123, 126, 132,
154, 157, 160, 170, 200, 208, 346
family events of, 113
help and support from, 255, 259–260,
267–274
visits to meetings of, 272–273
multiples:
as adventure, 20
closeness of, 324–325
labeling of, 240–241, 298–301
meeting, after delivery of, 67
more to do with, 19–20
as mutual comforts, 307–309
points of view of, 17–18
rare opportunity of, 351–353
telling them apart, 218–223, 227, 333,
340
uniqueness of, 111, 325

names and naming, 115–118
naps, 54, 193–194, 196, 234, 248
National Organization of Mothers of
Twins Clubs (NOMOTC), 269–
270
nausea and vomiting, 26, 36–37, 55
necrotizing enterocolitis (NEC), 99
neighbors, help and support from, 254–
257
Nelson, Waldo E., 27n, 30n
neonatal deaths, 103–106
neonatal intensive-care units (NICUs), 39–
40, 235
annual parties for graduates of, 102
breastfeeding in, 120, 124, 132
description of, 83–91
difficulties in leaving, 90–91
discharge from, 93
jargon of, 84
premies and, 80–93, 96, 102

379

INDEX

for identical twins, 29
and telling siblings about pregnancies, 76
*see also specific tests*
*Textbook of Pediatrics* (Nelson), 27*n*, 30*n*
thank you notes, 70, 233, 257
Thatcher, Margaret, 346
toilet training, 200–202
toys, 151–152, 178–179, 312, 313, 321
transverse lie presentation, 57, 65
Triplet Connection, The, 42, 275, 348
triplets, 29–30, 44, 49, 157, 311–312
Turner's Syndrome, 359
Twinless Twins International, 106
twins, 27–31
  adoption of, 32–33
  in families of twins, 323
  fraternal, 27, 29–31
  identical, 27–29
  individuality of, 305–308
  overlapping, 133
  super-, 29–30
*Twins*, 54, 132, 155, 266
Twins Day Festival, 276
Twin Services, 275–276
Twins Foundation, The, 275
twin transfusion syndrome, 29, 56
two facing forward on a lap position, 150
two in seats position, 150
two sideways on a lap position, 149–150

ultrasound, *see* sonograms
umbilical hernias, 100

undescended testicles, 100
urine and urination, 38, 55, 140, 201–202, 203
uterus:
  bed rest and, 50
  breastfeeding and, 122
  HUAMs and, 47–49
  and sexual activity during pregnancies, 44
  in single vs. multiple pregnancies, 36

vaginal birth, *see* deliveries of multiples
vanishing twin phenomenon, 31
vans, 160
videotapes, 222, 286
vitamin and mineral supplements, 45, 54, 140

walkers, 173, 183
walking tours, 113, 179
water, 45, 139
weight gain, 41, 55
  breastfeeding and, 127, 129, 140–141
  in premies, 92
  as sign of multiple pregnancies, 25–26, 30, 36
*Where the Wild Things Are* (Sendak), 177
*With a Daughter's Eye* (Bateson), 202
work, 70, 131

X rays, 31–32

# $\mathscr{A}$BOUT THE AUTHOR

Betty Rothbart, M.S.W., received her Bachelor of Arts in English education and theatre arts and her Master of Social Work from the University of Pittsburgh. A psychiatric social worker who has counseled parents and families, she currently writes health and sexuality education curricula and trains teachers for the New York City Board of Education.

She is adjunct professor at the Bank Street College of Education, where she teaches adolescent development and sexuality education. She has taught writing to health professionals at the Hunter College School of Health Sciences and sexuality education and writing at a Fordham University program for low-income New York City teenagers.

She coauthored with physicians *The Hernia Book* (Consumer Reports Books, 1993), *Your Pregnancy: Reassuring Answers to the Questions of Mothers-to-Be* (William Morrow and Company, 1992), and *Hemorrhoids* (Consumer Reports Books, 1991). She also wrote *Frontiers in Fertility* (Planned Parenthood Federation of America, 1985).

She has served as a consultant and writer/editor on bioethics,

ABOUT THE AUTHOR

family planning, adoption, HIV/AIDS services, and organizational governance for the Planned Parenthood Federation of America, the National Center for Children in Poverty, the AIDS Resource Center of New York City, and other organizations.

She is a member of the American Society of Journalists and Authors, the Authors Guild, and the Society of Children's Book Writers and Illustrators. She lives with her husband and children in Brooklyn, New York.

Dear Reader,

I would love to hear from you about your own experiences with multiples.

I would also appreciate your feedback about this book. What did you find most helpful? What do you suggest changing or adding in future editions?

Please write to:

Betty Rothbart, M.S.W.
Author, *Multiple Blessings*
c/o William Morrow and Company, Inc.
1350 Avenue of the Americas
New York, N.Y. 10019